Flying High with Gringo Billy

Billy and Kay Dekle

FLYING HIGH
with
GRINGO BILLY

a smuggler and his wife

encompass
EDITIONS

© Copyright 2022 by Billy and Kay Dekle.
All rights reserved.

No part of this book may be reproduced, copied or used in any form or manner whatsoever without written permission, except for the purposes of brief quotations in reviews and critical articles. For reader comments, orders, press and media inquiries:

Published by EnCompass Editions, Canada
www.encompasseditions.com

ISBN: 978-1-927664-19-3
Printed in the U.S.A.

Cataloguing in Publication Program (CIP) information available from Library and Archives Canada at www.collectionscanada.gc.ca

We dedicate this book to our children
and grandchildren.

Kim, Amy, Hayden and Marlee,
may God bless you with happy memories
for the rest of your lives.
We love you.

Daddy and Mama, Papa and Mimi.

In Appreciation

We owe a debt of gratitude to the people who devoted their time and patience to the evolution of this book over a span of thirty years. Billy's parents urged him to begin a handwritten account of events in his hopeless situation and diligently transcribed and preserved his writing. Years later, Kay's good friend and colleague, Michele Roundtree, made huge editorial contributions. Finally, publisher Robert Buckland devoted a year to helping us arrive at our final draft. We wouldn't have produced this book without any and all of you.

Prologue One

I remember that boy the way he was then. Nothing like me. He was the opposite of me in almost every way. First time I laid eyes on him, he came out with the worst pick-up line I ever heard. My mama had just bought me a brand new 1969 Plymouth Road Runner for my eighteenth and I'd just pulled up to the pumps at the old Amoco station. This boy a bit older than me, he's in the other lane and he comes up and says, "What you got under the hood there?" I say, "I don't know. It's got that big number written on it. I guess you can tell." "A 383," he says. "Guess so," I say. The attendant put some gas in and I drive off.

I was dating another guy at the time and eventually that guy and I got engaged. Turned out we didn't stay engaged though and Billy kept coming around. He was sort of cute and funny, sort of a bad-boy type who wouldn't take no for an answer. Turned out I liked that. He talked a lot about airplanes because he ran the little airport here in Lake City. Once or twice, he took me up flying with him. It was okay but I preferred staying on the ground.

We started getting serious and talking about getting married and so on. What I wanted from marriage was a house with a white picket fence and a nice lawn, a baby, a family. Ozzie and Harriet, like. For Billy though, work came first and I know now what he wanted from marriage. He wanted to take me off the market so he knew I was *his*, even if he wasn't ready to settle down. Whatever I wanted — the house, the fence, the baby — he was fine with that as long as he could get on with his work and have a pretty good time. We did get married and we got a single-wide mobile home at Hill's Trailer Park. My mama's family didn't have much but after my mama and daddy got divorced, she married well — twice. So, I'd never lacked for anything — clothes, jewelry, cars, whatever. I'd got a Plymouth Barracuda for my sixteenth birthday so a person couldn't expect me to live for long in a single-wide mobile home. We bought a house across the street from Billy's parents and then we bought a better house across the street from that first one. You know how it is when you're young and you've always pretty much had what you wanted. That was true for Billy too. He didn't want to say no to me or himself. Trouble was, what he made at the airport wasn't enough to keep us afloat and buy all the things we wanted. We had our first baby and certainly we didn't have enough money then. Billy went to work for his dad who ran a grassing company and has big contract with the government. But the contract ended and his dad wasn't as good at business as we all thought. He went bankrupt and Billy was left with a mountain of bills. A friend with a paving company hired him but the hours were long and the pay was less. We were both tired and struggling. We couldn't seem to get what we needed from one another. We'd get mad and Billy, he'd just up and go to the bar.

I thought we could borrow from Peter to pay Paul, but Billy figured we'd borrowed enough from Peter and from Paul. He had a better idea, he said. "No," I said. He did it anyway. He was a good, kind man who'd never hurt a fly but if he thought something was alright with him, he couldn't see why it shouldn't be alright with everybody else. For him, this was true of women and true of smuggling and true of just about everything.

Now we had money but those were lonely years, anxious years. The long, long hours — days often — of waiting, not knowing whether he was alive or dead. It got worse and worse and I couldn't see a way out. I thought of doing nothing. I thought of taking my own life. Finally, I thought of divorce. Billy was mad as hell when I told him. He thought I'd tell the lawyers about the smuggling but, really, he was just in shock. He couldn't believe his charm and lies weren't working.

I married Bryan. He was everything I'd hoped that Billy would be. He was a good father and a good husband, but one evening I overheard my two daughters in the bath. Five-year-old Amy was asking seven-year-old Kim why Daddy couldn't just come and live with us. Kim explained that Mama was married to Bryan now and Bryan wouldn't let Daddy live with us. Neither of them said anything for a minute. I stood stopped in my tracks in the hall. "Then I guess we'll have to get rid of Bryan," Amy said.

I had everything I wanted and all I had to do was break up my family. Then Billy started coming back around to see me. He was hurt and lonely, just like I'd been for years. When I told my husband I was going back to Billy, he said, "You know he hasn't changed. He'll hurt you again." And I said, "I know. But I've got to give him a chance."

There was something about Billy I can't describe. Maybe it was his attitude, maybe it was his smell. Whatever it was, there was something about him and it sparked something in my heart even though my head was calling out "Not good!" So two years later, we remarried. That's when I started drinking like all his buddies and went back to playing softball with the Lake City team. I worked at the school and I raised my two daughters. Billy was a bit better behaved, I'll give him that. He kept any women out of sight and I had all the money a person could want.

It was only a matter of time, of course, before he slipped up. Not with me — not more than he ever had — but with the law. His second arrest came in 1984 and they gave him a couple of years and he was gone. I protected our girls from thinking anything bad was wrong. We'd go and visit their daddy in prison and he kind of took it in his stride because that was his nature. And then he was back home and I was back to being that wife at that picket fence and life was about as normal as it ever had been.

Prologue Two

I remember going out to the parking lot, still wondering how Freddie could be out of money. The math was baffling, no doubt about it. I'd have to ask him for an explanation when I handed him the loan. I opened the trunk and reached into my overnight bag, grabbed the wad of cash, the cocaine, and the pot. I closed the trunk, opened the driver's door, dropped the thousand in a litterbag, stuck the pot under the fold-down armrest and put the cocaine in my pants pocket. I closed the door and turned to walk back into the restaurant.

A non-descript man about my build was walking towards me. He started taking large strides and then he was at a full run less than twenty feet from me and then he was pointing a large-caliber semi-automatic pistol at me. He was excited, maybe even scared. We made eye contact.

"Put your hands up in the air! Don't move!"

Law enforcement had been the last thing on my mind. I experienced an impulse to run away from this scene, it was so unreal. I looked around the parking lot. Faces were coming out from behind unmarked cars, all of them in a blur. Plain-clothed law enforcement officers, weapons drawn and pointed at me, circled from every direction. It would be suicide to run. Even if the first guy missed, they couldn't all miss. And anyway, I was very, very tired of running.

I slowly raised my hands and looked over to Bennigan's windows. I didn't see any of my friends now and a kind of fog of unreality wrapped around me as the cops closed in. Visibility was almost nil.

"Okay," I could hear a voice. "Okay, guys. Stop it. This is crazy. Course Jim Lang oughta go to prison. Course he oughta. But not Billy Dekle. Billy Dekle, guys, see, he just needs to go home."

It was *my* voice though.

1

"Maybe that's how the Cubans do it in Miami but we're farming folks up here."

I'd borrowed my mother's Buick and it was less than an hour on I-75 from my place in Lake City to Gainesville. I pulled into the front parking lot of the Holiday Inn at nine and right there was the new Ford Ranger Frenchie said he'd be driving. I don't know why he hadn't put it in the underground garage but at least he didn't bring his yellow 911 Porsche. He was all smiles when I walked into the restaurant.

"Eh, buddy! Salut!" He waved from his booth at the back and even from the door I could see the flash of his fat Rolex. They wouldn't let him wear stuff like that in prison and he hadn't been full on with the bling when we'd met up in Daytona a couple of months earlier. But the guy was a mover — a superb dresser with a big house in Coconut Grove and a sailboat and a busy surf shop — an actual businessman. All a front of course.

"Hey, comment ça va, Billy?" He got up and we shook hands. He was wearing a light blue pinstripe and a sort of shocking pink shirt open at the neck. You could see his gold crucifix bouncing around in his chest hair. Guess that was left over from being a Catholic. "You okay, Billy?"

"Not okay like you, Frenchie, but hey, still okay." I was actually down to my last thousand. "Good to see you, man."

"Never mind da Frenchie, eh, Gringo?" He put on a theatrical frown. "Never mind it. Son of a gun, eh, Billy? Frenchie bullshit. Come on, sit down 'ere."

He flashed his smile and I sat down. He was a Quebecker with this real strong accent and he hated being confused with "dem frogs" from France. He liked to be called Rob, which happened to be his real name.

"That's okay, Frenchie. Rob it is."

"So, where's yer boy? Da flipflop kid you tole me. Da blondie."

"Glen? Don't worry about Glen. He's totally no good at early morning anything."

"Yeah, seem so. But you, you know him pretty good?"

"For sure."

"Better 'n me."

I wasn't sure what that meant. He narrowed his eyes a bit and looked down at his menu. I liked Frenchie. We'd been together in the Tallahassee pen but he'd been suspicious of Freddie, another friend I'd met there — a West Florida crop duster. They both trusted me but somehow they didn't trust one another. Then it turned out we were all three released a couple of months apart in the spring of 1986. Inside, we'd rarely talked about a smuggle but something was understood between us and I wanted to bring them both in on this first project. Neither knew the other was involved.

"I'm buyin' da breakfast," Frenchie said. "What you like?"

We both had bacon and eggs and talked about the surf shop and the weather, especially the weather. Only at one point did he lean in close.

"So dat's good now, de Navajo, no?"

"Yeah. Far as I can tell."

"An' de bladder," He leaned back and grinned. "She good, eh?"

"Yeah. Can you keep your voice down, Frenchie?" Only smugglers used bladder tanks to extend the range of their aircraft.

I glanced around but there was nobody close.

"Listen, Rob, you found a Navajo and I like Navajos. And the bladder was a good idea for sure. But you told me this plane was perfect and what happened? It lost power on the runway during the first take-off in Miami and that could have been ugly. Really." I noticed he was staring hard at his remaining egg, but this had to be said. "We dropped a week there. Then I'm finally bringing the plane back here from Miami and I discover the locker tank transfer pump wasn't working at all. How would that have turned out, somewhere over the Caribbean?"

"Tabernac," he muttered. It was some sort of Quebec swear word. "I do what I can, man."

"Okay, Frenchie. I know you do. And you came up with the bladder tank as a solution, which was great."

"Tanks."

"No. You came up with one tank."

"Yeah. Tanks dat you appreciate what I do. Tanks."

Sometimes his damn accent just threw me.

"But the bladder tank has a manual pump, Frenchie, which means I have to pay another man to sit in the right-hand seat and operate the pump. Okay — never mind. I *am* grateful." And I was. He'd done his best.

What I didn't tell him was that the man in the right-hand seat would be Freddie, because, as I say, those two guys didn't really trust one another. I wanted Freddie to be on the team in some capacity because I really liked the man. He was from an upper-middle-class family, always looking sharp even when he wasn't trying to. He was well-built and decently handsome and if he couldn't get a woman with his looks, he'd get them with his gab. Most important, he was a skillful and successful crop-duster pilot.

"Okay. Dat's good," Frenchie said. Like a lot of people, he just wanted to be appreciated.

"But next time, please Rob, scare the shit out of those mechanics, will you? Everything's lined up and waiting and its already the sixth of December. This has to happen in the next ten days."

There were some awkward seconds of silence.

"So where you want to go now, Billy?"

"We'll go to the interchange at I-75 and Newbery Road near here. There's plenty of tourist traffic and a bunch of public phones."

"Hey, good, good. Okay."

"We'll make the Belize call from there."

"Okay."

We finished up and while Frenchie was paying, a black F-150 Ford pickup pulled into the lot. Glen jumped out of the cab and I could see his grin from where I stood. I couldn't help admiring the kid's spirit and spunk, him being a federal fugitive who'd managed to hit the bushes when the DEA came down on their sailboat during an unloading in North Carolina. He'd been on the lam ever since.

I met him as he was coming in the door.

"Hey guys!" he almost shouted. "Where are you going?"

I gave him a friendly scowl. "None of your business, Glen." We laughed and he and Frenchie shook hands.

"Guys, Listen. Know I'm late but I'm starved. Really. Gotta eat."

"Hey, Mr. Glen." Frenchie raised his eyebrows. "You're way too late, man. We got business."

Glen was maybe ten years younger than Frenchie and me and at least an inch shorter, but he was lean and tanned and muscular. He looked like the Beach Boys probably wanted to look but he was a great off-loader and a great distribution manager. He'd never had a real job in his life and, yeah, he always wore flipflops.

"No! Lemme get something — please!"

"Glen," I said. "We're going together to the interchange at I-75. You can grab something there. Let's use your truck."

"Hm." Frenchie looked across the lot to the Ford. "Big truck, dat. What you come in, Billy?"

"I borrowed my mom's Buick."

Glen laughed. "Wow! That's yours, Billy? A Buick Regal? They still make them?"

"Perfect," Frenchie said. "Dat Buick, 'e just, like, for Gramma, dat Buick. Dat's perfect."

We got in mom's car with Glen in the back seat still grumbling about his stomach.

"How're we going to call Belize?" he asked.

I took my Crown Royal bag of quarters out of the glove compartment and held it up.

"Cool," Glen said. "I'm thinking about two eggs sunny side up and a pile of fries."

"What's dis?" Frenchie asked. He'd spotted my police scanner on the floor of the passenger's side. He picked it up and turned it over.

"Bearcat," I said. "Top of the line."

"Sacre bleu!" He caressed the scanner. "I wan' one of dees, man. One dat can do de FBI."

"The Bearcat can do that." I started the engine.

"Yeah. But de DEA. Ha ha, I wanna 'ear de DEA."

"It covers them too."

"An' de customs guys."

"It can do all that. Just turn it on. It'll scan the frequencies automatically."

I started to pull out onto 13th Street. The Bearcat locked instantly onto a live channel. I must have had the volume set pretty high because a voice crackled out loud and distorted.

"Blue on blue Buick pulling out of the parking lot onto 13th Street," it said.

An instant lump formed in my throat. "That's us!" I gasped.

The scanner sort of jumped in Frenchie's hands like he'd picked up a hot skillet. "Non!" he yelled.

I threw the car into reverse.

"They're backing up into the parking lot," the scanner boomed.

"No!" Frenchie yelled again. "No! Shit!"

He threw the scanner on the floor, opened the door and was out, sprinting through the parking lot with Glen right behind him. I gripped the wheel and felt their panic shift the lump in my throat. If I had been in any car other than my mother's, I would have bailed too. The seconds ticked by. I thought of my mom — they'd wreck her car for sure. I thought of my wife — she wouldn't tolerate another bust.

I rolled back out onto University Street in slow motion. The light at the University Avenue intersection was red. I stopped, hesitated, my foot hovering above the gas pedal. I couldn't see anything that looked like a cop ahead or in the rearview. Seconds crawled by and the light stayed red. What had gone wrong? Could we be busted for just *talking* about smuggling? Of course we could. I glared at the light. I knew Gainesville and the college neighborhoods this side of I-75. Could I lose them there?

A crackle of static. The scanner was lying on the floor, silent, off frequency. I picked it up and scrolled with one hand through the channels. A voice barked suddenly from the speaker. They had my tag number. Where were they? The light turned green.

I shot across 13th Street and headed west on University. Three blocks further and a silver-colored car in the rearview mirror was getting closer so I hung a hard-right at the Purple Porpoise Bar and Grill and entered a subdivision of student apartments. I veered into the parking lot of one and pulled in behind the building. My heart rate was off the charts and I was struggling to steady my breathing. I sat there frozen, watching the street, listening. The scanner was babbling with confusion. It was clear now that there were a number of cars filled with Feds looking for my mom's Buick and it was clear they'd lost me. My breathing started to return to normal but my hands were sweaty on the wheel. Would they search every street? Would there be roadblocks? A silver-colored T-Bird sped by and in that instant, I saw the driver's head turn and he looked right at me. My heart stopped. There was nothing left now but make a run for it. I backed up and shot into the street. The T-bird wasn't there but his voice broke through the scanner static.

"Ah, yeah. Buick in a parking lot on Second Avenue." Static. "Didn't see the street number." Static. "Three story beige apartment building. Going back there now." I turned in the direction he'd come from and headed west with my foot on the gas. At the first intersection, I turned north back onto a road near the same apartment complex and sped down a long hill with a major intersection at the bottom. I thumbed my right turn signal and pulled into the right lane. As I reached the intersection the light turned to caution and I swerved left across all lanes and went west again about a quarter mile. I turned right into another subdivision, pulled into a side street and up into an empty driveway.

The scanner chatter was chaotic. I sat in the driveway, listening, trying to breathe evenly. The Feds were making confused sounds and those were good sounds. I waited a few minutes then eased out of the driveway, crept through the subdivision and headed north using a couple of secondary streets and farm-to-market roads. I joined County Road 231— open and empty, generally unpatrolled — and twenty minutes out I pulled into the village of Brooker where there was a pay phone in the old store by the post office. I called the Gainesville Holiday Inn and asked for Frenchie's room. Someone answered.

"Who's this?" I demanded.

"It's Ray." A nervous voice. "Who's this?"

"Oh yeah. Ray. You drove Frenchie up, right?"

"Who's this?"

"Listen, Ray. The shit's hit the fan and everybody's scattered. You wanna do the same. When you get hooked up with Frenchie, tell him I'll be back in touch in a day or so."

"Who *is* this?"

"Frenchie'll know who it is. Beat it, Ray."

I called Kay and asked her to go next door to my parents' house. She understood and I called there a minute later.

"What's wrong?" she asked right off.

"Nothing." I sort of laughed. "How can you tell?"

"Your voice. I can hear your voice and you told me to go next door."

"Baby Love. It's okay, Baby. There was a little problem in Gainesville this morning and I'm ... looks like I'm under surveillance. You noticed anything suspicious?"

There was silence, then a deep, contemplative breath.

"Everything seems normal around the house," she said. I could hear the edge of tension in her voice.

"Okay. I'll call back in a couple of hours. If you notice anything, tell me to pick up some milk from the store. I'll go to Uncle JE's house and get him to drive Mom's car back. If everything's cool, just say supper's almost ready."

There was silence.

"Baby Love?"

"I hear you, Billy," she said.

I continued north twelve miles to Lake Butler and went in for gas. Less than an hour had passed since I'd slipped out of Gainesville, so I went over to the Full House Lounge and had a couple of beers for lunch. Didn't see anybody I wanted to talk to, so I drove around for a bit, passed Dekle Cemetery, passed the Union County Jail where Dad's dad had been sheriff and ended up out on Highway 100 west of town. Not for the first time, I turned down toward our old farm on Road 237 and drove by the house pretty slow. I wondered who was living there now. Saw those damn pecan trees were still standing in the side yard. Bob and I used to break our backs filling croker sacks with pecans for Dad. Not much else had changed in twenty-five years. The field of corn stalks where Bob and I used to hunt quail looked pretty much the same. I'd been so proud of my 20-gauge — other kids just had BB guns — I'd shoot anything that moved — except livestock, of course.

I parked up the road where the old Lake City to Palatka railway had cut through and I walked back in a few hundred yards on the rusty rails to the bridge over the New River. I looked down into the pool where I'd learned to swim. It was still deep and dark like always. The New River swamp was infested with water moccasins but the pool was generally better, and Bob and I would jump in after working all afternoon putting in fence rows. Bob was eighteen months older than me. Now he was the assistant state attorney in Florida's Third Judicial Circuit. Bob was the good brother and I was the bad brother. He was still my brother though.

I sat there maybe an hour trying to decide what I'd do if they had our house in Lake City surrounded. Finally, I drove back into Lake Butler and called Kay.

"Supper'll be ready about five," she said and there was the hint of relief in her voice. It seemed the setup in Gainesville had been for surveillance and I wasn't the target. Who was? It had to be Glen or Frenchie, but I figured the Feds would have me added to their list after that morning's adventure. I'd have to take extra care, of course. Otherwise, I couldn't see any real problems except I was out of money and had a terrible itch to get back in the air.

"I'll be there, Baby Love," I told her.

"Of course you will," she said.

Kim and Amy looked up from the kitchen table where they were doing their homework. Something was steaming on the stove.

"Hi Daddy," they said, almost in unison.

"Hi. Where's your mom?"

"She's here," Kim turned back to her notebook. She was fourteen now.

"What's that on your eyes, Kim?"

She looked up again, maybe just a little saucy.

"Mascara," she said with a little attitude.

Kay came into the kitchen.

"I was in the bedroom folding clothes," she said. That was her happy and relieved tone of voice. She came over and kissed me. "I'm glad you're okay."

"Sure, I'm okay, Baby Love. What's for supper?"

"Pork chops and acre peas." She drew back and smiled and then her smile disappeared, and she turned and went to the stove.

"Good," I said. "That's good. I'm real hungry."

"I bet," she said. She picked up a package from the counter and swallowed something.

"What's that, Baby?"

"*My* appetizers."

"What's that?"

"Tums. I've grown to love 'em."

The girls were washing the dishes and Kay gestured me with her eyes. I knew this wasn't going to be good but we went down to the bedroom and she shut the door.

"What happened?"

"Baby Love, it was nothing. Really, I promise." But I told her the story anyway.

"So, you're two months out of prison and you're under surveillance? That's nothing?"

Her eyes were burning into me and I had this crazy impulse to make a run for it.

"It wasn't me, I told you."

"So, who were they after then?"

"Come on, Baby Love. Just guys I know. Just talking business ideas."

"Just talking business with guys the Feds are watching."

"I didn't know the Feds were watching them, Kay."

"In your mother's car, you were trying to hook up with known criminals and you on parole."

"Kay! Listen! I would never do anything that would cause you or the girls any harm. You know that."

"Billy, I do know that. I do. But you're a damn fool and I know that too. I've already divorced you once, Billy. Please don't make me do it again."

I saw red.

"Stop the divorce talk, Kay! Nobody's divorcing nobody."

"Then you stop!"

"Stop what?"

"Stop … what you are doing."

"You don't know what I do!"

"Yes, I do, Billy and so does half of this town. And I know what you're going to do. You're going to go down to Tom's Place now and get drunk and play pinball and come home at one in the morning."

"I am not, Kay, and you don't know what I do!"

November 14, 1986

I know what I said tonight was right. Billy left after our argument and he's probably sitting on his favorite bar stool right now talking to Tom about how women just don't understand men. I fear we're headed right back down the same path — him flying pot and carousing around with the wrong friends. Nothing like starting the weekend out with a good fight that leaves you sitting at home alone!

I sat in the parking lot at Tom's Place. Tom had been one of my co-defendants in the so-called racketeering case. He was twelve years my senior, a man I looked up to and he was well-liked by most everyone in Lake City. Six years earlier he'd been transporting a J-50 Beechcraft Bonanza for me from Columbus, Indiana when he lost an engine on take-off and went into a VMC roll. He had enough altitude to complete the roll all the way and cut the power to the good engine, but the dead engine kicked back in and he nearly rolled the other way before he cut it too, then hit the ground more or less flat. The severe injury to his right foot left him with a slight limp. The man was a pilot, no question, but it was a miracle he'd survived and he'd spent a year in the hospital. He'd traveled any distance to see me when I was doing time and I always said I would never find a better business partner or friend. Now I'd frequent his bar — not always, but especially on quiet nights when maybe I felt like talking smuggling. His gentle, fun-loving nature made him a natural for running a bar. He was easy to talk to and a man you knew you could trust the first time you met him. His place was pretty big, with a bar and dance floor downstairs and pinball and pool tables and another bar upstairs. There was always a crowd on Friday and Saturday nights, and I sat in the car listening to the music for some time but I can't say how long exactly. Sometime before eleven I pulled out and drove over to the Longhorn, a little dive bar I liked on US 90 East.

"Geoffrey Bodine!" Ricky Saunders was shouting when I came it. "It was fuckin' Geoffrey Bodine!"

"It fuckin' was not!" Darrell Swane was sitting across the corner table from Ricky. "It was Bill Elliot! He was *the* champion, man!"

"No it fuckin' wasn't Bill Elliot!"

"It *was*!"

"It was way back in February, Darrell. You've forgotten, you asshole."

"Hey, Billy!" Ricky waved at me.

"Hey there, Billy!" Darrell waved too.

Up at the bar there were maybe three or four others — and Chris, of course, who was tending. Ricky and Darrell were all smiles and loud talk, as they often were at this hour, but also because they could normally count on me for a few rounds and some serious tokes out in the parking lot.

"Billy, tell this jerk who won NASCAR this year."

"Matter of fact, Darrell, I was busy at the time. I don't rightly remember."

"Oh yeah, Right. Anyway, it was Bill Elliot."

Problem was, I wasn't rolling in it anymore and I'd have to make an effort to keep up appearances.

"What'll it be guys?"

It cost me a few rounds, but the upside was that when these boys had been drinking all night, they'd appear to forget how good I was at pinball. The betting generally started at ten bucks a game but this night we were soon up to fifty. I let Ricky win one and finished off with a couple of hundred-dollar wins. I bought the last round to soften the blow.

"Hey, Billy," Darrell said. "I saw something — where'd I see that? — in the paper about Bob again. Looks like ole Ted Bundy's going to the chair at last."

"Looks like it."

"That was Bob got him, Ricky. That was Billy's brother Bob all the way, wasn't it, Billy?"

"Yeah. He was the chief prosecutor."

"Hey, that sucker Bundy's gonna fry for sure, ain't he, Billy?"

"Looks like it."

"And that Bob's something else."

Yes, that Bob was the good brother. And the smart one.

November 20, 1986. Lake City.

The girls are out for Thanksgiving break and we're leaving right after lunch at Billy's parent's house to go to my mother's house in west Florida until Sunday. Can't wait. No smuggling, no bars, no worries. My mom's place is in the middle of nowhere on land that my stepfather grows pine trees on. The kids love it. They take the lawn mowers out and explore the land, which is on the river. They stay gone for hours, just riding. The river is muddy and not really swimmable, but they still have a blast just wading and fishing in the stocked pond near the house. When we get back, I have the Falconette Christmas party that I need to start planning. I love Christmas and all the celebrations. Our party will be thirty-five girls and their parents. I love being involved with the dance team. It keeps my mind off what Billy is doing and on Kim and Amy and what they are doing in school. We have the Christmas parade coming up too and a performance downtown, so we will be practicing three days a week after school. Kim is one of the captains this year. She's doing a great job.

Doc Philpot sat himself down just outside his hangar at the Lake City airport and I was careful not to laugh at the sight of him.

"Lord, I do wish they'd make aviation fuel cans smaller," he said. He actually mopped his brow with a stained handkerchief, though it could not have been later than nine in the morning. He was a big man in his fifties — maybe six-two — but his 300-pound bulk hung over both sides of the bench.

"Good exercise, Doc," I told him. "Anyway, we only got maybe sixty gallons more."

It was three days before my planned flight to Belize on the seventeenth and we had Frenchie's Navajo stashed in Doc's hangar at the Lake City airport. He'd been a student of mine back in my days as a flight instructor, and him being a doctor he could afford a plane and hangar of his own. There was nothing strange about our hanging around at the airport and after the Gainesville stumbles of two weeks earlier I was being highly particular about the details. I'd worked too hard — we'd all worked too hard — for mistakes now. I'd set up my contacts in Central America for high quality marijuana and a crew to load my plane, I'd organized an unloading crew in Florida and a stash house to keep it in, I'd established a trusted distribution network through Glen to off-load it without delay, and I had a fearless and reliable pilot to do the flying — me. I'd ironed out every crease and screw-up.

When Doc got tired of lugging fuel, he and I went over the equipment one piece at a time, checked the Navajo's engine and systems again, checked the bladder to be sure we had all the necessary fittings to plumb it in correctly.

"I do hope you have nothing planned for this afternoon," Doc said. He was back on the bench. "I have patients to see."

"No, I don't have anything for us to do. You do that, Doc. I have a date with my parole officer."

He shifted his bulk and shot me a glance.

"You never have occasion to mention me, of course."

"No, I don't, Doc. And I never mention our smuggling operation either. My parole officer would disapprove."

"Heh, heh," he chuckled.

I chuckled back, but it was really the thought of Doc with his patients that always amused me. The man presented as a human edition of the giant sloth, a sloth who worked in a used car lot and slept in his clothes with a shirt pocket full of pens. Even his slow, gentlemanly southern drawl was a little sloth-like. And yet Doc was awful smart — even shrewd — and owned a slew of properties around Lake City and had a reputable medical practice if you didn't count the one time he was charged with Medicare fraud, which by the way he beat. Prosperous as he was, he was noticeably thrifty — no flashy jewelry or cars for Doc.

"Billy, look at me, son." He put on his best more-in-sadness-than-anger expression. I knew what was coming. "What do you see?"

I sure wasn't going to tell him *that*, but he answered his own question.

"You see a worried man. Why?"

"You're breaking the law?"

"No, no. I'm worried because this plane was supposed to be here for two days and it's been weeks now."

"Come on. Doc. You know the story."

"Billy, my boy. We had an arrangement, and that arrangement was for me to provide you with an invaluable — an almost irreplaceable, I would say — asset: a secure hangar. In return, you would pay me a modest $5000. That $5000 combines the rental of the hangar *and* the risk associated with your venture. Am I right?"

"You could break it down like that, sure."

"Now Billy, both those considerations are tied to time. Time is increasing but my compensation is not."

"I get it, Doc. You want more money at the end. I understand and I agree. How's that?"

Doc looked away for a moment, like he was frustrated.

"It's not me, dear boy, it's the logic of the thing that needs addressing. I'm just following the logic."

And so it would go. The man just loved to bargain and deal. Money seemed to mean a lot to him but it was my belief that if the money was everything, he wouldn't have been out here hauling fuel cans. Doc Philpot just plain-out liked the excitement of breaking the law, getting away with it, and getting paid to do it. We had a kindred commonality in that regard.

December 11, 1986

Well, the Christmas party for the dance team was a success. I love the girls and their parents. It keeps me sane. My daddy and stepmother helped with the party at the Shrine Club, where Dad's a member. Getting that marked off the list was a biggie. Billy had an out-of-town meeting with some of his associates. I had too much to worry about with the party to argue with him about attending, I'll draw the line in the sand on something else!

December 15, 1986

It's getting close to my birthday and Billy knows how I feel about birthdays and Christmas. I can feel my uneasiness building by the minute. He says he'll be home, but I'm no fool. He's on the verge of a deal and I know it's 50/50 on whether he'll be with me. I hate my life! Today's the last day of school, Friday. Maybe I can finish Christmas shopping for the girls this weekend. I have just about maxed out all three credit cards, but Christmas is the one time of year that I'm happy — happy to see Kim and Amy's faces on Christmas morning. Even though Kim is 14 and Amy 12, they enjoy it as much as I do. It makes me feel like a normal family. We're far from that.

I served nine months of a two-year plea-bargain sentence for a 1981 RICO — the organized importation of marijuana, in my case — conviction. While I was on probation, the Feds hit me with charges of possession of marijuana with intent to distribute and conspiracy to possess with intent to distribute. I faced ten years' federal time, five years on each charge, but a federal judge threw out the possession charge because the prosecution could not produce a witness. I was found guilty of the conspiracy charge and sentenced to five years. After serving twenty months I was placed on parole, but since this federal conviction violated the terms of my state probation, I was paroled to the Florida State Department of Corrections to finish the remainder of my two-year RICO sentence. I served a total of 28 months and it was while I was in Tallahassee serving my federal conspiracy sentence that I met Frenchie and Freddie. I was released on five years parole in September.

Jackson was my parole officer. His office was in the Federal building in Jacksonville, FL and when he stepped out into the hall to call me in, he was always polite about it. I appreciated that in Jackson. He wasn't the pushy sort, just your standard suit-type cop, big guy but not a smart ass.

"How's it going, Billy?" He always started like that.

"Pretty well. Well as can be expected."

"Everything okay at home?"

"Oh yeah. Well as can be expected." I added a friendly chuckle and Jackson smiled.

"And how is the job search coming?"

"Well, y'all know how it is, officer, it's hard. I mean, they like me and all, until the part where I tell them I'm a convicted felon and that sort of chills them like."

"You've got experience in, hm, roadwork, I believe." He was looking at my file.

"Yes I do, but most of my experience is in flying, as you know, and I can't do that because they took away my license."

"Hm. So what is it you're actually doing at the moment?"

"Oh, I'm busy. I'm busy working for my uncle on his farm. I've got plenty of farm experience. I grew up on a farm."

"Where's that farm, you said?"

"Just outside Wellborn."

"And your uncle pays you."

"He pays me what he can."

"And you do anything else?"

"Well, let me see. I do odd jobs for a doctor friend of mine. He's got properties he rents here and there. I help him sometimes."

"Right. And what's that doctor's name again?"

"He's, ah, he's Dr. John Philpot. I help him."

I didn't like that but what was I to say?

Officer Jackson spent a long time just looking at the file and I suppose he was reading. Finally, he looked up.

"Well, Billy, that's fine. But look, I need you to get yourself a real job. I know it's difficult these days, but that's what the board wants to see — what we call a third-party employer. Do you know what I mean by that?"

"I surely do, officer."

"An arm's length employer. That's what they want."

"Yes sir."

"Billy, you're a nice man, it seems. Believe me, I don't want to see your ass in a sling. I just want you to keep out of trouble."

"Me too, officer. Thank you. That's what I want too."

"So you keep on looking, okay?"

"I surely will."

I thought about Officer Jackson while I was driving home. I knew he was doing his best to hang onto that government job until his far-off pension day. I understood him and in fact I would have loved to have told him the truth — that I *did* have a real job and that I got up every morning for my three-mile run at seven and then started to work at my job and I worked at it hard except maybe for a noontime break for a few beers and smoking a little pot and then I'd go back to work, generally until three in the afternoon. Officer Jackson would understand if I told him but then I'd probably spend the rest of my life in prison and if I was ever to go to prison again, it would have to be for something more serious than telling the truth.

That night Doc and I flew to Miami in his own plane and picked up the down payment from Frenchie. Miami was well out of my parole travel district but that wasn't too much of a worry. Central America would be way, way out of my parole travel district.

"Tabernac!" Frenchie handed over the bundle at the Opa Locka airport outside Miami. "Me, I'm givin' dis guy I don''ardly know $40,000. Make sure you spend it all in de one place, non, Billy?"

"I'll look after your money, Frenchie. You just say your rosary or whatever for me."

"Bullshit, de rosary!" he snorted. French Canadians used to be big Catholics, I guess, but they got over that. "Jus' be careful wid my money!"

December 16, 1986. Lake City.

Something is going on with Billy and the law. Why does he feel that I need to watch the house for surveillance? I can't take this again. My nerves are shot. Whatever is going on, it's enough to make Billy nervous. He isn't telling me anything and I don't know these people he's dealing with now. The only guy I really know now is Buddy, and I trust Buddy. I'm starting to get that feeling in the pit of my stomach again. My tension headaches I know will start again soon. Good thing I still have my Xanax that the doctor prescribed. I hadn't needed them in the past few years with Billy in prison. I'm sure they're still good. He's staying in the bars again and we're arguing continuously. Why do I live in this? Why do I allow my children to live in this? His personality has changed since he came home this time. He's more brash, more overconfident about smuggling. I'm scared, scared for him and for us. It's a couple of days before my birthday, and I can tell by the action that he's going to go down on another trip. He came into the kitchen this morning after he'd taken the girls to school. I'd fixed breakfast, his favorite meal of the day, and I said, Billy, I know you're about to leave on a trip, and my birthday is the 18th. You haven't been home for one of those in over two years. You aren't going to miss this one too, are you? He grabbed me around my waist and pulled me close. I love you, he said. You know I'd never miss your birthday on purpose. I said, yes, but again, Billy, you aren't going to miss my birthday, are you? He said he'd be back by tomorrow and at the latest the next day. So, no sleep for me tonight, maybe not tomorrow either. It's hard to not show my anxiety around the girls. But I can do it, I always do. It wouldn't be fair to tell them where he really is and worry them. Those nightmares are for me and me alone.

Before dawn on the morning of the 17th, I drove one of Doc's old cars out to the motel on I-75 where I had Freddie bedded down. We got to the deserted Lake City airport while it was still dark, about 5:30, and opened the doors of Doc's hangar. We pulled the aircraft out.

The Navajo is a highly capable twin-engine cabin-class aircraft powered by counter-rotating twin Lycoming TSIO-540 engines. Navajos had been one of my favorites for smuggling before my bust because of their sturdy undercarriage, their ability to take off and land in a comparatively short distance, their speed, and their load capacity. The Nyack wing locker tanks were empty because of the pump problem but the night before Doc and I had filled the big black bladder tank on the floor behind the pilot and co-pilot seat with enough aviation fuel to see me to my destination.

Freddie was craning his neck at the sky. I was glad to have him in the co-pilot's seat even if his only job would be pumping fuel from the bladder tank. He didn't have any instrument or multi-engine rating and I had more flying experience, but the man was a crop duster, and the general opinion was that you'd not find a better stick and rudder pilot anywhere. He was also known to have a gigantic drug problem, though he was cold sober that morning.

"Looks like a bit of clouds," he said.

I looked up too. "I see a few stars."

"Really?"

"There's just enough clouds to keep it interesting."

I climbed in and closed the doors and ran through my preflight procedures while Freddie fiddled with the bladder pump bulb in his lap.

"Got the map?" he asked.

I took out the little hand-drawn sketch that my man Ruben had sent up from Belize. The town of Orange Walk was in the north of the country just over the border from Yucatan. I knew it well enough. The map showed a road running west from Orange Walk and passing through a settlement with an old wooden water tower like the kind you see in old western movies. Not far past the settlement a narrow lime-rock road ran south a mile or so and through a large sugar cane field. The guys would be waiting there with the trucks. I handed the map to Freddie, who smoothed it on his leg and looked at it for a long time.

"What's our distance, Billy?"

"I don't know. Near eight hundred miles but don't worry. We'll find it." At that point in my career, I could have pretty much made my way to any place in Latin America, drunk and in the dark.

I cranked the engines. They ran smoothly and I taxied out and turned onto the 10/28 runway. There was just a hint of daylight in the east as I pushed the throttles forward.

A rush of gratitude and euphoria washed over me. It was like the first time again, back at the controls of an airplane after two and a half years. How many nights had I dreamed about the acceleration, the effortless lift into a starry sky, the rush of excitement flowing through me as I climbed over the clouds? Now, I was not only flying again but flying on a job. A beautiful morning was approaching and as I pulled back on the yoke, I totally forgot Freddie was there for a minute. It was just us in the brightening sky — the airplane and me.

I leveled off at 12,000 feet, well above the cloud layer and below a brilliant canopy of stars. I set the engines up to cruise power and began to lean the fuel-air mixture for optimum economy. I pulled the mixture back until the exhaust gas temperature was peaking, then enriched the mixture until it settled down at 25 degrees on the rich side of peak. I could see the header pipes glowing cherry red through the louvers on the side of the cowling.

We were over the Gulf when the sun rose. Central America lay five hours ahead.

"Oh boy!" Freddie was almost hopping in his seat. "We *are* in the money, man. I can feel it in my *bones*, man!"

The sun was already pretty high off to our left and the Gulf was glittering like it was a field of diamonds two miles below us.

"Remember you and me, man? Remember us walking the track in the recreation yard and plotting and dreaming about this day?"

"I surely do, Freddie."

"Well, here it is, man! It's great, isn't it?"

"Yes, it is, Freddie. Mind giving the bladder a few more pumps? Let's keep the tank levels up. Wanna be on the safe side."

"Right, right." He worked the pump a bit, then unfolded the little paper map again.

"Your friend Ruben ain't much of a map drawer, is he, Billy?"

"Nope."

"But it's enough for you, right?"

"Yep."

I could just make out the northern coast of the Yucatan peninsula on the horizon. From there, we'd be over jungle most of the way, heading for a lime-rock road in the middle of nowhere, Belize. I strongly favored the middle of nowhere. Even if the police knew about the operation, if they weren't already there when we arrived, we could do our work and be gone before they could respond. I wouldn't risk a repeat of Jamaica, busted with a load of pot at a real airport on the edge of a real town.

The two of us lapsed into our own thoughts, with just the muffled roar of the engines outside the cabin.

"This will be your first time on a bus, won't it, Billy?"

Mom was packing my lunch — three ham sandwiches, which were my favorite, and an apple, which I could throw away later. I had my bag by the door and in the bag were two copies of *Motor Trend* magazine because I knew Reggie and Rodney liked muscle cars and maybe they didn't have these issues.

"I'll wrap some celery stalks in tin foil for you too. Celery's nice after a sandwich. It cleans your teeth sort of."

"Sure."

I was sixteen that summer and my cousins Reggie and Rodney were seventeen and fifteen. They were the sons of my dad's sister Frances and we'd always been close. Summer's past, we'd usually meet at my grandfather's house in Fort Myers down on the west coast of Florida. But then Big Daddy retired and moved back up to Lake Butler, where he'd been sheriff back in the forties, and my cousins moved to Miami. I hadn't seen them for a couple of years, and I was pretty excited, not that it showed.

Dad came into the kitchen and started looking in the refrigerator.

"You be careful, Billy," Mom said. "You've never been in a big city before."

"And you pay some heed to your cousin Reggie," Dad said. He was gnawing on a drumstick left over from supper. "That boy has got some sense and he's now at Miami Dade College. You follow his example."

"Sure, Dad."

"Time you got past this cowboy stuff and started thinking like an adult. You're sixteen now."

I'd never thought there was much wrong with being a cowboy. It sounded pretty dangerous to me. It sounded fun. That was stuff I liked.

"Your aunt Frances is good enough to have you for a week and I'd appreciate it, Billy, if you'd put that week to good use.

You talk to those cousins of yours about what they're going to do with their lives. Listen to what they have to say."

"Sure, Dad."

Reggie and Rodney picked me up at the bus station and I found Miami to be a pretty big place compared to Lake Butler and Lake City. I sat in the back seat and they showed me the town and thanked me for the copies of Motor Trend magazines and at some point, Reggie told me he was taking flight training at Burnside Ott Aviation Academy. I didn't quite get it.

"You're taking courses or something?" At least I could tell Dad I talked to Reggie about education and all that.

"Aviation academy," Reggie repeated.

"You study what there?"

"Flying. You learn to fly."

I guess I was silent a bit while I chewed on that. Then I must have laughed.

"How can you do that? You're just out of high school. You can't fly an airplane. What do you do, look at pictures or something?"

Reggie looked at me and raised his eyebrows in the rear-view mirror.

"Billy. Did you just fall off the back of a turnip wagon? I'm studying aviation because I'm learning to fly airplanes."

"But you haven't even graduated from college, Reg. You just started."

"College hasn't got a damn thing to do with it, Billy. Flying is like riding a horse. You don't need to go to college. You just have to want to learn. And have the guts."

"You don't have to join the air force?"

"Are you kidding? I've already soloed. You know what that is, right?"

"Sure, I think so."

"It's when you've had a certain amount of instruction from your teacher and he thinks you're ready and you climb into the cockpit alone and take off alone and fly around and then land, all on your own."

"You've done that?"

"Yep, and I've finished my night flying dual instruction and I'm now scheduled for my first night solo flight."

"When's that?"

"Tonight."

"Wow."

"'Course I've only got a student certificate and I can't carry passengers. But if nobody knew somebody was on board, nobody would mind, right?"

"You kidding?"

"No. You got the nerve, Billy?"

"You know I do."

It was July so we had to arrive at the Tamiami airfield after 8:00 for a night flight. We sat in Reggie's car for a bit and laid our plans and then he told me how he wanted to be an airline pilot someday. He got out and went into the office. At 8:30 I left the car and went around behind the row of hangars Reggie had pointed out to me, waited maybe ten minutes between the third and fourth hangar. I was wearing dark jeans and my black t-shirt. The wing lights flashed on a small plane about a hundred yards out in the field and I heard the engine roar into life. I looked towards the office and there was nobody in sight. I ran across the field, behind the plane like Reggie had told me, ducked under the right wing, opened the door, climbed in. Reggie showed me how to fasten my seat harness.

"You wanna go flying?" he yelled.

"Why not?" I yelled.

We rolled forward.

I guess I'd always known that when you're up in the air, things on the ground would be below you and look a lot smaller. I guess I'd have always figured that the streetlights and house lights would sparkle like jewels in the night. But what I could never have known was the thrill of it and I didn't have any words for that.

We flew all over Miami that evening while Reggie shot night landings at most of the Miami-area airports. He even let me take the controls of the Cessna 150, as it was called, and for a few minutes he became my flight instructor. Afterwards, we drove out to Miami International and parked off the approach end of the active runway. The big commercial jets soared just over our heads for their landings. I was a boy transformed.

Dad met me at the bus station.

"So? So how'd it go with Reggie and Rod?"

"Good. It went good. I'm starting my flying lessons right away. I'm going to be a pilot."

He didn't say anything for a minute. Then:

"What about your cowboy thing?"

"I'm going to be a pilot, Dad."

On August 14, 1966 I took my first flying lesson and on August 25, after seven hours of dual instruction, I took my first solo flight. During my senior year of high school, Dad sold the farm in Union County and bought me a second-hand Champion Citabria, an aerobatic aircraft. The guy who sold us the plane refused to show me how to do loops and rolls, but the summer of 1969, Reggie came up from Miami. A pilot there had taught him how to do loops, rolls, and spins. Reggie taught me.

Thing is, Reggie and I were sort of kindred spirits. We both carried the risk gene.

I recognized Orange Walk ahead and began my descent, passed over the town at about 2000 feet and banked right to follow the road west. The water tower was easy to spot in the middle of a tiny one-eyed settlement and the lime-rock road just past it stood out — a white ribbon against the green of the cane. I turned south and watched for the trucks. I'd been picking up loads in this area since the early eighties and I knew it well. Johnny was my main connection, being the local dealer who Glen and the other beach boys from Daytona used. Johnny was probably mostly Mayan, short with black hair and a black mustache. He had a small sawmill near Orange Walk and a farm where he grew aloe. Like most of us, he had quite the white powder habit. He was also a sugar daddy to as many ladies as he could afford. I liked the guy and trusted him.

"Is that them?" Freddie was pressing his face against his window as I banked low and tight. A half dozen guys were standing by two vehicles. A couple of them waved up at us.

"That's them."

I came in north to south, touched down, throttled the engines back to a purr and taxied towards a spot the team seemed to have widened out. A couple of kids were standing in the ditch with their bikes near the sugar cane and they ducked down under my right wing as we passed. They were maybe ten years old, likely from the settlement. They smiled and waved.

I killed the engines and we climbed out.

"Hey Gringo!" Tommy was first in line when I opened the door, and he gave me a big hug. "Good to see you, man! Where you been? It's been what? Two years, man, no?"

He knew for sure where I'd been.

"Where's Johnny?"

Tommy was the son of one of Johnny's girlfriends and pretty much family — young, heavy-set, easy-going, some sort of mixture of Hispanic and Mayan.

"He's keeping back case there's problems. Plenty of heat now, Gringo, and Johnny, he's got the connections."

Gaston was there too — stocky, strong, Mayan heritage — he'd been on Johnny's crew from the first day I worked with them. He was Johnny's leadman — quiet, serious, dependable. And there was Keith, a slender black man, a truly agreeable personality and a talented airplane packer. A talented airplane packer has a knack for getting the most pot in an airplane in the shortest amount of time. This is important when the cops might be buzzing down some local road in your direction and Keith also had this knack for connecting with the growers of the best pot at the best price.

I handed the remainder of the down payment for the load to Tommy and we all pitched in to push the Navajo around. The crew rushed to fuel and load. I had Freddie supervise and make sure the tanks were full and the fuel caps properly secured. Meanwhile I climbed onto the wings to check the oil levels. Number one engine was one quart low, normal for a five-hour flight and not low enough to waste time topping out. Number two engine was seven quarts low. I wiped the dipstick. "Shit," I said to nobody in particular. I checked it again. Seven quarts low.

There was no way a healthy engine would burn well over a quart of oil an hour. Did I even have enough oil to refill the number two engine? I jumped down and climbed into the cabin. I had six quarts of aviation oil stashed there, more than I'd normally bring but barely enough if — and this was a big if — the oil burn didn't get any worse on the return trip.

I told Freddie, keeping my voice down. He nodded.

"Can we make it?" he asked.

"We're gonna soon find out."

The crew finished fueling and loading 1,200 pounds of pot and the plane sat in a nose-high/tail-low squat. I'd never figured a weight-and-balance on this type of load, but even an untrained eye could tell we were overloaded and the center of gravity way past its rearward limit. I knew the Piper Navajo was a capable flying machine. Properly balanced and in the right hands, it would have no problem taking off from this makeshift airstrip. Properly balanced.

Freddie and I said our goodbyes to the loading crew and climbed aboard through the rear airstair door. We crawled over the load of pot to the cockpit and secured ourselves.

"Billy." I heard Freddie sort of clear his throat. "Are we going to be able to take off out of here with this load?"

It was a reasonable question, and the man *was* a crop-dusting pilot. I flipped the ignition switches.

"We'll find out."

I cranked the engines, gave the mags a quick check and cycled the propellers. Everything felt okay. I held the brakes and ran the engines up to full power. I released the brakes and we rolled forward.

"She's slow," Freddie said. "Real slow."

If we happened to lose power on one of the engines just after takeoff and were below a certain speed, the airplane would simply roll over from the asymmetrical thrust of the engine that was still developing power. That critical speed is known as VMC and when airspeed is below VMC you haven't got enough air passing over the rudder and ailerons to offset the rolling. That's what cost my partner Tom a year in the hospital and Tom was both skilled and lucky.

VMC is figured with the airplane loaded at gross weight and the center of gravity at its rearward limit. For an overloaded and out-of-balance airplane, the book on VMC was out the window. We were attempting take-off in an effectively experimental airplane. As we rolled, our speed was 40 knots and our lift-off speed would be about 70 knots. My eyes were glued to the narrow road as I worked the rudder pedals to keep us on it, judging speed more from feel than the airspeed indicator. Fifty knots. Fifty-five knots.

"Christ!" Freddie yelled. "What's that?"

Ahead of us, the two kids we'd seen earlier came up from the ditch on bicycles and pulled out into the middle of the road. They were side by side, peddling as fast as they could, racing us. I could hardly believe what I was seeing. They had a pretty good head start but we were closing on them fast.

"What the hell?" Freddie yelled.

They'll get out of the way, I thought.

"Get out of the way!" I said out loud. Did they think they were going to outrun the airplane, pedaling as fast as they could, looking back over their shoulders, checking to see how quickly we were gaining on them?

Seventy knots. Too late to turn back.

"We're going to hit them!" Freddie might have shouted. I could hardly hear him above the howl of the engines. I pulled back on the yoke and the Navajo's nose lifted and the boys hit the ditches and disappeared under our wings.

We leveled off at 14,000 feet. With the power and fuel-air mixture set for our return flight, we just had to stay on course and pump a little fuel every so often from the bladder out to the main tank, but after about an hour, I got to thinking about the quality of our cargo. I pulled out my Silver Falcon pocket-knife, turned in my seat, cut about a foot-long slit in the plastic wrap of a bale, and dug out a few buds. They passed the nose and eyeball test while my co-pilot watched with intense interest.

"Freddie, howzabout you roll us a sample joint?"

The man was grinning widely as he cleaned out the twigs and rolled an expert spliff, which he lit and handed to me with ceremony. I took a serious toke. Freddie eyed it greedily.

"Hey, Billy, you being an experienced, safety-conscious pilot, I guess you've been, like, reluctant to smoke marijuana while at the controls of a multi-engine aircraft."

"You're right, Fredrick." I topped up with a second toke. "I was always of that opinion in the past. But circumstances, see, they've forced a new way of thinking and I can now safely say I'm a highly experienced pot-smoking pilot. In fact, this little ritual — I call it the breaking of the bale — this has become an important part of our product assessment and in this case, I'm prepared to give you a professional opinion: we haven't wasted our time."

Freddie now joined me in the sampling and for a few minutes he was silent.

"Jeez, you're right," is all he said.

At this point we were well into the northern part of the Yucatan peninsula. I again took control of the sample.

"You'll notice," I said, "how carefully I inhale. There's a reason for this."

"What's the reason, pilot?"

"It's so that I do not get too high."

"You don't want to gain too much altitude."

"I don't, co-pilot. It's important that I'm at the proper altitude when we approach our destination. We could face any number of challenges at that point."

"Of course."

"I remember, for instance, one return trip in a single-engine airplane. I was over water at an altitude of 10,000 feet and working my way around some large developing thunderstorms while enjoying a sample of product. Suddenly, at a certain point, my mental altimeter told me that I was too high. You're probably thinking, where could the harm be in that? But the problem was that my ears had become highly sensitive to every sound of the engine and airframe. I in fact had acquired super hearing. Maybe medical scientists can explain how this happens, but I could hear every misfire of a spark plug. I could hear the valves opening and closing. I could hear the airframe making little creaking noises caused by the turbulence. These were all noises that I preferred not to hear, especially with hundreds of miles of water to traverse before reaching my destination airstrip."

"Sounds alarming, pilot. What did you do about it?"

"The only thing I could do, the thing I'm doing now. I eased back on the inhaling."

"Sounds sensible."

"Works for me."

For a while we flew along without speaking. Freddie must have lapsed into his own thoughts, because his eyes were shut, and he was slumped a little in his seat. Then he roused himself.

"Wow, Billy!" He was shaking his head. "This is *great*, isn't it? I mean, wow, man — making some real money again and, you know, flying planes and chasing women and not worrying about anybody nagging us. It's living the dream, ain't it?"

"I like it, Freddie."

"I like it," Kay said. "I've always liked the Wayside."

It was May 1978 and a young waitress with good legs was showing us to our table. I looked around. The Wayside Restaurant was wood-paneled, as places were in those days, and most of the customers were lawyer and doctor types wearing shirts and ties. It was about as high class as you could get in Lake City.

"We haven't been here in a long, long time, Billy. What put it in your head to take me out for dinner? And come home straight from work?"

I was trying to concentrate on the menu. The Wayside was a steak and seafood place, but good steak and seafood.

"Hm? What's this all about, Billy?"

I made myself look up.

"Baby Love, you know I feel bad about us not having enough money to go places and also you know how bad I feel about borrowing thousands from your step-dad to pay bills. We need to enjoy ourselves sometimes. That's important too."

"It is, Billy, and I do enjoy being alone with you."

She was smiling but she was also looking at me pretty steady and I was feeling anxious inside. I just knew this wasn't going to go as smooth as my conversation with Mike, who was my friend and my boss at the paving company. He'd been totally supportive when I told him about the plan.

I ordered a medium-rare sirloin and so did Kay.

"So," I said. "Kim's birthday is coming up next week, right? What are we going to do about that?"

"I'm going to have three of her friends over and we'll have a cake and I've got a bunch of games for them to play and, you know, a few little presents."

"Well, that sounds really good."

"You probably won't be there, will you?"

"I'd like to be, Baby Love. Maybe I will be."

It went like that while we ate our meal. My gut was in a bit of a knot. I couldn't put it off any longer.

"Baby Love, I figured out how I can get us out of the hole." It came out of my mouth like that, almost before I'd thought what to say. "I've got a plan."

She looked at me intently.

"What are you saying, Billy?"

"Baby Love, remember when those FBI and DEA came out to the airport and tried to get me to set up that guy?"

"Sort of."

"Well, I went to see him the other day."

"See who? The FBI guy?"

"No, Tom, the guy they wanted me to set up. You know, the one who owns Tom's Place."

She didn't say a thing. She'd ordered a slice of key lime pie and the first piece was on her fork. She put the fork down real slow.

"Billy, I will leave you," she said softly. "I will divorce you if you do that."

"Do what, Baby Love? I haven't even told you what the plan is."

Thing is, I knew how much she loved me, and I was confident she'd never go to that extreme. She'd threatened it many times on account of my continual drinking and partying nights, but she'd always get over it when I promised to do better. Anyway, she herself had promised never to break up our family, and I was banking on that.

"What's your plan?"

This was the moment of truth. I leaned in a little and dropped my voice.

"It's just one run, Baby. Just one run and I'll net a hundred thousand dollars. A hundred grand! Think about that."

"Billy." Her voice was almost a whisper and her eyes were getting fiery. "I *am* thinking and I'm not stupid. I know what you're talking about and there's no way you're going to make a hundred thousand dollars with one run of anything.

"No, Baby. It's you who's wrong! That's the beauty of the plan! We're going to do ten tons. Tons! There'll be three of us and I'm going to fly a DC-7!"

"A what?"

"A DC-7. A big four-engine airliner."

"To where?"

"Colombia."

"Oh God!" She fell back in her seat. "Oh God. I'm with a crazy man!" She sat up, then leaned forward and shot glances left and right.

"Billy, you listen to me and get real. You've never flown anything like that. You'll crash and die and where's that going to get us?"

"Kay! Airplanes are all basically the same. They're just like cars, right? I mean, some are bigger than others, sure, but they still fly the same."

"They're... Good God! Billy, they're not like cars! They go in the *sky*!"

"Shh!" I knew this was going to be tricky. "Look Kay, I'll make this one run. We can pay off our debts and I will be done with it. I can use the money to start a legit business and we can get off this living paycheck to paycheck for the rest of our life."

She was shaking her head with every word I was saying. Her tears fell on the key lime pie and I knew the conversation at the restaurant was over. We drove home in silence and I went next door to ask Mom to keep Kim and little Amy for the rest of the night. Kay and I talked into the wee hours. I held her and promised over and over this would be the only time. She understood she wasn't going to change my mind, but she was scared. To my surprise, I was too. I knew nothing about Colombia and nothing about flying something like a DC-7.

Course, all that had happened eight years earlier. I'd flown thousands of miles since then, served two prison sentences and had a hell of a lot of fun. I was a wiser man now.

We passed above the beaches west of Isla Mujeres and were northbound out over the Gulf of Mexico. I was in a peaceful, maybe complacent frame of mind as I reviewed my plans for our arrival at a tiny, abandoned grass airstrip in the south end of Suwannee County, just west of the town of O'Brien. Plan A was a carefully laid out plan that would entail intersecting the Florida coast near Cedar Key and proceeding to the Hatchbend boat landing on the Suwannee River for what we call a "fly-over." My fly-over crew on the ground would give us a visual on the plane and advise by radio that we were in the clear and it was safe to land.

Plan B would be put into action in the unlikely event that during the fly-over, the ground crew reported that I was being tailed, possibly by eager DEA agents in their own plane. I would then look for the biggest clouds around and hide in those clouds until I'd shaken off the tailing aircraft, presumably piloted by a person less skillful than myself. In the even more unlikely event that Plan B did not work, we would go to Plan C.

Plan C would entail landing the Navajo on the road leading down to the Hatchbend boat landing, jumping out, abandoning the airplane and load, and running into the woods toward the Suwannee River. On the banks of the Suwannee, we had a small canoe with an outboard motor hidden in the bushes. Once in the canoe we would motor downriver about four miles to the mouth of the Santa Fe River. Just a short distance past the mouth of the Santa Fe we would jump out of the canoe, abandoning it to drift down stream. We would then proceed to where we had a pickup truck parked and so make good our getaway.

We did not want to enact Plan C, or Plan B for that matter, but both were preferable to winging it in the course of a chase, and overwhelmingly preferable to capture. Plan C was a particularly good strategy, not just because it was my plan, but because going within fifteen minutes from an airplane to a canoe to a pickup truck would get us away from the location before the law could establish communications and had the further advantage of crossing two or three different county jurisdictions.

I took a final, reassuring toke and glanced at the oil gauge. It appeared to have moved. I said nothing but made a mental note of where the needle was. Fifteen minutes later it was clear that the oil pressure was steadily falling — still well within the green arc, but no doubt on its way to yellow and then to red. Whatever had caused the engine to burn the large quantity of oil on the trip down was most likely getting worse.

I looked over at Freddie, who might have been snoozing a little.

"Freddie, the right engine oil pressure is dropping. We may have a problem."

He sat up straight and stared at the gauge.

"Can we make it with only the left engine?" Freddie was a good crop duster but not an experienced long-haul man. I shook my head.

"We're still very heavy with fuel. If the right engine blew, we couldn't maintain altitude with only one engine. You add the fuel load to 1,200 pounds of pot, it's just too much weight."

"Jesus. What can we do?"

"We'll have to land or lighten our load."

"Land?" He looked down at the Gulf of Mexico almost three miles below us.

"Right. But that's why it's so good you're with me, Freddie. You can crawl over the pot to the back of the cabin and open the airstair door and throw bales out."

"Oh my God."

"Not *all* of it. Only enough to stay in the air with a single engine."

Freddie stared somberly at the oil gauge.

"Freddie," I said. "Look, we've got an ailing right engine and several hundred miles to go, but otherwise this is a good day, right? I've waited for this day for years and I don't plan on letting a sick engine spoil it for me."

"Really?"

"Really. And remember, these Lycoming engines are famous. The bastards are legendary. They can take any amount of abuse and keep turning."

"Shit. That's good to know, Billy. Real good."

But even at that moment I was noticing the manifold pressure gauge. It had been dropping a few inches for a minute or so and then returning to its original power setting for a few minutes more before dropping again. Manifold pressure is a direct indicator of how much power an engine is producing. Now we had was an engine burning oil and significant power surges, though the RPMs remained the same thanks to the aircraft's constant speed props and the prop governors.

I wasn't an airplane mechanic by any means, but I did have a general understanding of the workings of this type of engine and that understanding might keep us above the water. To start with, I understood that turbo chargers make high altitude air thicker by compressing it, allowing the engine to develop power that normally would only be produced in the thicker air at lower altitudes. The turbo charger has a bearing that is lubricated by oil from the engine, and if the bearing was failing, power surges would result. The oil meant to lubricate the bearing was probably leaking past and bleeding out our exhaust as a trail of smoke. The only thing we could do was to reduce power and nurse the engine along. Maybe the oil would last until we landed.

But when the pressure fell into the yellow arc, I had a strong suspicion this wasn't going to happen. This right engine just couldn't last until we reached land. I looked to the north across the expanse of the Gulf to where the Florida coast would appear on the horizon in an hour. What if I nursed the engine until the oil pressure reached the red arc line, then shut it down before any damage was done and continued with the left engine alone? Maneuvering the aircraft around for landing would be the most dangerous phase of our single-engine flight and if I made a miscalculation — came up short of the runway, for example — I could still hope to restart the right engine and have the extra power to slow my descent and reach the grass runway. Nobody taught this procedure during my multi-engine instruction course. I couldn't remember reading about it in any book when I received my multi-engine instructor's rating because it certainly wasn't a by-the-book procedure.

As the oil pressure moved toward the bottom of the yellow arc, I reduced the power to the right engine. Surely this would slow the oil burn. We were currently about 125 miles from the coast in the direction of Cedar Key. We'd burned off a considerable amount of fuel and with this burn went a lot of weight. Maybe Freddie wouldn't have to risk falling out the airstair door.

Beside me, he was looking intently out the front windshield and I couldn't blame him. But for me the last 100 miles or so was always the fun part of a trip. I was getting close to the end of a long day *and* it was the low-level flying phase that keeps us below land-based radar. Flying low gives you a real sense of just how fast you're moving and as a bonus you're down there with interesting stuff: schools of dolphins, large areas of seaweed. In fact, just ahead, a big flock of sea birds were all sitting on the water.

"Watch this," I said.

These birds never let you just fly over them and, sure enough, as soon as they saw us, hundreds of them jumped up and took flight.

"That's crazy!" Freddie laughed. "They're trying to outrun the plane, just like those kids!"

And just like the kids, they flew as fast as they could until we caught up to them, then dove down into the water all at once.

"They think we're a monster predator," I said. "They try to outfly us. They can't, so they hope they can outswim us." And for both of us, the birds were a welcome distraction.

I'd normally fly the low-level leg five to ten feet above the water, but this time I held the altitude to a minimum of 100 feet. If the right engine failed, I could just maintain altitude and cross the shoreline above the trees. The oil pressure was now about a needle's width from entering the red arc.

We flew over the little fishing port of Cedar Key at 100 feet, then climbed to 1,500 feet so as not to attract more attention than necessary. I knew my fly-over crew would be waiting at the field by now, with Big B as their foreman. Big B was Bruce Wilson Sr., a former fishing boat captain in his fifties but now a fugitive like young Glen. He was a big guy — a 300-pounder like Doc Philpot — but as neat and casual as Doc was disheveled and slightly unsavory. Big B was my man at the time for a job like this, dependable and organized, always with a day planner in his hip pocket. About 25 miles from Hatchbend, I called him on the handheld two-meter ham radio I used to communicate with my crew without resorting to the monitored aviation frequencies. There was no response. A few minutes later, I tried again with no success. On the third try, Big B's voice crackled through.

"I've got contact with the unloading crew. Over."

I felt a little wave of relief wash over me. Everything depended on everything else and anything could go wrong anytime.

"Listen, B. We've got a little engine problem here. I'm gonna need someone at the unloading site to go to the nearest store and buy six quarts of oil. I'll have to have it at the site when we land. Over."

"What kind of oil? Over."

Fair question but this was no time for a shopping experience.

"Motor oil. Over."

a smuggler and his wife

A few minutes later we were over Hatchbend and Big B assured me that there were no panting DEA agents on my tail. I made radio contact with the unloading crew minutes away from landing so it was clear that the oil could not be at the strip when I landed. I decided to pull the power back on the bad engine to just a little above an idle — a level called "zero thrust" such that it produced neither thrust nor drag, but just rode along, hopefully without damage. I could see the strip ahead now to the east of the Suwannee and I was certainly not going to shut down the engine now. I held at 1,500 feet and flew west and then north of the airstrip. A long straight-in approach would draw less attention than a circling approach but in fact I was also killing time waiting for the oil to arrive. Less time on the ground the better. I banked again, about a mile out.

"We got the oil and it's on the way. Over."

"Thank you. We're landing."

Like a lot of Suwannee County farmers, Don Boyd had a chicken operation and grew tobacco on his 300 acres. It was no way to get rich, but Don did better than many, raising a family and finding the spare time and money to earn his private pilot's license. On this late afternoon in December, he'd stopped the tractor on the lane from the back acres because there was a pulley that kept squealing and he didn't want another broken belt. He was squinting at that belt when a plane passed overhead in descent at about seven or eight hundred feet. Don looked up as it disappeared behind the trees. It was a twin-engine plane; some sort of cabin class machine and it was either crashing or heading into the old, abandoned grass airstrip two fields over. Don picked up the mike of his CB radio and called his wife.

"Ellie, you hear that? What? Well, turn down the TV. That *plane*. Hear that? It was headed to the old grass airfield and nobody lands there, especially a big plane. What? Well, it *is* my business because they flew right over *my head*. Ellie, you call Grant at the sheriff's office right now and you tell him to get a couple of officers over there and pronto. I'm pretty darn sure they'll find something of interest."

He put the mike down and listened. If there had been a crash, there would have been an explosion of some sort. There was nothing. He picked up the mike again.

"Ellie, you call Grant. Well, call him now, 'fore it's too late. I'm coming back and get the truck. Something's going on."

I taxied to the end of the runway, turned around for a quick getaway and left the engines running. A Ford pickup truck with a camper top was parked at the side of the field. We could load a little over 200 pounds in the car and the remainder onto the bed of the pickup truck, and while we were loading the last bales on the truck, the car arrived with the oil. We quickly juggled the loads. The vehicles raced away for the stash house.

"Hey!" Freddie called. "They left without the bladder tank!"

"Never mind, man! We'll throw it in the woods and come back for it. Just get it out of the plane!"

I jumped up on the wing and climbed to the back of the engine cowling, removed the oil filler cap and began pouring the oil into the engine as fast as possible. Freddie dragged the bladder out of the cabin because if someone checked at an actual airport, that thing would be a dead giveaway that we were smugglers.

The oiling job had been streamlined by the new plastic oil cans. You could now just remove the filler cap, stick the neck of the can in the port and squeeze as hard as you could. Like the Loran C navigation systems that some planes were now equipped with, and the plastic bags we used for money instead of paper ones, these technical miracles since I'd gone to prison were making a smuggler's life so much easier.

I looked up as I was emptying the last oil can. At the other end of the runway, a pickup truck was bearing down on us. I screwed the cap on, jumped off the wing, and ran back to the airstair door.

"Freddie! Company's coming! Get in! We gotta leave *now*!"

I scrambled up to the cockpit and was in the left seat and we'd started rolling while Freddie was still shutting the door. Seemed the truck's driver intended to block our take-off.

My fellow pot smugglers considered our profession non-violent, just as I did, so we never carried any form of weapons. I could only hope whoever was coming down the runway didn't have a gun either but I had no plans to interview him. Freddie hunkered down in the back and I gunned the engines. The driver stopped in the middle of the runway while I was running a desperate calculation. Did I have enough runway to get airborne? I didn't like the math and dropped the flaps to short-field take-off settings. Surely this guy had as much sense as the kids on the bicycles. As though he read my mind, the truck suddenly reversed. This was not his day to be a hero.

The Navajo lifted off the grass strip with the oil pressure on the right engine well within the green arc. I retracted the landing gear and flew out over the trees. It felt good to be airborne again. I fastened my seat belt and was beginning to relax when Freddie came through from the now empty cabin.

"The cabin door is open," he said.

I almost laughed. "What?"

"You took off so fast, I couldn't get it closed."

Who could blame him?

"Just be careful not to fall out, man. I wouldn't be able to go back for you."

The open door was actually no problem. I'd simply fly a little slower than normal airspeed to avoid stressing the hinges. We'd be fine until we reached New Smyrna Beach. This run was history as far as I was concerned. We needed to vacuum out the residue left in the cabin and reinstall the seats before dropping the aircraft at a maintenance facility in New Smyrna Beach. We would then rent an automobile, go home, and call it a day.

Freddie used the six battery-powered vacuum cleaners on the cabin carpet and reinstalled the seats that the unloading crew had thrown in the back of the plane after the pot was unloaded. As we were flying over a large forest in the Palatka area, he tossed the six vacuum cleaners out the open door. I made sure he also tossed the bed sheet we'd lined the floor of the cabin with. If we were checked at the New Smyrna airport, we'd be a clean airplane.

We arrived at twilight and taxied over to a small maintenance facility. It was after hours and no one was around, we took a short walk to a corner store and called a taxi to come pick us up. During the wait for the taxi, I beeped a happy Frenchie and told him of our success.

"We're on our way to the stash house," I said. "I'll give you a call first thing in the morning and we'll coordinate the loading of your cars with your share of the pot."

"C'est beau, mon chum!" He actually laughed out loud. "I can smell dat good weed from 'ere!"

My clothes were covered with oil from my haste in putting the oil in the right engine of the Navajo, so I felt I needed to explain to our taxi driver that our car had broken down on the road. The driver dropped us at the Daytona Airport where we rented a car for the three-hour drive to Lake City.

Before leaving Daytona, I made a phone call to the stash house just to confirm that the pot had reached there safely. My old friend Buddy and one of my unloaders, answered the phone.

"Hey!" I cackled "How's it going, Buddy?".

"Not so good, man." I instantly hated his tone. "Not so good."

"What do you mean, 'not so good'?"

"Right. I mean, the big truck broke down, but the Ford is okay."

"Fine. What's the plan? Is it fixed?"

"The big truck?"

"Yes. The big truck. Are you fixing the big truck right now?"

"The big truck can't be fixed, Billy."

"Fix it anyway, Buddy. Come on, man! We gotta fix that truck! We ..."

"Billy, you don't understand, Billy."

"I damn well do understand! I'll be there in three hours and we'll get the big truck fixed!"

December 17, 1986

It's nearly 11:00 pm. The girls are fast asleep. They look so peaceful with not a care in the world. I tried to read but my mind keeps trying to imagine where in the flight he might be. Is he still in Belize? Over the gulf? Unloading? He isn't home, although he could walk in at any minute. I'm listening for vehicles driving by on Pine Street or a door slamming shut. I'm imagining the key in the door. In the past all my anxiety ceases when the door finally does opens and shuts, and I hear his footsteps coming down the hall. It's a relief I long for tonight.

We drove more or less in silence to Lake City and out to Buddy's house three miles west of town as fast as the speed limit would allow. No use drawing attention.

We sat in Buddy's kitchen. He was the level-headed one and had been waiting patiently to relay the story. I'd known him longer than the rest and trusted this man — "my Indian friend" as I called him — with my life. He fixed me with his dark eyes and in his soft-spoken voice told the story.

As they were leaving the strip, police radios became active on the scanners and they heard sheriff deputies being dispatched to the abandoned airstrip. Upon learning that the sheriff's men were on the way to their location, the troops defaulted to full-blown panic.

For Glen, who'd been with me and Frenchie in Gainesville that day of the chase, it was like the recurrence of an awful nightmare. Buddy led in the Ford with Glen and Big B's son following close behind in the truck. Buddy knew where the stash house was, but Glen didn't. As Buddy raced toward it, Glen was gunning the truck to keep pace but fell further and further behind in the truck. He missed a curve and the truck crashed into the ditch with such force that it knocked the right front tire off its rim. The truck was down and the spare tire and jack were under a half ton of pot. Buddy wouldn't abandon Glen but he had to dump his load first, so he'd be clean. He crossed over U.S. 129, still on a dirt road, and stashed his cargo behind a windrow of brush. As soon as he crossed 129 again, he ran into Big B headed to rescue Glen and Little B. After a quick exchange confirming their location, Buddy started home. Big B reached Glen and his son, who jumped into his car, abandoning the truck and its cargo. Buddy said they didn't have time to change the tire or even try to switch the load to the trunk of Big B's car. Police were in the area, and as it was, they were lucky to not be spotted.

A flat tire had done us in.

"Where's the pot you saved?"

Buddy hesitated. "It's still where I stashed it in the woods."

"Well, *guys*." I looked to Freddie for support. "Let's go get it ... now!"

"Billy, listen. It's not worth the risk, man. It'll be all right. Leave it until tomorrow."

"Tomorrow? Buddy, I've spent months planning this and since I got out of bed almost a day ago, I've flown to Central America and back with a sick engine. I'm definitely not leaving the little bit of pot we've got so's a few cops or someone else could find and split it up between them in the woods. We need to go get it."

I was tired. It was two in the morning and it took us forty minutes to get there by dirt back roads. We were two miles from the airstrip and for sure the only set of headlights in the woods, visible at a great distance. If there were any lawmen still lurking, they'd check out those headlights.

"Okay." I sighed. "You're right, Buddy. Let's leave it for now."

He gave me that reassuring nod that only a good friend can give when he wants to offer a little hope in a bad situation.

I woke up the next morning about nine and beeped Frenchie. He called right back, all happy, and I gave him the news. For a moment he was silent and I thought the line was dead. Then I heard him mutter "Sacra*ment!*" — one of his Quebec swear words.

"Yeah," I said. "It's bad, all right."

"Osti de tabarnac de sacra*ment*, Billy!"

"I *know!*" I offered.

"De câlice de ciboire de criss de *marde!*"

"Well, that's how *I* feel too."

December 18, 1986

I'm 36 today. I feel 56.

Billy didn't miss my birthday but from what I can tell, the load didn't go off as planned. He's tense and aggravated but he's home at least and I can sleep tonight. He took me out to eat but shortly after we got home, he went out again.

I spent the day with Kay and took her out for her birthday. Due to the disaster of a load, I couldn't treat her to a nice gift the way I would have liked. Christmas was going to be a little skinny as well.

That night I and my friend Ronnie drove out to the hidden bales while there was still traffic on the nearby roads. We hauled it to his house and weighed it. Just shy of 150 pounds. The other thousand and fifty pounds were a write-off. I called Frenchie.

"We only saved 150 pounds, but it is now in a secure place."

"Tabernac," is all he said at first, then, "You gotta come to Miami, Billy. You gotta tell da Cubans whad happen. Dos guys, der ugly sometime, you know?"

So, it was Miami Cubans who'd provided the plane. They'd need proof we'd lost most of the load, so I went to Live Oak and bought a copy of the Suwannee Democrat with my fingers crossed. On page one there was a little story headlined "Hot tip busts over 1000 pounds of pot." I packed an overnight bag and caught a plane to Miami. I got a motel room near the airport and beeped Frenchie. When he arrived, I gave him the newspaper and went over the details including the problem with the airplane.

"We godda get de top dollar, Billy. After dis shit, we godda."

"Totally agree, Frenchie. That's your specialty, right?"

"Oui oui. Da top dollar. I tink I get da bes' price in Boston an' in Canada. You go back to da nord Florida. I'll send ya da driver to get de pot and haul it dere."

"Sounds good."

"Whad about da plane? De Cubans, dey wan' me to look after der airplane, for sure."

"We will. I'll have my mechanic up at New Smyrna Beach fix it. We'll go for another load as soon as possible."

"Dat's it! Dat's real good, Billy. Anudder load an' quick!"

I flew home that afternoon and the next day, I drove over to the New Smyrna Beach Airport and talked to George, my mechanic. The Navajo was probably going to need a new turbo charger in the right engine and a new transfer fuel pump for the nacelle tanks. George said to give him a week.

During that week, after Frenchie's man showed up to get the pot and take it north for sale, I met with Doc Philpot and paid him his $5000 for the use of the hangar. He counted it real slow.

"You know, Billy, you're getting an awful bargain here."

"How so, Doc?"

"You think about it. Think what you're getting. A beautiful hangar close to your base, a willing assistant, a master of discretion."

"You're right, Doc. And don't forget the pain in the ass, too."

"I do feel unappreciated, Billy. I must confess that."

"Doc." I massaged my forehead. "Doc, you're the only one who got paid everything he asked for. The rest of us took major haircuts. Please just count your money."

"It appears satisfactory, Billy."

"I hope so, Doc, 'cause I'm going to need your hangar again in short order."

December 23, 1986

Credit cards held out and I finished all my shopping this afternoon. Bought Billy some clothes for Christmas. I wish I could buy him the world, make him happy. Can't wait until the 25th. We're leaving after lunch for west Florida again, this time for a week. We're staying with mama until the 2nd of January. My little family will be together for a week, I am so happy. Just family, no intrusions. Just happy thoughts, happy times. My sister and her family will be there too.

December 28, 1986

Billy showed the girls and my nieces how to shoot a rifle. That lesson lasted about 10 minutes at best. He had them all lined up 14, 12, 9 and 6 beside the pond for a briefing about guns. He gave them the safely lesson and they listened although all they wanted to do was shoot the gun. The first time the gun barrel swung around in the air the gun show was over. They are girls and their attention span is brief before they are on to something new. No boys to hope to teach to hunt —, hahahaha. He is relaxed when we're here, and this is when I know why I came back. I love him so. We are staying in the little house across from the main house — the Love Shack, as he calls it. It has a bedroom, kitchen, bathroom and small living area. It's cold at night but cozy at the same time.

I called Freddie to arrange a meeting at the rest area on I-10 at the Chattahoochee River.

"We're going again right away." I told him. "Before New Year even, as soon as the plane's ready. You up for it?"

"Of course, man."

"All we need is a suitable spot to unload but I'm a bit worried about some of my old places."

"Oh, man. Why didn't you ask me before? I know a ton of duster strips in west Florida. Why don't y'all drive out this way and look at my selection?"

"I think I will, Freddie."

"And if you have a little bit of money, Billy, that will sure help."

"Would three thousand sound okay?"

"Sounds right to me, under the circumstances."

Good thing I had kept a couple of bales back when Frenchie's man picked up the pot. I was able to pay Doc, Buddy, Freddie, and myself a little for our effort. He was generally pretty easy to get along with, Freddie. I knew all three thousand would be gone on blow in a week or so, but that was the man's weakness and I understood it too well.

When we met a few days later, we spent the afternoon touring old duster strips and settled on one deep in the forest along the Florida/Alabama state line, in a cotton field owned by Joe, a farmer friend of Freddie's. For a fee, Joe would post himself down at the end of the only dirt road access and deflect the curiosity of anyone who happened along. Joe liked the extra money he would be getting to help supplement his farming ventures. I liked Joe's laid-back demeanor. He would make a perfect addition to our group.

So, we had a nice airstrip for our next load. Frenchie was busy putting the money together. We had the airplane repairs going forward. We had our pot selling in Boston. Flat tire aside, things were looking up. I could already feel that bump as I set the Navajo down on the West Florida strip with 1,200 pounds of pot in the cabin.

Here was a chance to take a week off before going to pick up the Navajo and I spent most of that week around the house, getting out every morning for a run of three or four miles, a habit I'd acquired while in prison. The rest of the day I'd spend working around the house, cooking a pork loin on the grill or just being with Kay.

Buddy drove me to New Smyrna Beach to pick up the Navajo. It wasn't on the ramp so I assumed it was in the hangar being worked on. I was used to disappointments, but I'd just about had my fill of them, even if it was a single day of delay. When I entered the lobby, I spotted George right away, talking to a customer. He saw me and nodded his head towards his private office.

"Don't tell me," I laughed as I walked in. "You're doing such a great job, it's going to take another day, right?"

George shut the door.

"Actually, Billy, we've had your plane ready for almost three days. I've had it parked on the ramp."

"Oh yeah? Great. I didn't see it there."

"You didn't. Because this morning three federal agents — U.S. Customs and DEA —showed up. They advised me they'd been searching everywhere for that Navajo for weeks and they informed me that the airplane had been awful busy the day it arrived here."

"Busy?"

"They asked me a ton of questions about you, Billy, but I told them I hardly knew you. They requested the keys from my mechanic and this pilot they had with them flew away in your plane."

"Flew away," I repeated weakly.

"That's why it's not on the ramp," said George.

"Tabernac," Frenchie whispered on the phone when I finally called him from the pay phone.

We were both silent for a full half-minute.

"I godda have proof," he finally said.

"What sort of proof?"

"Da newspaper article."

"Another one? What if it's not in the paper?"

"It better be. For me. An' not jus' me."

I returned to New Smyrna Beach a few days later and went straight to the office of the *Observer* paper. My heart was in my throat as I leafed through the latest edition. There it was, on page seven. "Airplane seized at local airport." From there I drove straight to the Gainesville airport and boarded a flight to Miami, checked into the same motel, and waited for Frenchie to arrive. He studied the paper and seemed to take it like a man.

"Ting is, dough, de Cubans want dat farmer's name an' address."

"The one who called the sheriff?"

"Oui. Dey wanna burn 'im out."

"Frenchie. You know that can't happen. Maybe that's how

the Cubans do it in Miami but we're farming folks up here. We don't burn people's houses for reporting an airplane."

"Teach 'im a lesson, dey say."

"No no, Frenchie. Listen, I can stay for the meeting with the Cubans if you want. Talk to them, like."

"Tanks, Billy," he sighed, "but it's okay. Dis is de big-time merde, but I fix it. Tanks for de newspaper. Dey'll believe me now."

While he was struggling with whatever conscience he had, what was really on my mind was getting back to Lake City right away and meeting with Doc. I'd rent his Cessna 210 for the trip. No stopping now.

2

"Doc, you're saying there's something I don't realize about something I do realize?"

I returned to Lake City and went straight to Doc's house. He came to the door bleary eyed and wearing only his pajama bottoms, which wasn't an inspiring sight at that early hour.

"Good morning, young Dekle," he said. He scratched at a two-day stubble of beard and shuffled off in the direction of his kitchen. "Can I assume you're here on account of yet another criminal adventure?"

"You're right, Doc. Is that coffee I smell?"

"It is. And no doubt you're looking to take further advantage of your friend by renting his hangar at some rate far below market."

"Wrong, Doc. That's not why I'm here."

"You don't say. Welcome, then."

"Doc, I'm here because I want to rent your airplane and I intend to pay you generously for it."

"Oh, do you? And why would you want to do that and what would that generous offer be?"

"Customs have seized the Navajo and I'm afraid we'll never see that little plane again. That's why I need you to rent me your Cessna 210 for just one trip for the sum of $40,000. That's double the going rate and half the market value of your plane."

"I do believe you're right Billy, and indeed, I am sorry about your Navajo. I'm also sorry to tell you that the answer is no. And I'm forced to remind you, there's no going price on risking a man's medical career. You take milk, right?"

I sat down at his messy kitchen table because I wanted him to know I meant business.

"Black, Doc. Okay, so three years ago, when you purchased your airplane, I rented it from you and I paid you $25,000 for one trip. Remember that part of that money, $15,000 in fact, was an advance paid up front for your down payment on the airplane and at that time, you were mighty grateful, and you promised to let me rent it for a total of five trips."

"Perfectly true, Billy. All true."

"Then after the first trip you said you'd made a bad deal. You told me about the terrible pressure and worry you were under while I was away on the trip. I was dodging thunderstorms over Central America and the worry was killing you. What did I say, Doc? I laughed and said, no problem. I'll let you chicken out of the deal."

"Very generous of you Billy. Very generous. I still cluck with gratitude."

"So, Doc, how could a businessman like you turn down such a deal as I'm offering?"

"Excellent question, young Billy. Allow me to enlighten you as to my reasoning, which is purely mathematical. On that occasion, if anything had gone wrong, the only ones who would have lost anything would have been you and the finance company. But now, after three years, I've made three years' worth of payments. I've installed a factory re-manufactured engine and paid for it out of my own pocket."

"I appreciate that, Doc."

"So who is now the biggest investor in the airplane?"

"You are."

"See, Billy, my dear young friend, I had no problem gambling with your money and the finance company's money, but only a fool would gamble with his own money. It's just bad arithmetic."

a smuggler and his wife

Frenchie asked for a couple of days and, bless him, in two days he called back to say he'd located a Cessna 310 and a Cessna 210. The 210 was a single engine aircraft and the 310 was a twin. The 210 was almost as fast and would haul almost as much as a 310. The weakest point of the 310 is its undercarriage and I'd be afraid to take it into the unimproved strips we were using, fearful that the gear wouldn't hold up.

I checked the airline schedule the next day for an evening flight to Miami and beeped Frenchie but he didn't respond and neither did his pilot, Ruben, a Cuban American who spoke fluent Spanish and English. The man was rated in helicopter and Lear Jet. His attitude was like that of Val Kilmer's character, Iceman, in Top Gun: a cocky know-it-all. He'd tried to tell me how to fly a load the first time I met him.

I decided to cancel my trip to Miami until we'd made contact. For the remainder of the week and through the weekend I kept trying to beep Frenchie and Ruben. Finally, on Tuesday of the following week, Ruben returned my beep.

"Ruben, man. Wow, I was worried about you. Where are you?"

"At my mom and dad's."

"You didn't return my beeps."

"Didn't get 'em, Billy."

"So, where you been, man?"

"Jail. I'm out on bail."

Oh oh.

"And Frenchie?"

"No bail."

"The Feds thought it was me who piloted the Navajo into Suwannee County. They'd had it under surveillance at the Opalocka Airport the whole time. Remember I was running up the engines for you before you picked it up. They took a ton of pictures of me and that Navajo."

Ruben was sitting on a bench in the lounge area of the airport. I'd flown into Miami on Eastern Airlines that morning.

"Yep." he shook his head. "All that heat you guys ran into at the Holiday Inn in Gainesville came from Frenchie."

"Our little deal?" I was amazed. "It hadn't even happened."

"No, no, no. Frenchie was part of a major weapons operation, Billy. But the deal had been infiltrated by government agents. Their surveillance of Frenchie, that's what caused them to stumble onto our pot operation."

I understood. Frenchie's weapons play plus the farmer reporting the plane and our losing the pot because of the flat tire — that explained why they'd made such an effort to locate the Navajo.

Ruben looked glum.

"It doesn't look good for Frenchie, Billy."

"Well, it depends what they've got on him."

"What they've got? They've got videos of him in a warehouse filled with machine guns and rocket launchers and grenades. They've got videos of him walking up and down aisles filled with heavy-duty weapons and saying, 'I'll take dese and dese and dese.' They tried to arrest him leaving the warehouse and he managed to get to his car and attempt a get-a-way. Woulda looked good on Miami Vice."

We sat in silence for a while.

"What you gonna do now, Ruben?"

"Probably go to jail. Any ideas?"

The Florida countryside glided by below. I stared out the airliner window and pondered my situation. I was fresh out of prison. I'd lost my first load of pot. I'd lost our airplane. I'd lost most of my money. I'd lost a partner to jail.

I'd always liked a challenge.

January 15, 1987

Kim has a boy who likes her and is hanging out around the house. Billy loves to aggravate her about him. He's a skateboarder and Billy tells her "that boy is doing all kinds of tricks out there, you better go out there before he breaks his neck." I know it won't be long before she will be wanting to date. They are growing up too fast.

January 17, 1987

Billy heard that one of the new partners got arrested. He's easily agitated and goes to the bar nearly every night now. I feel like our relationship is slowly dying. What am I doing wrong? Why can I not keep him at home? Almost sixteen years with this man and I still don't know what it is that can hold his attention for longer than a day. Is every marriage like this? Is this all there is to life?

January 20, 1987

I started taking the girls, Kim, Amy and Amy Douberly, Kim's best friend, to Denise Carol Modeling School in Jacksonville. They're all doing very well in the class. The school teaches them runway modeling and etiquette classes. Every other Saturday we drive the 60 miles and spend four hours in class. Billy goes with me sometimes but bores easily, so he leaves me and goes to, who knows, a bar, a strip club. Maybe he's setting up his next deal. It's easier on the girls for me not to ask. They hate the arguing and who can blame them? I hated when my parents argued before they divorced. I said I wouldn't do that to my kids. It's hard to keep promises until you remember why you are trying to keep them.

I remember that afternoon in 1957. Debbie was a toddler maybe one at the most. I was six. My parents were fighting again in the small duplex that we lived in on Camp Street. My mother was yelling about a divorce and my dad was yelling back at her. Their fighting had become an everyday event. I hated it. I crawled under the kitchen table. I could hear Debbie crying in her crib as my dad slammed the door and left. Even at that age I knew something dreadful had just happened. I somehow knew it was something that was no good for our family.

A pilot trying to smuggle without an airplane was like a cowboy trying to round up cattle without a horse. Who did I know who had an airplane?

"Doc, now here's an idea, a real idea. You and I draft up some paperwork that proves you're leasing your Cessna to me. You'd have absolutely no legal responsibility should I get caught and in the unlikely case I *was* caught, I'd just tell the authorities I stole the airplane."

Doc was in his favorite easy chair, munching on Pringles, his preferred brand.

"There's no risk for you here, Doc. None I can see."

He continued to munch.

"Know what, Doc? There's no known case where someone was convicted because his or her airplane was stolen and used for smuggling. Are you aware of that?"

Doc finally set down the bag, probably because it was empty.

"Billy, dear boy." He actually looked sorry. "I've got way too much money in that plane."

The two of us sat a minute without speaking while I waited for him to qualify this. Finally, he spoke.

"What I don't understand is, why you don't just *steal* an airplane?"

I was always against stealing, including airplanes. I'd passed up many opportunities to steal a plane or fly loads in a stolen one. I'd even turned down trips when the owner warned that if I got caught, he'd report the airplane as stolen. Other times, people had said "Here's my airplane. Steal it because I don't want it back. When you finish, just burn it." But I drew the line at making any deal involving an additional crime. And Doc knew this.

These feelings, however, mostly ruled prior to my incarceration. For most people serving time, prison has the opposite effect to the effect the system and the judges intend. My moral compass had changed. The crime of thievery was a minor offense in the prison world. So, my response to Doc was not a list of moral dilemmas. Instead, I pointed out to Doc that finding an airplane parked on a ramp that would have the needed range for overseas flight, was full of fuel, able to carry the load, and ready to be picked up at the exact time the load was ready — that would be next to impossible. For a couple of minutes, we sat again in silence.

"Now what might work," I said, "would be to select several likely airplanes in advance. Then when the load was ready for pick-up, I could get one of the selected planes and take it to a hangar and make a complete inspection, and bladder it and fuel it up and so on."

I looked at Doc inquiringly, but he was getting out of his chair. He shuffled into the kitchen and opened the fridge.

"The trouble with these products," he said, "is they put too much salt in 'em and salt makes you thirsty and you drink too much water and water's no good for you."

"Problem is," I called, "I don't have the hangar needed for this plan."

He came back with a tall glass of cold tea and sat down again.

"No hangar, you say?" I caught just a hint of a smile. "For a fee, of course, you could use *my* hangar."

"Really?"

"I'll even help you find an airplane."

So, he would help me steal a plane but he wouldn't let me use his for a load. Doc maintained a unique way of weighing money against risk. I couldn't fathom his math, but I liked the way the answer came out.

February 1, 1987

I'm concentrating on competition with the dance team. We're practicing every day after school. Before long we need to begin Saturday practices. Having thirty-five girls to love helps take the pressure off our home life. The girls on the team are like my daughters to me. I can be a part of their lives. I love it and them. No one asks about Billy and what he does but they have to wonder — the parents I mean. They all know who Billy is and it's a small town. I can tell by his demeanor that things in his smuggling world aren't going well. He never really gives me the details because he believes this protects me. But not knowing always leaves me with unanswered questions and builds doubts in our relationship. I pick up bits and pieces from conversations, but I don't know most of his so-called associates.

Will I ever have a normal life? What happens in other people's lives? Do their husbands leave in the middle of the night and then days later suddenly come back, like they were on a business trip? Except in my case my husband may never come back.

This is slowly killing me.

A morning early in February. I beeped Glen and brought him up to speed. He loved the plan.

"Okay Billy. Now listen. I've got access to some real magic here."

"I could use some magic."

"This here magic is a magic key ring."

"How magic is it?"

"This key ring contains twenty keys and those twenty keys — or one of them anyway — can open the door and turn on the ignition in most any airplane you'll find."

"That *is* magic," I admitted. "Where *is* that magical ring?"

"A friend of mine is in possession of it, but jeez, Billy. I just remembered you're totally against stealing airplanes, right?"

"It's all circumstances, Glen. Just talk to your friend about that key ring. Tell him you intend to use its powers to do good."

Freddie and I met at an I-10 rest area just east of the Chattahoochee River about halfway between Pensacola and Lake City. I had to tell him about the bust of Frenchie and Ruben in Miami.

"Wait a minute." Freddie shook his head. "You mean it was our pal Frenchie from Tallahassee Federal supplied the Navajo?"

"It was, and I'm afraid our Canadian friend is in serious trouble."

"Wow, man."

"Weapons trafficking. Bad."

"Yeah, yeah. Sure. But Billy, did he know I was involved in the flat tire load?"

"Did you know who my Miami connection was, Freddie?"

"No."

"Right. And my Miami connection didn't know who my co-pilot was."

"I was never sure about Frenchie, Billy. Not really sure."

"If Frenchie weakened and started talking, he could only turn up Glen and me and Glen is already a fugitive."

"But what about you, Billy?"

"You know what Frenchie always said. 'De Canadians, dey don' talk.'"

Which didn't prove altogether true.

Doc seemed to be experiencing something like joy.

"A hangar," he almost burbled when I filled him in. "*That's the indispensable asset* — a hangar for your stolen plane. You are so fortunate, my boy, that you've got a friend like me who has a hangar and is willing to take these risks for a simple fee."

"Yeah, thanks, Doc. It's great."

"Furthermore Billy — and I've never made this offer before — furthermore, I am — and this too for a simple fee — very happy to assist you in locating an airplane to steal."

"You're an amazingly generous man, Doc."

Actually, apart from the thrill factor, tax-free cash without having to invest a penny or risk any of his own assets was exactly Doc's idea of good business. The man was stoked.

"Okay, Doc, so here's how it goes. First, we locate four or five good prospects and then return at night to match up the right keys. Second, we get the load scheduled. Third, the night before the trip, we get the airplane and run it to your hangar. Fourth, we install the extra fuel bladder. Fifth, we go after the load."

"Superb planning, Billy. Now, I want to earn my fee fairly. What's my role?"

"Your role is to scout around smaller airports that have little or no security and target Cessna 210s, Piper-Aztecs, Navajos or anything suitable for just one quick trip. I'll meanwhile obtain the magic key ring I told you about."

February 10, 1987

I may have to kill Kim before she ever reaches 16. She has a mouth on her that begs to be slapped. How can two girls be so different? Amy is laid back, easy going. Kim is just like me, Billy says — fiery hot. Between her and Billy I'm going crazy. No one tells you how hard it is to raise children. We go to church every Sunday and I try to do what is right but Lord, it is trying at times. I guess I was much like Kim when I was her age. My stepmother was 15 years older than me and I gave her a fit with my mouth. Karma gets you sometimes. I wish Billy took more time with the girls. I feel like I am raising them by myself.

I'm remembering 1971. I'd gone with Billy to a refresher course in Tallahassee for his flight instructor's rating in late August. We'd been married a little over 6 months. I wanted children. I knew we — Billy and I — were still learning to be adults but all my friends were pregnant or already had children. Isn't that what you are supposed to do after marriage? Billy cut me off every time I'd talk about it. I guess I pushed the issue too much. He thought it would take time away from us and away from him. But I continued to bring it up every time I got the chance.

I'd been by the pool all day thinking about it and when Billy got back to the room I waited until he got out of the shower before I began the conversation.

"So, when we have a baby do you want a boy or girl?"

I thought that I was being casual about it.

"Don't care."

"Well, you must care. Do you not want a baby?"

"If you want one."

He was sitting at the desk reviewing the lesson the instructor had given that day. He got up as I was still talking about babies and went to the suitcase. He picked up my pack of birth control pills and walked to the motel bathroom.

"What are you doing?"

He began pushing out the pills one by one into the toilet.

"Hey, Billy! Those are my birth control pills!"

"Yeah, I know. If you keep taking them then all you are going to do is keep talking about babies, so this is the only way to stop talking about it."

I did a little freak out because I suppose the realization that I might now really get pregnant set in. We were laughing about it within the hour as we crawled into the bed that night. I figured what the heck, I could get the prescription filled next month anyway. Little did I know. Kimberlee would be on the way before that.

It goes almost without saying that Glen's friends wanted in on the deal and were now holding the keys for ransom. This was the fee phase of any deal. They wanted in on the deal in exchange. Fees, fees, fees. But it turned out that the man with the key ring was Big B, the boat captain I'd used on the flat tire load. I had a feel for Big B and told Glen I'd pay no extra fee for the ring of keys but would happily pay Big B to work on the unloading crew.

"If he doesn't like that he can take his keys and go get his own load and we'll work for him as *his* unloading crew."

As I suspected, Big B relinquished the key ring. It didn't take a rocket scientist to figure out it wasn't going to do him any good to hang on to them. With that taken care of, I laid plans for the next load.

The unloading site that Freddie got for us in West Florida would cost a landing fee, but I'd gladly pay where safety was involved.

A final logistical challenge: it's one thing to fly out of an airport with a stolen airplane, but the wise man will not land that stolen airplane back in an airport. I decided to leave the plane at the unloading site. But that site couldn't be Joe's field because it would bring the heat down on him. We needed a strip in the real boonies but the strip didn't need to be long enough to take off from. Our only interest was landing and we'd be happy to give the police something to do, give the locals something to talk about. Perfect.

I was starting to feel the best I'd felt since the earlier disaster. We had direction. We had a plan.

Doc reported back the next afternoon that he had located many potential targets and he was ready to go forward.

"What? You don't have the keys yet? Come on Billy! Let's get moving on this!"

The man was pushing, ready, and that was a quality I liked. I explained that Big B was the holder of the keys and he didn't want to let them go without knowing what was in it for him.

"I understand," said Doc, which was an understatement for sure.

Our anniversary was close and I needed to get something for Kay, even something small. My thoughts slipped back to a day in February 1971 when I was as sick as I'd ever been in my life. It was 2:45 pm and I was behind the First Baptist Church throwing up for the third time in thirty minutes — dry heaves mostly. My brother Bob was shaking his head watching me. The night before about a dozen of my friends had thrown me a bachelor party, tying one on for my last night of freedom. The whiskey had flowed like water. We were bulldogging cows off the hood of a pickup truck; we were so drunk. Bob was the designated driver and finally got me home around 4:00 am.

Mom tried to get me to eat something in the morning but just the thought of food made me start throwing up. I'd been hung over before but never like this. Several hundred people were to attend the wedding. The thought of Kay killing me if I didn't or couldn't show up entered my head at several points. Mrs. Summers, the wedding director, finally found us and told me we had to start. As I walked into the side door of the church with Bob and the preacher, I saw the church was full, even the balcony had people in it.

"Lord, please don't let me throw up in front of these people," I prayed in my misery. "And Lord, especially don't let me throw up on Kay's dress."

I made it through the ceremony and even managed a smile for the hundreds of pictures people took. On the ride to the Woman's Club, Kay looked at me.

"What is wrong with you, Billy?"

I confessed that I was sick from the night before and I'd almost thrown up on the preacher's shoes.

"You had better hold it together through this reception, Mr. Dekle. And you force the cake and champagne down, too. You understand?"

I was to fly us to Freeport, Bahamas for the first night of our honeymoon but I knew after taking off from Lake City that was not going to happen. I put the airplane down at the Ocala airport thirty minutes after takeoff and we spent our first night in a small motel just off I-75. I managed to consummate the marriage, but it was definitely not my best performance. Kay reminds me of it every so often. I don't always use the best judgement and it could have been the end before we ever got started. But I ended up with the best wife a man could have.

February 20, 1987

Well, we've made it 16 years today. I guess that year total depends on if you're counting the years we were divorced or not. Billy doesn't count them, so he says 16 years. Wow, if I had known now what I didn't know then, would I have walked down that aisle? I was so naïve; I don't know if I really had any idea what life was all about then. Hell, do I know what it's about now? I've heard Billy tell me so many times, "Baby Love, everything is going to be all right," I guess I just put one foot in front of the other and don't think about it much anymore. It doesn't really matter anyway. Life goes on and you have to get up and face whatever the devil throws at you that day. Sometimes God says, "That's enough, you sorry good-for-nothing devil!" Then a person sees the sunlight and knows everything will be okay. I wish there were more of those days. I worry about the possibility of being alone. What if he's incarcerated again? How would I make ends meet? He doesn't think about how his decisions affect other people, nor do I think he cares. He doesn't intentionally mean to hurt me, but he does. The smuggling, his increasing addiction, the unfaithfulness — they face me daily. This — and raising two teenage girls and living like I'm in a glass house — it's all driving me nuts. I need an outlet, someone to confide in. I feel like the steel ball in a pinball machine. I bounce from one side to the other, band-aiding one problem and moving to the next until someday I finally drop like the ball in the hole.

When Glen wasn't organizing a deal, he was surfing the Atlantic and soaking up the sun in Daytona. I told him I needed the keys. He smiled.

"Okay, man. Great. Just give me two days and beep me."

His nonchalance — the opposite of Doc and the essence of the very drug we were trying to smuggle — was calming. It takes many types to make a team.

March 15, 1987

I've been substituting at the middle school and high school lately trying to earn some extra cash. I know many of the teachers because I worked in the system before I divorced Billy in the late 70s. Billy's mother is also a teacher, so I stay booked up. I don't make as much as I would if I was a certified teacher, but it helps between Billy's deals, which haven't been going so well. If he isn't being followed by the law, his airplane is being confiscated or he loses a load. I try not to be involved but with Dr. Creepy coming by the house all the time, I can't help but overhear some of the crazy shit going on. Between Dr. Creepy and this pilot Freddie from west Florida, Billy stays on the go. I've quit asking where he's going. Better not to know.

March 28, 1987

The girls are on spring break and we've gone over to the beach and down to the river skiing and wakeboarding. We finished the tryouts for the next year's dance team before school let out and Kim made the high school dance team. I will miss her not being on my team but Amy will be the co-captain next year so we'll be together. Billy has been home all week; he does his morning run and then we have breakfast together. We're getting along much better than last month. I just pray it continues.

I spent a few days hanging out at home that early April and the weather was still nice in north Florida. I ran four miles every morning, then I helped Kay cook and generally enjoyed the time with my family. Preparing food and cooking was something I loved doing, especially with Kay, always a time of joyful torment for me: home with my girl, but knowing a job was on the horizon. The settled calm before the anticipated rush. Doc dropped by every night for a visit and gave Kay the creeps, but he'd been busy shopping for more planes and wanted me to check them out.

"Some things can't be forced, Doc."

Two days later, I met Glen at the Lake City Holiday Inn and he had the key ring. It was an ordinary key ring — a large round metal loop with probably 15 to 20 keys the size that open filing cabinets.

"And hey, Billy." He gave me a wink. "Seems like Big B is ready to work on the unloading crew."

So everyone involved was satisfied and onboard.

Glen and I drove an old Buick Riviera that belonged to Big B for several hours to a farmhouse in the Bristol and Blountstown area west of Tallahassee. Our contact man, Sal, was a member of a hunting club that had access to large tracts of land owned by a paper company. At a truck stop, Glen bought a road map that had all the dirt roads, campgrounds, and parks shown on it. We were looking for a straight spot long enough to land an airplane on. After zeroing in on several prospective sites we took Sal's 4-wheel drive pickup and drove through the woods for over two hours. Every straightaway we found was ether too sandy or the tree line was too close to the road. Finding a suitable spot was looking like a bigger job than we anticipated. Three or four miles east of Bristol in the Telogia Creek area, we turned off highway 20 and drove about 200 yards through a heavy wooded area and suddenly we entered a big clearing where the road went for about a mile over straight and smooth land. It looked almost too good to be true.

We headed home. One little problem: how were we going to come up with the down payment for our cargo?

"I can see if I can talk Johnny into fronting the load without a down payment." Glen suggested. "Or maybe I can talk some prospective buyers into an upfront loan."

The kid's easy way of things was just what was needed for that kind of tricky negotiation.

April 2, 1987

Amy wanted to know why that doctor keeps coming by the house to see her daddy? Is daddy sick? I wanted to say, no. your daddy isn't, but the doctor is! That man gives me the creeps. He's like a leech. When I open the door, I just roll my eyes and yell "Billy!" I don't even acknowledge he is standing there anymore. Billy thinks it's funny, I don't.

April 3, 1987

Doc is coming by the house every day — sometimes two and three times a day. I know a deal is about to happen, but I don't trust that man or this guy Freddie from west Florida. I hate it that Billy does. They are going to get him caught but nothing I can say will stop Billy and I'm afraid he's experimenting with more and more drugs. His friends out west are pulling him farther away from us.

I've signed a short-term contract with the school system until the end of term. One of the teachers will be out and I'll have her classes for the next month and a half. I'm excited. I do love teaching and it will be a good income for us. I'm practicing dance three times a week at the middle school, so my calendar stays full. Not much time for anything else.

Doc had visited the Ocala Airport and seen several Cessna 210s parked on the ramp. We spent part of the day planning and late that night he picked me up at my house and we flew to Ocala. Instead of just landing and taxiing up to the ramp, Doc shot a few touch-and-go landings.

"This is a waste of time, Doc."

"A reconnaissance operation, my boy. Can't have too much information."

More like old Doc was starring in his own private action movie.

"You ready to go in and try the keys?" he finally asked, then banked and landed, taxied to the ramp and parked his plane in the transit area between two other airplanes. We sat for a few minutes discussing strategy and waiting to see if anyone was going to come out of the buildings. If someone were there, we'd just buy some gas, leave for the next airport and try again.

After ten minutes of knocking on doors, it was apparent that we were the only people at the Ocala Airport that night. We gave it a little more time, then broke out our key ring and started to work. There were three 210s sitting on the ramp and I started with the one least visible. I tried all twenty keys with no luck. I started again, going slower that time, jiggling the keys up and down, pulling them out a fraction of an inch to turn them. Just as I decided the keys had no magic, the lock turned. I climbed into the cockpit and jiggled the key in the magneto switch.

In 45 minutes, I had keys marked for three Cessna 210s and a Cessna 182 RG. These sporty little airplanes didn't have enough range to safely get us back from Belize to our West Florida dirt road, but a bladder tank would solve that, even if it would take extra time and work in an already very busy night. All in all, we were satisfied.

Doc was the only one who made any real money out of the flat tire fiasco and I wanted to find a place this time for Freddie, who was ready to risk his ass. These planes were all going to require a bladder tank. Glen was my principal partner and I approached him about it.

"Glen, listen, man. I'm going to have to go down and steal the airplane, bring it back to Doc's hangar, install the bladder, and fill it with fuel. I'll be exhausted. Fourteen hours of hard flying isn't a wise thing to do in such a state. What do you think about me getting everything ready and Freddie flying the trip?"

"Hey, dude. Whatever you think is best, man."

He ran his fingers through his blonde hair and grinned. In some situations, an easygoing nature is a huge asset.

When Freddie and I met the next day we drove out to the dirt road near Telogia Creek. On the way I brought him up to date on our progress and proposed he join us.

"Shit, Billy. I'm totally aboard. You know that man." Freddie, impulsive with just the right amount of crazy, never took much time to decide. We spent an hour so he could get a fix on the surroundings.

"I could find this in the dark, man."

I dropped him back at his house.

"Stay close to the phone, Freddie!" I shouted as I drove away. "And keep your overnight bag packed!"

I beeped Glen to let him know that everything was set on our end and he needed to contact Johnny in Belize. He called back within a minute.

"News flash, Billy! Johnny's agreed to front us a 700-pound load — no down payment!"

"We're off and running then!"

a smuggler and his wife

The landing strip in Belize was a long, wide road on private land that I'd used many times, years earlier. I could easily mark it on a map for Freddie and give him the landmarks to look for. One of the biggest problems for a pilot going south of the border for a load was finding the right strip to land on. In Colombia, out on the Peninsula de La Guajira, there were many strips for landing. If a pilot selected the wrong one, it could cost him his life. The people of Belize possessed a more mellow mentality but locating the right strip remained critical for any pilot. At the very least, he didn't want to be short on fuel, flying around in circles, burning gas, attracting attention.

For all that, I was getting the right vibes about this load. We had a good plan, a good airplane, a good strip on both ends, and a good pilot. I called Freddie. He'd be in Lake City no later than the following evening. I passed this on to Glen and told him I'd call back around noon the next day. By that time, he should have confirmed the deal with Johnny and the mission would be a go. Doc's little eyes were meanwhile glittering with excitement. He said he'd pick me up at my house shortly before noon. I headed home to be with Kay and my girls for the rest of the day.

Doc came by on schedule. We then drove by one of his vacant rental houses where he'd allowed me to store our smuggling equipment. We checked the fuel bladder, pump, hoses, filters, valves, and all connector fittings to be sure we had everything. I confirmed that the police scanner batteries were in good shape and looked over the packs of aeronautical charts to make sure they covered the areas we needed.

We located a large bank of pay phones and I beeped Glen. The phone rang a minute later. Glen had talked with Johnny and everything was on go for the next morning at nine, Belize time. This is one-time zone different from our zone. It would be 10:00 a.m. in Lake City. In a Cessna 210, from Lake City to Belize would be a six-hour trip plus or minus a few minutes. This meant Freddie needed to take off by 3 a.m. at the latest. I figured if we could get

81

the plane to Doc's hangar by midnight, we should have plenty of time to install the bladder and fuel it for a 3 a.m. takeoff.

Doc took me home with a promise to be at my house by five that evening. Three hours later Freddie rang and gave me his location and room number and twenty minutes after that I was knocking at his door. With a world aeronautical chart, we went over the location of the road in Belize that he would be using as a landing and loading strip and the landmarks he'd be looking for in the area.

"Get some rest, buddy." I patted his shoulder. I want you to be alert for your 3 a.m. takeoff."

Doc picked me up at five. We retrieved the smuggling equipment from the vacant house and drove to the Lake City airport. On our way to the hangars, we noticed one of the middle doors was open just down from Doc's hangar. Inside was a Cessna 210, her sporty white frame reflecting the headlights of passersby.

"Hell, Doc," I said. "We don't have to go to Ocala. There's our airplane right there."

"No, Billy." Doc's tone was firm. "You'd be crazy to take that airplane and bring the heat right here to Lake City."

"You're right, you're right." I sat back in my seat. "We need to stick to our plan."

I was a little disappointed, but we pulled Doc's plane out of his hangar, jumped in and took off. We arrived at the Ocala Airport traffic pattern shortly before midnight. Just as before, Doc wanted to shoot touch-and-go landings, a ploy he felt justified our presence, before making a full stop landing and going straight up to the airplanes. On our first couple of touch and go landings it looked as if the airport was deserted.

"Doc, please. We're wasting valuable time circling the airport. Land this sucker."

Below, a set of headlights appeared and started moving slowly between the rows of airplanes. We flew close enough to see that

a smuggler and his wife

it was a county deputy sheriff's car. We made a few more rounds keeping our eyes on the deputy, hoping that he would leave. He parked on the ramp between two airplanes and stayed put.

It was getting late.

"Doc," I pleaded. "Let's go back to Lake City and get the Cessna 210. It's just waiting for us in that open hangar."

But Doc hung onto the yoke of his plane and he had a determined look I rarely saw.

"Billy, my boy, a good idea must give way to a better idea. I was through the Leesburg airport a few days ago and I saw one of the airplanes there that we matched a key to in Ocala."

"Really?"

"I'm confident."

"Okay then. Leesburg it is. Let's go right now."

He banked to the south and away we went, landing at a dead Leesburg Airport well after midnight. He taxied over to the buildings and parked. A routine knocking on all the office doors proved we had the airport to ourselves. Doc pointed the airplane out and handed me the matching key, then posted himself as a lookout at a safe distance. I walked straight up to the airplane and untied the rope tie-downs that secured it to the ground in case of gusty winds. I inserted the key into the door lock on the pilot's side door. Nothing happened. I jiggled it up and down and side-to-side to unlock the door; it still didn't work. I retied the airplane and with some effort walked calmly back over to Doc.

"You gave me the wrong key, Doc."

"That's impossible, Billy."

"Doc?" I raised my voice a decibel. "If I have the right key, then we have the wrong airplane. Which is it?"

He dug out another key.

"Yeah, yeah. Maybe you're right. This is the key."

I walked back over to the airplane but didn't untie anything. I tried the new key. No luck. Suddenly Doc whistled and began walking my way. There were some headlights at the other end of the airport working their way towards us. The airplane was sitting next to a service road with a wooded area on the other side. We walked a short distance into the woods and took up a vantage point that allowed us to observe the approaching headlights. A local police car was making its rounds.

"Doc, listen," I hissed. "I'm almost positive we never tried keys on this airplane before." "This airplane has a different kind of wing tank drain plug, a plug like I've never seen. The drain plug on this plane has a threaded stud bolt screwed into the bottom of the fuel tank. Any drain plugs I've seen before had a head that a wrench would fit so it could be turned."

"What's the significance?"

"We've got a problem even if we do find keys that fit. We gotta get this baby back to your hangar and see if our bladder hookup is compatible with the drain sump. Give me all the keys. Oh man. We're running way behind."

The patrolman took his time finishing his rounds. Doc gave me all the keys and after only a few tries I was in the cockpit and had the magneto switch on. I jumped back out, untied the tie-downs, got back in, and started the engine.

"Hustle it, Doc!" I yelled.

I rolled down the taxiway to the runway for takeoff. My newly acquired airplane was a late model Cessna 182 RG — clean, well equipped, a high-dollar single-engine general aviation aircraft and basically a little brother to the Cessna 210. The 210 is a six-seater where the 182 has only four seats but both have retractable landing gear. The 210 has a more powerful engine, which employs a Continental IO-520 and produces from 285 to 310 horsepower. The Cessna 182 RG gets its 235 horsepower from a Lycoming IO-540 engine. The numbers 520 and 540 represent the size of the engine displacement in cubic inches.

After a routine takeoff from Leesburg airport, I headed back to Lake City. The airplane performed flawlessly, though of course we could fit 150 pounds less pot in the cabin. Still, I was flying it and the price was right. My biggest problem now was the clock. It was getting close to 2 a.m. We wouldn't be able to meet our 3 a.m. departure time.

On the flight to Lake City, I found myself mesmerized — I often experienced this — by the beauty of the stars above and the twinkling of the world's lights below. Doc landed first and opened the hangar door as I swung the 182 around in front of the door and shut down the engine. We pushed the airplane into his hangar and quickly closed the door. I grabbed the tools and speedily went to work removing the seats so the bladder would lie on the floor.

All us smugglers had a soft spot for bladder tanks and I'd used one as recently as the flat tire occasion. We couldn't conduct our business without them because your average private plane owner doesn't often fly to another continent for the fun of it. These specialized accessories are like waterbeds made of very tough black rubber and rigged to feed fuel to a wing tank. As the fuel leaves, the bladder collapses in on itself. The bladder has two holes, one about 2 ½ inches, used to fill it, and another 3/8-inch hole used to attach the feed line to the airplane tank. My favored method of connecting the long-range fuel bladder to a Cessna 210 or 182 was to drill a half-inch hole through the side of the airplane or through the Plexiglas side window. I'd attach one end of the fuel line to the small outlet hole in the bladder and stick the other end through the hole in the side window and run the hose outside to connect to the sump drain on the wing tank. Before connecting it to the wing tank I'd splice in an on/off valve to prevent fuel from gravity feeding down from the wing tank to the bladder and I'd also splice into the line a fuel filter and a pump in order to pump fuel from the bladder up to the wing tank. Operating the bladder is simple: burn the fuel out of the wing tank, open the valve and turn on the pump to refill the wing tank. Once full, close the valve, turn off the pump and repeat the procedure as necessary.

As soon as I had the seats out, I positioned the bladder in the airplane. With the vice-grip pliers, I started to remove the stud from the bottom of the wing at the drain location. The late fall air had a stickiness to it and the longer I worked the more humid it felt. Soon we'll know if this trip is going to happen, I thought to myself. Everything now hinged on whether the fitting was compatible in size and whether it would thread to the fitting on the end of my fuel line. If not, we had no choice but to cancel the trip for one day and find a fitting that would work.

I focused my attention, locked onto the fitting with the vice-grip pliers and started to turn. The stud would not budge. I tried harder and could see the jaws of the vice-grips cutting into the stud. To my dismay it still would not move. I never dreamed that a stud would be that difficult to remove. After more tries, the pliers only cut deeper and started removing the threads from the stud. The pliers slipped along with my grip and any hope of this trip happening. I went to the stud on the other wing tank with the same results. It was now evident that the vise-grips would not do the job. What we needed was a Stillson pipe wrench and we didn't have one. I hung my head, sweat dripped from my brow. I looked at Doc.

"We're going to have to delay the trip for a day until we get the right tools to remove the stud." I tried to sound resolved. "Guess the people in Leesburg probably won't miss this airplane for one day."

Doc was scowling.

"Billy, there's no way this stolen rig is staying in my hangar for even one day. It's out of here before daylight."

"Wow, Doc. I see you can be a determined old coot."

"I can indeed."

"Stubborn, even."

"That too."

For sure there was no changing his mind and he might even be right. It really would be stupid for him to get caught with a stolen airplane in his hangar, especially when all we had to do was go and get another one. For now, we were out of time and the airplane had to go.

"Where are we going to take it?" I wondered aloud. Cross City? Williston? Back to Leesburg?"

Doc stepped in and I could see he was relishing taking command.

"No. Let's do Keystone."

"Keystone?"

"Because of its proximity to Jacksonville. The FBI will be sure to think that whoever was responsible was from Jacksonville. That'll take any heat away from Lake City." His mind was set and I agreed.

"Okay, Doc. Let's get going so we can get back to Lake City before daylight catches us."

"And maintain radio silence on the way," he suggested, which did seem sensible. I was flying a stolen aircraft.

I got in the 182 RG, cranked it up and took off with my friend right behind me. The flight to Keystone was uneventful with a clear sky and unlimited visibility. One couldn't ask for a more beautiful night for flying. I shook my head. Such a shame that we could not get the stud out of the wing tank. I trailed behind Doc two or three miles and saw him touch down at Keystone. He immediately keyed his mike twice on frequency 122.8, the Unicom frequency, our all-clear signal. I made a straight in, blackout approach. There was enough moonlight, no need of landing lights or taxi lights. The airport was silent as I rolled to the end of the runway and I counted eight deer feeding on the grass at the side. We were alone. I pulled up beside Doc on the taxiway and shut down the 182. I sprayed the inside of the cabin with the powder-type

87

fire extinguisher to leave a thick coat of white all over the interior of the plane. So much for fingerprints or any other evidence that I may have overlooked. I was of course wearing my golf gloves. I climbed into Doc's plane and took the empty extinguisher canister with me. He took off and remained low, just over the treetops. Instead of turning towards Lake City he turned south.

Where are you going, Doc, and why ain't you climbing?"

"I'm avoiding radar so as not to be traced back to Lake City."

The man was certainly our security detail for the night.

As we flew south of Keystone at tree top level, we passed over Lake Geneva. I opened the side window and tossed the fire-extinguisher. Doc made a loop around the lake and headed towards Gainesville and then Lake City, never climbing above tree level.

We arrived back before daybreak and stored Doc's airplane in his hangar. Before leaving, I stopped at the open hangar, the one with the 210 inside. On impulse, I tried one of my keys on the door and it worked. I tried it on the magneto switch, and it worked again. I locked the door again.

"This is the airplane we are going to use," I said.

His face fell a bit as he realized he'd won several points that night, but I'd won the match.

"Cheer up, Doc. I was sure of this one from the start and of course you're welcome to help me bladder the plane. Yeah, true, I won't need your hangar because this one comes with its own, but hey, there's more adventures coming up."

"I was prepared to make you a great deal," he muttered.

"I'm sure you were, Doc. But save it — I'll need it another time."

a smuggler and his wife

I drove out to the motel, woke Freddie, and brought him up to speed before I went home. By this time, it was daylight, so I beeped Glen and gave him the bad news and then the good news.

"I have another plane in a hangar at the Lake City airport," I explained. "I'm dead tired and need to get a few hours' sleep but after that I'll be back up and running. Tell Johnny and his crew not to get discouraged. This is going to happen tomorrow for sure."

April 14, 1987

I should know by now that when Billy goes on a pot run, maybe 7 or 8 hours after he's left, I might hear the key in the door and he's walking down the hall. The deal fell through, the airplane malfunctioned, the load wasn't ready, he couldn't get in touch with somebody. When he leaves I place my mind in robot mode: let no one see you're worried, show no emotion, don't let the kids see you're worried if he doesn't come home on schedule. Then suddenly, there he is, back home. I get irritated and start complaining and he says, "Why are you complaining? I'm home. You didn't want me to go in the first place, did you? Make up your mind."

Well, hell no, Billy. I didn't want you to go but I don't want to be on some emotional roller coaster ride either, you idiot!

I slept four or five hours until shortly after noon. I woke in problem-solving mode. The 210 was already in its own hangar so we could use Doc's hangar for staging. The hangar doors faced U.S. Highway 90 and the plane would be visible to car traffic. I decided to loosen a sheet of siding on the back of the hangar to provide temporary access.

Doc and I met about an hour later at another one of his vacant rental houses. I asked him to go out to the airport and see exactly how the siding was attached because we would need tools to remove it.

"Billy, I don't say you're a fool but you're committing a crime in your own backyard."

"I understand, Doc. Please don't tell on me. Just do this recon please."

He went off grumbling but returned with good news. The sheet-metal siding was attached with small screws with nut-type heads accessible from the outside. I dispatched him to a hardware store to buy the tools.

It was 10 p.m. when Doc picked me up. We went to a pay phone and called Freddie. He'd be on standby until we were ready to take off. Doc and I rode out to the airport, where everything seemed quiet. He drove right on by.

"Doc, you just missed the turn off."

"Billy, we need to look things over really good before we drive into the parking lot. Do not argue, please."

He drove about three miles past the turn off and turned around. The entire area was dead quiet. We headed back and Doc drove past the entrance again.

"Doc, what are you doing? We need to get to work!"

"I think I saw a set of headlights and I don't want anyone see us pulling into the parking lot."

I was losing patience.

"Man, no one will care or even remember your car driving up to this airport. But if someone sees us driving back and forth in front of the entrance road, speeding up and slowing down, they just might remember that kind of strange behavior."

As though he hadn't heard a word, Doc drove back past the airport another three miles and then finally turned around. As we begin our run for the third pass, we were on the verge of a full-fledged argument. I took a deep breath.

"Doc?" — my tone was calm — "Doc, please turn in and let's get started doing what we need to do before time becomes a factor."

He was either listening to me or satisfied that the coast was clear. He parked next to the access gate that leads to the ramp and hangars. As soon as he stopped the engine, and before I could get out, he said, "Don't get out."

"What do you mean, don't get out?"

"We need to sit in the car five minutes to make sure no one is around."

Well, we were in the parking lot. I decided not to protest. It became apparent that we were the only people on the general aviation side of the airport that night.

"Billy, I think the time is right for us to go now." We both got out and met at the trunk of the car. Doc had his big key chain in hand, which must have held 40 or 50 keys, and he quickly located the trunk key. I reached in, grabbed the bladder, the hose, and the fuel pump. He took the tools and a police scanner and closed the trunk. We then went through the gate and out to Doc's hangar. He cracked one of the doors just enough for us to pass through. We went inside and organized our tools and equipment, then turned on the scanner.

The front door to the hangar with our target airplane was closed and secured with a padlock. We were prepared for that; it posed no problem since we had a set of three-foot bolt-cutters. The lock in fact was an advantage for us because we would be working behind a secured door.

We took out our electric screwdriver and installed the proper fitting that adapted to the nut-head screws securing the siding to the hangar. I slipped out of the door, went around to the back of the hangars, stepped off the distance I felt was the back center of our target hangar, located a seam in the siding and removed the sheet metal screws. I pulled the siding sheet out enough to shine a flashlight into the hangar and was relieved to see the 210 inside. I removed more screws and entered the hangar. With the proper key I opened the door to the cab of the 210 and tried the key in the magneto switch to ensure that there would be no problem cranking the engine. I turned on the master switch and checked the fuel gauges. They both indicated well below half-full. I'd dared to hope we'd only have to install and fill the 50-gallon bladder because many pilots fill their tanks at the end of the day to prevent condensation. Unfortunately, not the owner of this little 210. Time was ticking.

Doc had a 55-gallon drum of fuel in his hangar that he'd drained from his fuel tanks over the past week in anticipation of our needing to fill the bladder. Now we'd have to drain more fuel from his plane.

I quickly removed the seats and started drilling the one-inch hole in the passenger's rear side Plexiglass window. I was feeling an urgency while I worked and pushed the hand drill right through the window leaving a big, jagged hole. There was going be a little wind noise. We'd live with that. I returned to Doc's hangar for the bladder and some fuel. He'd pumped two five-gallon cans full of aviation gas from the drum. I glanced at my watch. The time was 11:45 pm, which gave us sufficient time to have the airplane ready for a 3 a.m. departure. Doc returned with me and carried gas cans to the other hangar while I carried the bladder, hoses, and pump. We entered through the back and I positioned the bladder out flat on the floor of the aircraft. Working quickly, I ran the fuel line through the hole in the window and removed the drain plug from the wing tank. Gas began pouring out of the hole and running down my arms, drenching my clothes until I'd finally screwed in the line fitting. I entered the passenger cabin and held the filler neck of the bladder so that Doc could start pouring in the fuel.

There were noises and voices outside. We froze. I met Doc's eyes. My heart sort of kicked my stomach just before my brain caused my body to respond. I could see Doc's body tense up. Slowly, silently I put down the gas can and listened. I climbed out of the airplane, trying to move weightlessly with each step.

"Doc," I mouthed almost silently. "Turn on the scanner."

I listened for a few minutes then eased out through the siding, walked around the backside and peeked around the corner. A half-dozen kids were riding up and down the ramp on skateboards. I exhaled. They were having the time of their lives and so was I. I slipped back into the hangar, where Doc stood in a sort of paralytic shock.

"We've got a job to do, Doc," I reminded him.

We resumed pouring fuel into the bladder. When the cans were empty, we went back to Doc's hangar and refilled the two cans plus two more and returned and poured 20 more gallons into the bladder. This brought the bladder fuel up to the 30-gallon level. Another trip emptied the drum and brought the bladder up to the 50-gallon mark. Outside, the skateboarders had either run out of energy or reached their curfew.

By 12:30 a.m. we still had to fill the wing tanks from five-gallon gas cans. The only fuel left since we emptied the 55-gallon drum was in the wing tanks of Doc's plane. Our only option was to use a piece of garden hose commonly known in our area as a "Georgia credit card" to siphon gas from Doc's airplane. This went quickly while the fuel level in Doc's tanks was high, but as the fuel level lowered, it ran slower and slower until it stopped. Doc's plane had been tapped out. With the clock approaching 1:30 a.m. we moved our siphoning operation to the ramp, where there was a low-wing airplane parked. Doc sucked gas from the hose and appeared to slosh it around in his mouth a bit before he spat it out.

"Hmm," he said quietly, "I do believe I prefer the cleaner taste of 100-octane low-lead over 80-octane."

We were dog tired and covered in gas and would have ignited with the smallest spark, but we were happy.

On the way to pick up my car we stopped at a pay phone and I called Freddie. Doc dropped me off at my car and we transferred the bolt cutters. I drove the short distance out to I-75 and met Freddie at his door. He was ready. We pulled back into the airport at 2:40 — perfect timing.

Just as I put the car in park at the airport, headlights appeared on the highway. Freddie and I sat in silence as they drew nearer. I squinted into the darkness. It was Doc. I couldn't blame the man for wanting to see the plane take off; he'd invested so much time and effort in our venture.

I grabbed the bolt cutters. We passed through the main gate and made a beeline down the ramp to the hangar door. I snipped the lock and lifted the center part of the hangar like a garage door. We slid open the two side doors and pulled the 210 straight out on to the ramp. Freddie hopped in the pilot's seat, which was the only secured seat; the others were stacked in back on top of the bladder, destined to become welcome additions to the furnishings of one of our loading crew's Belize residence. Freddie started the engine and we shook hands as I wished him luck. He closed the door and taxied to the runway. I closed the side doors and laughed quietly to see Doc still cruising up and down US 90. The middle door would not pull down. That was probably why it was open the night before when I spotted the plane in the hangar. I could hear Freddie running up the engine at the far end of the runway while I tried again to close the door with no success. I left it and made my way to my car. Freddie was in the air. It was a couple of minutes before 3 a.m.

A short distance from the airport Doc pulled alongside me and motioned for me to follow him. We arrived at one of his vacant rental houses and went in to talk.

"Why did you leave the hangar door open?"

"The door was jammed, so I left it."

"Hmm. So, what are your plans for the rest of the day?"

"I estimate Freddie will be in with the load around 4 p.m. I'm gonna be highly visible around town all day."

"Hmm." Doc had a certain look in his eye. I knew that look. "Ya know, Billy, I'm putting my liberty at risk here, not to mention my medical license."

What I did know was that these were not at the top of Doc's mind. Even if he were charged with a crime, he might well beat it in court. But his legal expenses would be high and the thought of high legal expenses was more frightening to Doc than the loss of his freedom. He rightfully saw himself as a key player in our operation. Knowing full well the answer to my question, I asked anyway.

"What are you getting at, Doc?"

"I helped you steal two airplanes, Billy. For that I should get double the pay."

"Double the pay?"

"At least."

"Doc, your help has been crucial to the operation, but it's three o'clock in the damn morning. The case is closed for now."

I made my way home, shaking my head.

April 15, 1987

I guess Freddie was running a load. I was glad but Billy was a nervous wreck. He'd come home after being gone all night and smelled like he'd taken a shower in gasoline. Even after the shower the smell was strong. He was irritable and couldn't sit still. Too bad he doesn't realize that what he's feeling is just a little of what I feel when he's gone. Hopefully, everything will go smooth and Freddie will start flying more.

Just after daylight I climbed out of my dirty gasoline-soaked cloths, showered, and put on my running shoes and shorts. As much as I would have liked to have climbed into bed with Kay for some rest, it would have to wait. This was the time of day for my routine four-mile run. That run must happen and I would pass many people out for their morning walk. I knew those people. They were my alibi.

I dressed and beeped Glen from a pay phone. He was of course happy that Freddie was on his way and assured me that he had everything ready.

I returned to my house for a much-needed nap but doubt set in when I woke. Despite Glen's ease and confidence, I knew that whatever could go wrong, would go wrong, and waiting was harder on my nerves than flying the load myself.

Shortly after 3 p.m. Doc came by and said that he had been keeping the airport under surveillance. No surprises.

"The airport employees worked on the door and freed it. They closed it and went back into the terminal building."

"Good work, Doc. They must have assumed that the owner of the plane was on a trip, so looks like nobody's discovered the theft. Excellent."

"What have you been doing, Billy? Have you heard anything?"

Nobody likes waiting but the man wasn't used to the tension that was part of our business.

"Like I said, Doc, I've been covering my tracks. I even made a credit card purchase. That's something I don't often do. Then I took a nap and watched some TV."

"But have you heard anything?"

"How could I hear anything? Freddie's in the air somewhere over the Gulf. Tell you what, I'll be beeping Glen at 7 p.m. Would you like to come along?"

"I most certainly would. I'll be back at 6:30 p.m."

At 6:30 p.m. sharp he was at the door and we drove to a

payphone at a county crossroad convenience store and beeped Glen. We walked around trying to look nonchalant for about ten minutes. The phone rang.

"It's Miller time!" Glen chirped. This was our code. I gave Doc a thumbs up.

"Tell Freddie as soon as he gets some rest to give me a call."

"Will do, Billy. By the way, the beer's already half gone, and we'll have the paperwork for it in a week and the rest in one more week. Uh, by the way, just under 800 pounds."

If anybody was listening, they must have wondered about 800 pounds of beer. But what the hell. A couple of days later I met a smiling Freddie at the Jacksonville International Airport. Good to see him.

"And you found the strip without any problem?"

"Yep."

"No glitches?"

"Well, Billy, dammit. You could have warned me about the British fighters."

"Really?"

"Two military jets buzzed us while we were loading. Spooked the hell out of me. The loading crew almost ran away but, course, they wouldn't have seen their pay if they'd done that. Man, I was in such a rush to get off the ground, I didn't put on the oil filler cap. I just broke ground on takeoff and oil started splattering all over the windshield. I made a tight turn back to the airstrip, landed and secured the oil cap and took right off again."

That's why they pay us smugglers the big bucks. The British had maintained a presence in Belize because of a long-standing border dispute between Guatemala and Belize but their air force never interfered with Belize civilians.

"Exciting," I chuckled. "They probably just picked up our plane on radar and dispatched jets to check it out."

May 2, 1987

I've always wondered why the girls never ask about their father's profession. After his arrest on our front porch in 1984, he was front page news, but they were at summer camp and didn't have the pleasure of seeing the FBI pulling him out the front door in his underwear. But the neighbors certainly did. Of course, the girls have heard talk at school, but I try to shelter them as much as possible. I myself experienced a different Lake City after the arrest as well. Even though I had broken no laws; I and some of my family members were treated as if we were the ones smuggling drugs. I learned over the years to get tough. If I was to survive in this life, I'd have to hold my own. One of our friends had a saying, "I wasn't born a bitch, but the world is making me one." I understand that now. I've found out quickly enough who my friends are and are not.

Several of Billy's attempts have been unsuccessful over the years, but even the unsuccessful ones have a bad effect on me. The least worrisome are the ones that Freddie flies. Billy gets the load ready and Freddie does the flying and Billy helps with the unloading. Not that this isn't worrisome but at least I know he won't end up in the sea. Problem is, they don't do this often because Billy can't stand the anxiety of not knowing what's happening. Imagine that! That's how I feel every time he walks out the door.

A week later I paid Freddie $40,000.00 for his services. A week after that, I paid the unloading crew. I gave Doc $20,000 — $5,000 more than we first agreed on — to cover the extra work he'd performed. He counted it slowly.

"Billy, son, I need you to know, I'm still entitled to double pay because I helped obtain two planes for you."

"Doc, my friend. We've been through this. You assisted in stealing two airplanes, but we only hauled one load. The money we make is based on the amount of pot we haul, not the number of airplanes we steal."

"But stealing airplanes is part of your business, son."

"No, Doc. Stealing airplanes is just an occasional improvisation. Hauling pot is us."

Thing was, I *knew* that more than anything, Doc enjoyed the challenge of seeing how high he could barter for his services. And once your counterpart knows your weakness, you're handicapped.

Glen and I were the last to get paid — $36,000 each after all expenses — my first real payday in years. Already, I could feel the juices rising. I knew I'd soon be winding up for another load.

May 20, 1987. Key West, Florida

Billy said he wanted to take me away somewhere, so we've driven down to the Keys, just him and I. The girls are at a Christian camp in O'Brien for two weeks, like they have been every year for the past eight years. Kim's going to be a counselor this year and both girls enjoy the camp but mostly it's a time when Billy and I can be alone. We go shopping and eat at great restaurants. Yesterday he rented a seaplane, and we flew to Fort Jefferson in the Dry Tortugas for the day and picnicked and snorkeled off the island. I know our time alone is going to end much too soon but this is also when I know he loves me. It'll be the clutter and confusion of our lives when we get back that will make that feeling fade.

Back in Lake City, I beeped Glen and arranged a meeting. Everyone likes a winner, and after our recent success, we were back in the winner's circle. Sure enough, one of Glen's buyers had access to an airplane we could rent.

"What kind of airplane?"

"A twin Piper Aztec. It sounds totally great."

I've said how Glen's general demeanor was nonchalant but now he couldn't hide his enthusiasm.

"How much for one trip?"

"They want the rent in pot — $25,000.00, payable when the load arrives. I'll get back in touch with them to arrange when and where."

"It does sound excellent, man, but we don't want to go through the same maintenance hassles we had with the Navajo."

"For sure Billy. I'll make it clean, man."

"We may be back in business, Glen."

I'd never flown a load in an Aztec, but it was one of my favorite airplanes. In fact, it was the airplane I'd flown when I took my multi-engine and instrument rating check rides. The Navajo was a good plane, but the Aztec wouldn't be bad either. Both planes had twin engines, but the Navajo had a larger cabin with a rear cabin access through an air stair door versus the over-the-wing loading door of the Aztec. The Navajo had a heavier gross weight and more modern design but for the smuggler, the only thing a Navajo had over an Aztec was its ability to carry several hundred pounds more pot and carry it faster.

I was working out the logistics before young Glen was out the door. We wouldn't pick the plane up until the load was ready because we didn't have anywhere to store it other than Doc's hangar and I only wanted it there long enough to take the seats out and fuel up. The longer we used Doc's hangar the more it would cost us. A load generates a large amount of cash but I still needed to keep an eye on expenses. Left unchecked, the cost of

a smuggler and his wife

Doc's hangar could approach or even surpass the airplane rental. We also needed to contact Johnny and tell him to start putting together a load of between 900 and 1,000 pounds. As to the unloading spot, we could use Joe's for a fee.

For the next three days, I followed my regular routine. We would get the girls to school and I would then take my four-mile run first thing in the morning. Around noon, Doc would drop by to shoot the bull, inquiring multiple times about the next job. On one of these occasions, I revealed to him that we'd already done a load since I'd seen him last.

"Yeah." I nodded with an expression more of sorrow than anger. "I wanted to use your hangar, but everyone was mad at ya."

The man looked crushed.

"They just don't understand business. What did they say?"

"They figured you'd charged us to assist in the theft of an airplane that we didn't even use."

"Billy, do any of you understand all the risk I'm taking on. I'm putting my MD license on the line, Billy."

I struggled to keep a somber demeanor.

"I know this tune, Doc, so you don't have to hum it."

"I'm serious, Billy."

"Doc, I know how valuable you are. We haven't done anything without you. We'll work again soon, and we'll need to rent your hangar."

"You didn't make a run without me?"

I couldn't help laughing then.

"It's good, Doc. You're in on these jobs."

He left happy.

After lunch, Kay and I watched TV and enjoy being together without the girls until school was out, then I went for a ride out into the countryside and toked up on the way. Since my return home from prison, Kay insisted that there would be no pot smoking or any other drugs in the house. She loved me, but she didn't approve of my conduct.

On day four, I got a beep from Glen. Johnny would be ready soon with a 1,000-pound load for us and Glen had a stash house out in the woods just off US Highway 231 between Panama City and Mariana. A full-size country boy named Big Bob lived on a large tract of hunting land as the caretaker. Apparently, the property was owned by an upper-level Florida politician but no one would ever suspect that the old farmhouse had one bedroom full of pot. Meanwhile, Glen's pot buyer confirmed that the Aztec was ready to be picked up at our discretion. The only remaining decision was where to land and unload. It was too soon to return to the dirt road where we'd abandoned the 210 and Joe's strip would cost a landing fee. Meanwhile I'd heard from other smugglers about an empty subdivision called Compass Lake, in the Marianna area. The following day we headed south on U.S. 231 and passed a billboard advertising lots for sale. To our dismay it boasted that quite a few lots had been sold and several houses were visible from the highway. It seemed like we'd driven a long way for nothing, but we were still equipped with our Florida Gazette campground and picnic area guidebook. The Compass Lake subdivision was crisscrossed with roads that continued for miles from Highway 231. We were faced with the unusual problem of having unlimited options. We could land on a clay road deep into the subdivision and far away from the paved road and any likely traffic, or we could land on a clay road close to a paved road that would enable a swift departure. At the point we'd spent over two hours driving back and forth over the subdivision roads in broad daylight and hadn't met a single vehicle, even on the paved road. Traffic in the area was practically non-existent. We'd land where our visit would be briefest and, as an unexpected bonus, we were only four miles from our stash house at Big Bob's.

May 27, 1987

Since they have started using the west Florida area to land, Billy is gone more and more. It may be for one-night or it may be for a couple of days. He told me the other night he's checking landing areas and making sure every little detail is taken care of. Whatever the reason he's gone a lot and he isn't flying in loads. I wish I knew the people he was dealing with. I wouldn't be so insecure. I know how Billy is and if the crowd is partying, so is he. They act like teenage boys with no responsibilities. I don't get that. At some point in life, you have to grow up!

The payphone was sprinkled with rain dots left from a passing summer shower and the air that Friday night was thick and sticky. A slight breeze was the only relief.

"Johnny, we're a go when you are."

Johnny's voice came through weakly. Sometimes the connection to Belize was flaky.

"Give me a few days, Gringo, and let's touch base. I should have all what you need by then."

Back in Lake City I called Doc.

"Looks like Sunday and Monday will be busy days for us, my friend."

Sunday morning. Glen and I met in Lake City and called Johnny, who had good news about the load. I called Doc and informed him that Glen and I were on our way to Sanford to get the Aztec and would be at his Lake City hangar shortly after dark.

Sunday evening. We arrived at the Sanford airport and spotted the Aztec right away. Glen parked in a space that gave us a good view of the airplane and we killed an hour by ordering a burger and relishing the way things were proceeding smoothly and as planned. I swallowed my last mouthful of burger, stuffed the wrappings in the bag, and climbed out.

"Glen, better hang around until I'm in the air."

I walked onto the ramp and climbed in the Aztec. A quick pre-flight inspection revealed that we were low on fuel. Why did it have to be like this? Even if I had enough to get to Lake City, Doc wouldn't have enough fuel in his hangar for a flight to Belize. I hurried over to Glen, who already had his motor running.

"Glen, go over to the office and arrange for fuel."

I returned to the plane and the pre-flight inspection to discover that the battery was dead. I could be in for a long night. Glen arrived with the line boy and filled the tanks, and the kid had a pair of jumper cables. I connected the cables, primed the left engine, set the magnetos, and engaged the starter. With only a couple of revolutions the engine fired. The oil pressure came alive and settled down into the green arc. Glen was standing behind the right wing, watching anxiously through the open door. I let the engine warm up for about a minute and was happy to see that the alternator was on-line and charging the batteries. I took a breath. If the right engine did as good as the left, this run might be smoother than the first.

I primed the right engine and hit the starter. It fired right up.

"Okay, man! Maybe all this old gal needed was a little gas in her tank and a little fire in her battery!" I waved him off. "See you tomorrow at Compass Lake, buddy!"

For five minutes the Aztec cut the evening sky like a duck across a pond. I was probably still smiling when I sensed her underbelly as struggling. I glanced at the indicators. When I'd retracted the landing gear, only two wheels had responded. The left main was in the down and locked position. I cycled the gear several times trying to get it to retract.

"No, Luck!" I said out loud. "No, Lady!"

Glen would be long gone from the airport. I had no choice

but to fly on with the wheel extended, checking the plane's performance all the way. Now I saw that the right engine cylinder head temperature was running so hot I had to open the cowl flap to cool it. This was likely just a magneto timing problem, which could be easily corrected by a competent mechanic. Count your blessings, I thought. Other than the gear and the cylinder head temp the old Aztec seemed to be in good condition. I flew to Lake City and radioed Doc.

"I've got equipment problems. I'm going to need you to pick me up back at the Sanford Airport." I circled Lake City and in just a few minutes Doc was airborne.

We tied down the Aztec where I'd found it and flew back to Lake City. I contacted Glen and told him about the repairs we needed. Glen said he'd also call Johnny in Belize and let him know we'd be delayed a few days.

Monday. It was back to my daily routine of taking the girls to school, doing a morning run, cooking and afternoon family time. Doc came by and we beeped Glen from a pay phone, but he didn't reply. We changed locations, dug out more quarters from my Crown Royal bag and beeped again from another payphone. We continued riding and beeping for another two hours.

"Just take me home, Doc. Glen's beeper batteries are either dead, or he's found himself a new girl and he's too busy to answer."

Tuesday, 8:30 a.m. Just after my run Doc came by and we went to beeping Glen again. I tried the answering service and left a message.

Friday. I called Glen's dad, Oscar, in Daytona.

"Oscar?"

"Yep."

"Oscar, it's me, Billy Dekle, Glen's friend."

"Oh yeah."

"Oscar, you heard anything from Glen?"

"Oh yeah."

"He okay?"

"Sorta. He's in jail."

"He ... he's in jail?"

"Some sort of problem with a plane. Messed up his plans. You know Glen — he went partyin' at a bar in Orlando and some bastard picked a fight with him and somebody else called the cops, some coward."

"Did ... did Glen hurt someone?"

"No. 'Course not. Some filthy rat friend of Glen's got busted couple of weeks before and turned up Glen's ID to the cops. Some fuckin' slime of a friend. The cops in the bar knew right away who Glen really was. He was Glen."

"Jesus, Oscar. I'm so sorry."

"He was a fugitive, you know."

"I know."

"He's a good boy, Glen."

"I know, Oscar."

"His friends are all filthy rotten slime."

Picture that old footage of World War I battlefields and the guys come out of their trenches and walk forward and you see one fall here and then one fall there. They don't twist or writhe or any of that movie stuff, they just fall down and the other guys, what can they do? They just keep walking forward. I don't say smugglers are soldiers or noble or anything, but we're doing our job and guys go down around us and what can we do? It's what happens and we all know it.

I gave Big B the bad news. He too had been trying to get in touch with Glen for the past few days. We agreed to meet face to face just outside the Oaks Mall in Gainesville two days later Big B showed up with a friend named Dog. I'd been hearing about Dog for years. Reputation as a wild man. He'd worked with us on

a smuggler and his wife

the last load, when his job assignment had been to go to Belize and make sure that the pot Johnny was fronting us was of adequate quality.

Could we put the run back together again without our busted comrade? If so, what job would each of us be responsible for? Big B said he'd get in touch with the Aztec owner, describe the mechanical problems and ask if he still wanted to make it available to us. Would the same deal apply? If so, could we use it as soon as it was repaired? Dog said that he wanted to stay on as a team member and was ready to go to Belize as soon as we gave him expense money for the trip. Big B would coordinate with the caretaker Big Bob at the stash house and the unloaders Glen had planned to use at Compass Lake. He would also get trucks, lookouts, radios and other necessary equipment.

I suggested it would be time well spent if we all went together with the unloading crew to our landing spot. I knew we could not afford another screw-up like the flat tire load.

"Dog," I said, because I was still lead man as far as I was concerned, "you remain on standby. If the plane owner is still in on the deal, I'll send you on to Belize as soon as I know that the Aztec is in the shop."

Dog reminded me of Colonel Sanders — tall, with a blondish gray mustache and goatee and long, blondish gray hair pulled back in a ponytail. He'd been smoothing that mustache and goatee with one hand as he listened to me talk. Now he nodded in agreement.

The following morning Big B came through Lake City, picked me up and we gathered the crew. At the landing spot I pointed out where I thought the lookouts should be stationed. We timed the drive over the dirt road back to the stash house. The crew seemed to be motivated and I was happy with the plan overall. Still, there was a nagging feeling I couldn't quite shake. Maybe it was Glen's bust or the fact that I had only just met Big B. Or the fact that I'd just met the unloading crew that day. Some instinct was playing chicken with my desire to complete this run. I squeezed my temples. I closed my eyes and scrolled through my doubts. "What's the real trouble?" I would be flying away in the airplane. Fine. I'd return with the pot and unload. Fine. I'd fly away again to stash the plane at an area airport. Fine. I wouldn't meet with them again until I'd made my way back. Hmm. These people had given me no reason to question their honesty, but would it be smart on my part to tempt them? A light went on. No, it would not. I couldn't let the pot out of my sight.

The solution came as Big B and I rode back to Lake City: the solution was Freddie. As soon as we arrived back in Lake City, Big B departed for the Orlando area to contact the Aztec owner and find when the Aztec could be ready. I made my own phone call to Freddie,

"I put it to you this way, friend. If you want in, you can choose your job. Job one: wait for me with the unloading crew and fly the Aztec away from Compass Lake after unload. Job one pays $5,000. Job two: co-pilot on the trip to Belize and then complete the fly-away. Job two pays $20,000."

"Uh *huh*," said Freddie. "Right. I'll take job two. I'll pack my bag and be waiting for your call."

For the first time since Glen's bad news, I felt my confidence creeping back. After a good night's sleep, I went through my regular routine with an early morning run and an afternoon movie with Kay. Doc came by and we went out and beeped Big B, who had good news. The Aztec was in the shop and we would be able to pick it up soon, maybe as early as the following evening.

June 8, 1987

More new partners for Billy. Evidently Glen, one of the Daytona boys, got himself arrested. More people I don't know and more people for Billy to try and trust with our future. The fun never ends in this world. Billy doesn't work on the weekends because he feels that more people are out and about. So, I always feel that if I can make it to Friday, I will have him home for at least a day or two. That is, unless he gets a wild hair to go get drunk. Anyway, we decided to take the boat down to the river today. It was so nice. We launched at Sandy Point and rode down the Santa Fe River to the Suwannee River and then all the way to the town of Suwannee at the gulf. We ate a sandwich and came back. The weather was beautiful until we were about two miles out from Sandy Point. A summer thunderstorm with lightening and pouring rain erupted. We loaded with not too much trouble but got drenched in the process. A lot of laughing and relieved sighs when we finally made it into the car and headed home.

We met in Tampa the next day at noon and put Dog on an afternoon flight to Cancun. Johnny would send a driver up from Orange Walk, Belize to pick up Dog. I gave him $15,000 cash in 50 and 100-dollar bills, instructed him to give Johnny $10,000 for the down payment and use the remaining $5,000 for his expenses.

"A high-quality load of pot and clean aviation fuel. Those are the musts, Dog."

"I won't let you down, Billy."

"I'll call you in Belize."

Wednesday. I called Dog the next afternoon in Belize. He reported that we'd be using the Pine Ridge strip, but they'd need at least two more days before they'd be ready.

"No Dog. Not the weekend. They need to be ready to see me Monday morning. Pine Ridge strip!"

This would give them plenty of time to get ready without having to rush. But my real consideration was that on weekends people were out taking drives in the countryside. All our reconnaissance work on Compass Lake area had been done on weekdays when there was no traffic. It would be foolish to bring the load in on a day for which we'd gathered zero intelligence.

I returned home to Kay and the family. We went grocery shopping (I'd always loved doing that with my girl), we'd plan meals, chat about our girls, take our time. Afterward, we went for a swim with the kids in my parent's pool — short-lived moments at home as husband and dad, my job a distant backdrop to our very normal life. I was in-tune with Kay as she moved through her daily chores and conversations with our daughters. I loved watching her. It made my mind drift as it always did to how much I loved and needed her. I would run my hands around her hips, surprising her from behind, kissing that sweet spot on her neck. She always warmed to me after some flirtatious resistance. But as the day of the job moved closer, my focus would begin to shift, and her warmth would begin to cool.

Sunday came around fast. I turned on the weather channel. A line of thunderstorm activity south of Belize was moving north. It looked okay — not good, but not bad either. I prepared the family a big breakfast. We all got dressed and went to church. When we arrived home, Doc was parked in my driveway waiting for me. I got out of our car, nodded to Kay, and got into the car with Doc. We drove south on 441 to I-75 near the town of Ellisville. I called Johnny from a pay phone.

"Hey, Gringo. Me and my crew are ready for the party at Pine Ridge at 8 a.m. I got three kegs of beer and all the party supplies. Don' be late!"

He had three 55-gallon drums of aviation fuel and the pot ready to go. Dog came on the line.

"Dog, how's the weather looking for the party?"

"Ah ... lesh shee. Shome clouds, shome blue shhkies... before there was a little rain and, like, lightning, but it shtopped ... the whhind ... by the time you get here, should be awright."

"*You* alright, man?"

"Ready to go."

I had nothing against a person drinking if they could control themselves. I didn't know Dog personally, but I had heard the stories from friends. The guy could lose it when he drank. From the phone conversation I could tell he was feeling good, but he seemed in control. I brushed off a few slurred words.

I called Freddie and instructed him to come to Lake City and check into the same motel. As soon as I returned from Sanford with the Aztec, I'd drop by the motel. Doc dropped me back off at my house.

Sunday evening had always been slow at the Lake City airport. Doc and I pulled his airplane from his hangar and we flew to Sanford. After landing, Doc bypassed an empty spot next to the Aztec and taxied to the end of the line of planes in the transit tie-down area. This was to give the area a good once over and spot any law enforcement surveillance. Fifteen minutes passed. Sanford airport on Sunday evening was almost as dead as Lake City. I was satisfied we could safely approach the Aztec.

"Doc, tune your radio frequency to 123.4, taxi out to the run-up area. I'll inspect the Aztec and fire it up, then I'll call you."

As soon as he cleared the parking area I walked over to the Aztec and quickly checked the fuel. I drained the sumps, untied the tie-down ropes, hopped in, cranked it and started to taxi out. I gave Doc the signal. As I reached the end of the taxiway, I gave the airplane a quick run-up, cycling the props, and checking the magnetos.

I lifted off with Doc near behind me and immediately checked that the landing gear retracted completely. It did, so some meaningful maintenance had been done on the plane. I climbed out to about 6,500 feet and leveled off. I closed the cowl flaps, leaned the fuel/air mixture and kept an eye on the cylinder head temperature.

A few minutes into level flight I radioed Doc that so far everything was performing, and it looked like we would be working late. I suggested he land first and if there were no spectators or skateboarders, I would come in. I was on the ground in a few minutes and we were pushing the Aztec into the hangar.

We refueled and removed the seats and Doc dropped me off at my house. I drove out to see Freddie at the motel, then home for a few hours' sleep. It seemed like I had just dozed off when the alarm went off at 1 a.m. I brushed my teeth, washed my face, got dressed and drove to the motel.

Freddie and I left the motel in separate cars as he followed me out to Buddy's house where we parked Freddie's car in the back yard. Buddy was a veteran of the flat tire disaster and a long-standing team member. He heard us and came outside, and we went over his job assignment. Buddy was our lifeline if we were tailed and had to ditch the airplane. He'd be on location at the fly-over spot no later than noon Monday, his 2-meter radio with a fully charged battery and the appropriate frequency pre-programmed.

The 2-meter radio that we used could hold about 15 different frequencies. You'd think that multiple frequencies would be an asset, but without fail and at the most critical times, one or more of the crewmembers would somehow get his radio on the wrong channel and cause major problems. Now I simply programmed the same frequency into all channel selections, so if a member changed channels inadvertently, he'd still be on the same frequency.

Buddy's other assignment was to pick up the airplane seats from Doc and give them to Big B, so they would be at the Compass Lake unloading site for re-installation in the Aztec as soon as the weed was offloaded. Seats missing from an airplane is what DEA, Customs, FDLE, and all our adversaries call the "profile" of a smuggler. To enjoy longevity in the smuggling business, a man had to know as much as possible about the smuggling profile and do everything in his power to avoid fitting that profile. If we were to park the Aztec at an airport without the seats, some good Samaritan — and there were a surprising number of good Samaritans out there — is going to call law enforcement and report a suspicious airplane. One call would be all that was necessary for the local police to spring into action. No seats equals a suspicious profile, which equals an investigation. DEA and Customs would then ask for the N number of the airplane, the equivalent of a car tag number. Feds could then run the N number through their computer and check the plane's registration. If a Fortune 500 corporation, or at the very least a known freight hauler was not associated with the registration, an agent would be quickly dispatched to the airport and our airplane would have more police buzzing around it than flies on a fresh cow-patty. In nine out of ten cases, before wrapping up their investigation, they would find some reason to place a law enforcement transponder bug on the plane. Any unauthorized alterations done to the airplane could result in its complete seizure.

Freddie and I drove to one of Doc's rental houses. I parked my car and got into one of Doc's vehicles. I didn't want my car to be seen parked at the airport and possibly have the law wondering if I had gone to Jamaica or Colombia for the day.

All quiet at the airport — not a skateboarder in sight. We parked and walked casually to Doc's hangar, opened the door and pushed the Aztec out, climbed in, buckled up and I cranked the engines. I taxied out to the runway and opened the throttles.

It was always a good feeling to lift off the ground and be on our way. It marked the beginning of a new mission even though much had been done to get us to that point. All the planning and preparation vital to a successful outcome, all of those painstaking steps were worthwhile at that moment of lift-off.

June 14, 1987

Billy's gone. He left and said, "I should be back in a couple of days. Don't worry if I'm not." What exactly does that mean? Don't worry if I'm not? Like, I'm leaving in an airplane with hundreds of gallons of gas lying on the floor and I'm crossing the ocean to an unfamiliar landing site where I'll meet people who'll load my plane with an illegal substance and I'll take off and then fly across an ocean and land and unload and maybe not get arrested. How does "don't worry" fit into that scenario? As I've been told, smuggling when successful is exciting for the active parties, it's mind-blowing, intense and satisfying — maybe even when it's not successful. The euphoria is similar to winning the Super Bowl. But for a smuggler's loved one, it can only be described as watching the man you love with all your heart jump off a cliff only to be saved miraculously by landing on a ledge, only to jump off again. I experience that same stab in my heart every time he walks out the door to go on a load and I experience that same relief each time he walks back in the door. This has played again and again since 1978, and now nine years later and dozens and dozens of trips, it is no easier. He takes my soul with him and I never know if he or my soul will ever return. His words never console me — they only begin the intense pain I feel.

He doesn't have a clue what his lifestyle is doing to me. It's fun and thrilling to him — it's torment and pain to me. I have only myself to blame. I'm the one who came back to him.

I remember maybe nine years ago, him flagging me down in the early morning traffic on Baya Avenue. "Where are you going?" he said. He was smiling because he knew where I was going, he just wanted to hear me say it. He could tell I was upset and he put his arms around me. It was my first experience as a smuggler's wife, and I hated the anxiety and helplessness I'd been feeling for all the two days since he'd left.

"I don't know" I said to him. "I don't know. It was foggy, and you're hours later than you told me to expect you. I was scared you'd crashed. I was going to the airport to see if the plane was there, if it was at least I would know you were home, you'd made it."

I remember him laughing. "This is why I love you —, always worrying about me. I told you not to worry. Everything is going to be alright."

From that first run to this run — it never gets easier.

The weather that night was good, with high, scattered clouds and almost unlimited visibility. We leveled off at 10,500 feet and the Aztec was performing perfectly. We cleared the west coast of Florida near Cedar Key. And our next landfall would be the northeastern tip of Mexico's Yucatan peninsula, which we'd reach right at daylight. The cruise over the Gulf was easy and pleasant, nothing to do except fly the plane, stay on course, monitor the engine gauges to be sure they remained within their limit, and enjoy the ride.

The lights of Cancun were ahead and just off to our left when a dark and distant early morning horizon to the south began to flicker like a giant's firework display.

"Jesus, Billy." Freddie looked over to me. "That's a storm, ain't it?"

"A line of storms, seems like. You get a lot of big electrical storms late June in Florida and the Caribbean. I'm not so surprised to run into one."

Not surprised but not happy either. The Aztec had no weather avoidance equipment, no radar or storm scope that could enable a pilot to pick the spots with the least activity. We would normally have several options. The safest choices — the recommended actions taught in flight schools — would be to land and wait for a thunderstorm to run its course or, if you unfortunately encountered one over open water, go around. Aviation textbooks do not address smuggling missions but landing at a Mexican airport would certainly result in our arrest and charges of illegal entry at the least. Ahead, the storm system had already formed a line and we didn't have enough fuel or time to go around it. Our realistic options were zero.

"Whatya going to do, Billy?"

Cancun was just below us now, the lightning slithering out of a climbing black wall ahead.

"Keep the wings level and stay on course if I can. Freddie, listen, man, secure as much loose stuff as you can. Then come back and tighten your seatbelt."

The sun was rising, and we were nearing the coastal town of Tulum when we entered the thunderstorm. Instantly heavy rain pounded us and a violent downdraft slammed us. My altimeter needle spun down 1,000 feet. Out of the downdraft, an updraft hoisted us 1,000 feet upwards in a few seconds. I could do nothing about the updrafts and downdrafts except ride with them. I couldn't hold altitude in a thunderstorm of that magnitude. My best piloting move in such severe turbulence was to slow the airplane to maneuvering speed so that it would stall before it was over-stressed to the point of structure failure. I could recover from a stall but if a critical part of the aircraft structure failed, recovery would probably be impossible and flight would be, er, discontinued. I was struggling just to keep the wings level, flying solely by instruments because the rain and clouds made it impossible to see outside. We had no idea what to expect: thunderstorms can produce hail and tornadoes — all grave hazards. Five minutes of buffeting and stomach drops seemed like an hour and then — suddenly — we were through the worst of it.

We flew on. Heavy rain and clouds but only light to moderate turbulence. We passed over the city of Chetumal on Mexico's southern border and entered northern Belize. The worst of the weather appeared to be behind us. Ahead, I could see lower-lying scattered clouds, the remnants of the passing line of thunderstorms. We began our decent and flew west of Orange Walk in route to the Pine Ridge, an area of scattered pine trees and grass.

"Where are the goddam trucks?" I asked Freddie, as if he knew. The trucks that transported the pot, the fuel, and the crew were critical markers for me. I circled, trying to distinguish a makeshift runway apart from main roads and paths. I couldn't see any possible landing strip for an airplane. Too many trees, too close together. On my third loop, scoping out the area from all angles, I noticed a couple of spots where the earth had been disturbed — spots where trees had been removed.

"How about there?" Freddie wondered.

"No!" I said. "No damn way they want me to land there!"

Freddie let out a little groan and we both adjusted ourselves in our seats as if to prepare for a second storm. My jaw was clenched.

"I can't believe it," I mumbled, probably incoherently. Dog had said proudly that the crew had worked out a new strip but of course he hadn't seen his work from up here. The pines were so thickly scattered amongst the grass pasture that it appeared impossible to land. It wasn't even clear that it *was* a landing strip or if it was, that there was enough room for our wings. I made a circling pattern to a short final approach and dropped down between the trees.

To my surprise, the Aztec squeezed in and settled gently. The removal of a few trees made all the difference, but most astonishing, we were miles from any main gravel road and in fact this was one of the best and safest smugglers strips I'd encountered anywhere.

I taxied back to what appeared to be the approach end of the strip and turned the plane to face in the direction of takeoff. The loading crew obviously delighted that their handiwork was a success.

"I thought you guys had lost your minds," I called. "Looks like I was wrong."

While the team raced to load and fuel, a crewmember and I sped down the strip in a pick-up truck, then made a slow return for a close visual inspection.

It was about 8:00 in the morning local time and the temperature and humidity was already sweltering. Sweat melted our shirts onto our backs and I was already anxious to be airborne again at a cooler altitude. The crew finished with their work and I was relieved to find that there had been no excessive oil-burn on the trip down. Freddie and I said our goodbyes, climbed aboard and cranked the engines. I conducted my usual routine with a quick run-up, checking the magnetos, and cycling the props. I set the flaps to approximately 15 degrees for takeoff and held the brakes while feeding in full throttle. I gave the oil pressure, the fuel pressure and the other engine temperature gauges a quick scan. I released the brakes. We rolled slowly forward.

A loaded take-off is the most dangerous part of a trip. The short untried strip, the soft ground, the high grass — they'd all impede the airplane's acceleration. I'd need nothing short of a maximum performance take-off.

"Maximum," I said out loud as we began to gather speed. I glanced at the airspeed needle. It was beginning to come alive with a bounce, but I knew I'd have to accomplish take-off more by the feel of the airplane than by watching my airspeed. All my attention was focused on keeping the plane tracking straight down the strip, keeping those wings from hitting an obstacle. Ahead, I scanned the runway for anything that could snag us at the point of liftoff from the pine-framed path, and all the while, I was mentally calculating whether I could clear those pines. If I saw at the last moment that it would be impossible to break ground in time to clear all obstacles, I'd have to chop the power and abort the takeoff. The objective would be a crash at a slower speed and to somewhat improved our chances of survival.

I was running rapidly out of strip.

"Pull up, Billy!" Freddie called but I couldn't risk a premature rotation. "Pull up!" Freddie called again.

I could feel the Aztec ready herself to fly. Very lightly, I applied back pressure on the elevators.

"Come on, baabyyyy!" I shouted over the engine roar. "Come on! We're talkin' now, you and me! We're talking now!"

A few yards before my bail point, the Aztec lifted herself off the ground. I immediately raised the landing gear and her climb abruptly improved. We skimmed over the tops of the pine trees.

"Pow! Pow! Pop!" like gunshots from nowhere. My heart jumped into my throat as the right engine cut off and back on again in rapid successions. I gripped the yoke and maintained a slow climb. If that engine didn't restart fully, I'd have no choice with this load and altitude but to cut the power on the good engine and crash straight ahead under as much control as possible.

"Crash under control" is one of those oxymoronic aviation terms that address impossible situations. Conventional twin-engine airplanes have a critical minimum airspeed — VMC — when one engine has lost power. In a textbook take-off a pilot accelerates the aircraft through VMC speed *before* lifting off. Unfortunately, textbooks are not written for situations such as that morning at Pine Ridge. The strip was too short for a textbook take-off because if I'd kept the Aztec on the ground until it accelerated through VMC I'd still be on the ground when I ran out of runway. Anyway, we were way over the certified gross weight for this airplane and it would be impossible to climb or even maintain altitude with only one engine operative. The chances of surviving a VMC roll crash would be practically zero and that was not an acceptable ending.

Our girl's belly skimmed the treetops, and I took a deep breath as all this washed over me. The pucker factor was maxed out. I met Freddie's eyes.

"Hold on," was all I said.

Freddie and I and 1,000 pounds of pot and 192 gallons of high-octane aviation fuel went spitting and sputtering over the ridge of pines. I prayed, "Lord, keep that right engine cutting back in long enough for me to turn around. Just let me land back on that strip."

I'd got barely enough altitude to attempt the turn back. I put my hand on the throttle and the right engine suddenly stopped cutting out. I made a climbing turn into the morning sky at about 400 feet, thanking God for every inch I gained. If the engine stopped now completely, I'd have a little time and height to choose my crash site. I leveled the wings on a tight downwind leg for the airstrip. The engine cut out again once, twice — then started running normally again. I extended the downwind leg and continued climbing through 1,000 feet. I could feel Freddie watching me intently. I glanced over at him and we both saw the question in one another's eyes.

"May as well see if she can get us back home," I said.

"May as well," Freddie repeated.

With every sputter from the first, I knew I might have only moments to live. My pumping adrenaline and all my years of flying allowed me to feel my way through each move as if I had synced with the controls of the Aztec. My body took over the mechanisms of flying while my mind contemplated all that was precious in this life. We climbed until leveling off at 6,000 feet.

Emotions had not kicked in yet, but I was beginning to get my wits about me again. The first couple of hours on the return trip would be over land, so I planned to keep my altitude relatively low and burn off a couple of hours of fuel — maybe 300 pounds of weight. After I'd lightened up, I could climb to around 11,500 feet for the over-water passage.

The Aztec performed perfectly.

"What do you think it was?" Freddie wondered.

It had felt like some sort of an ignition problem, but the fact that the IO-540 Lycoming engines on the Aztec were equipped with dual ignition systems made an ignition problem highly unlikely.

"It could have been water or trash in the fuel," I reasoned. The Aztec has four rubber bladder tanks and sometimes as these tanks age they develop wrinkles. These wrinkles can trap small amounts of water and trash and prevent these contaminants from reaching the sumps for draining. The Pine Ridge take-off, being a much rougher and bouncier takeoff than normal, probably dislodged some trash from the wrinkled bladders, which went to the right engine and caused it to go into a coughing spell until clean fuel flowed again.

By the time we reached Chetumal, Mexico, the line of thunderstorms had dissipated enough that we had little problem making small deviations around them and staying clear of anything too rough. We experienced some light rain and some little bumps here and there as we continued northeast along the Yucatan coast towards Cancun. I began a gentle cruise climb to 11,500 feet, a more comfortable altitude for the over-water flight. Cancun is even more beautiful from the air than it is from the ground — a view I enjoyed each and every time.

There was no adverse weather over the Gulf as far as the eye could see. Now that all the bad weather was behind us and our flying machine was performing perfectly, we leveled off at 11,500 feet. I turned to Freddie.

"It looks like smooth sailing ahead. I believe the time has come to break open one of those bales."

"Times past," said Freddie, "you would have brought that up sooner."

"Times past," I reminded him, "we didn't nearly die on take-off."

He got his pocket knife out and cut into a bale. We meanwhile continued heading north, northeast until we intercepted the 85-degree meridian of longitude, then turned due north over the Gulf of Mexico to break the Florida coast at Apalachicola, east of Eglin and Tyndall Air Force Base airspace. I thought it best that we keep a wide berth between us and those guys.

At the 85-degree line we started our descent to 1,000 feet at about 120 miles off the coast. I bled off altitude down to a high of about 50 feet and a low of five feet. Five feet was admittedly a little extreme but as I've explained, the low-level portion was the most pleasurable leg of a trip for me. And as a bonus, during daylight hours it was my habit to maneuver the aircraft around until I could see my shadow. Then, if I happened to see two shadows instead of one, it would be a sure sign that I had a tail and should go to Plan B, if I had a Plan B. And if I didn't have a Plan B, that would be the time to plan it.

On most trips, I could easily see schools of dolphins and sea birds at this point, and sport fishing boats and pleasure craft: welcome sights that meant land was near. When I passed close to these boats, Sunday sailors must have been thinking: what in the hell is that guy doing so far out flying so low? Or maybe they'd be hip enough to know.

We continued north, skimming over the Gulf until we were about a half mile from the beach. I climbed up to what I estimated would be about 20 feet under the tops of the trees and then held that altitude until probably 100 feet before the trees and then climbed to barely clear their tops. We passed over the beach and a coastal highway on a narrow strip of land that separated the beach from the bay. I descended to between five and ten feet of altitude and held this until we reached the tree line on the north end of the bay, where I again climbed to barely clear the treetops. All of this up and down would create an elusive, hard-to-identify effect for radar. About ten miles north I started a slow climb to 2,500 feet and held this altitude until I reached Compass Lake. In just minutes we were over the flyover spot and I gave Buddy a call. He answered immediately.

"I can hear the airplane but don't have sight yet."

I flew directly over Compass Lake and spotted Big B and the trucks.

"You're alone! Come on in!" Buddy radioed.

I made a wide left descending turn and rolled out on a long final approach to the subdivision road that we had predetermined to be the unloading site. I experienced a brief flashback to the Navajo load, and I hoped that there were no Good Samaritan farmers or other do-gooders watching me now.

Within seconds I touched down on a manicured clay street, landing as short as possible, turning around and taxiing back to the approach end of the street. I then turned back around on the cul-de-sac facing in the direction that I'd landed. I left the engines running so I could make a fast getaway if it became necessary. Freddie opened the cabin door and jumped out as I set the parking brakes. I climbed out with my 2-meter radio in hand. The unloading crew was nowhere in sight, but I could hear them communicating from one truck to the other and there seemed to be some confusion. We were at our most vulnerable now, on the ground with a plane full of pot and no friends in sight.

I broke in.

"Big B, what's your location?"

"I'm right here on the unloading road. Where are you?"

"*I'm* on the unloading road too and I'm waiting for ya'll. Ya'll got to get over here now!"

"Where is that?" He sounded irritated.

"I'm looking at a street sign and it says Cypress Ave."

"There's no such street by that name on my map, Billy!"

"Yes, there is, dammit, and I'm on it! It's the third street from where you turn off the paved road! When I flew over, you were a couple of roads south."

"Oh yeah. Yeah, right. I'm on my way. Be there in a minute."

Guys have spent years in prison for confusion like that. I turned to Freddie.

"Let's start unloading."

I remembered that we had also filled the forward nose cone baggage compartment with pot.

"Keep unloading from the cabin, Freddie. I'll go get the bales in the nose baggage compartment."

He nodded with a sign of caution in his eyes. Removing pot from the nose compartment while the engines were still running required some care because the right engine prop passes within a couple of inches of the baggage door when it's opened. It was bad enough having to work that close to the propeller, but the fact that the brakes were set with no one holding them was unnerving, especially with Freddie bouncing around inside the cabin as he went about unloading the airplane.

Big B and his crew pulled up and started loading the trucks as fast as possible.

"Freddie," I called over the roar of the propeller, "Take off! I'll be in touch with you sometime tomorrow!"

"Okay!" he shouted back. "I'll find some quiet airport and leave this old girl there. Be home waiting on your call."

He took off while we were still picking bales of pot up from the ground and loading the trucks. Within a minute he was over the horizon and we had everything loaded and were on our way to the stash house.

June 15, 1987

Doc came by today and he and Billy sat in the living room talking and laughing for over an hour. I listened as Billy conveyed every mile of the trip. What is it that excites a person when they face death? I don't think it would excite me. He told Doc about the violent thunderstorms, how the airplane lost power on takeoff and then getting high out over the gulf. They just laughed and laughed about each situation. How is that funny? I am sure after hearing about those adventures my imagination and dreams will be filled with new horrors about what could be going wrong when the one I love with all my heart is gone and I know nothing.

Within a couple of days my best buyer Mark had paid me what he owed for the pot that I'd fronted him. I'd paid Freddie his $20,00 and Doc his $10,000.

"Billy." Doc looked at his pile of cash with an expression of mild pain. "Billy, I'm sorry, son, but my reading of things is that I've been underpaid again."

"How so, Doc?"

"I believe you don't realize how my contribution is more vital to your operation than you realize. I'm risking my doctor's certificate *and* my liberty."

"Doc, you're saying there's something I don't realize about something I do realize?"

"In so many words, Billy, that's what I'm saying."

"You're saying you're risking two things."

"That's right."

"You're saying you're incurring double risk."

"That's how I see it."

"And deserve double money."

"That's it."

"Doc, you're absolutely right. I don't realize how your contribution is more vital to my operation than I realize. Would you like to keep the money anyway?"

I left him counting.

I got in touch with Glen's father and asked him to meet me in Palatka Florida, about halfway between Lake City and Daytona Beach. He told me Glen's legal situation didn't look good. I gave him $15,000.00 in cash.

"Tell Glen for me that we brought in the Aztec load. Tell him I know he was involved with it from the get-go and he should get something out of it."

"Yeah. Guess my Glen's got one friend who's not a louse," Glen's father said.

All expenses were paid, and I'd wound up with something close to $170,000.00. The pressure was off. Now to get the right engine fixed and bring in another load while I had the momentum on my side.

3

We exchanged satisfied compliments about this clever acquisition. But my mind was on that last kiss.

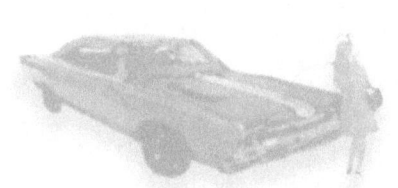

July 9, 1987

I'm writing this in Deland. I'm with the dance team for summer camp. Four long days and nights with the girls. We learn all the material and routines that we use during football season and for community events during the year. It is tiring for me and the girls but when we return, we are a team and a sisterhood. It forms bonds that all the girls have throughout their years on the team. Being their coach has strengthened me as a person and made me feel so appreciated. This is my third year, and I can't imagine not doing this.

July 17. 1987

We completed our summer practices today and I've given the dance team the rest of the summer off. The new school year will start just after Labor Day, a little more than a month away. Wow, Kim will be in the 10th grade, high school. Amy will be in the 8th and she is so excited about being one of the top officers on her dance team. Billy has done really well lately so I don't have to worry too much about school clothes — they'll be able to pick what they want. They've finished their modeling courses and they all three seem very confident and self-assured. I told Billy I wanted to take the girls and Amy Doub somewhere for a week before school starts. I found a place on Captiva Island, a condo owned by a tennis pro I was told. I'm looking forward to getting away. Kim is in love with the skateboard dude, as Billy calls him. She won't want to be gone for a week but oh well.

It was mid-July 1987. In less than a year we'd managed to lose to the police a Piper Navajo valued at around $250,000, approximately 1,000 pounds of pot valued at $550,000, and Glen, Frenchie, Ruben and two or three of Frenchie's Miami associates, all of questionable value but all in jail without bond. On the other hand — I preferred to look on the bright side — I'd completed two successful pot runs and stayed out of jail myself. Getting my head above water.

Big B was still standing, and we decided to have Robert's Aztec fixed. But B knew that Robert also had a single-engine Cessna 206 he was willing to rent. We could make another run in this 206 while the Aztec was being repaired, and now I had a little reserve, I could invest in the luxury of a paid-for landing site rather than a hit-and-run road or field. In fact, I had an almost perfect site in the Blackwater Forest area of the Florida panhandle: Joe's field, several hundred acres notched out of the forest and surrounded for miles by nothing but trees and dirt roads. No one could observe us or call the police, or if they did, it would take them at least 30 minutes to arrive on the scene. We'd be long gone.

Doc's hangar would be part of the plan and I offered Freddie the chance to unload or to make extra money by flying. Money was a lure to Freddie, but for him as for us all, money wasn't the whole story. More money meant more risk, which meant more of the euphoric rush we were chasing.

I'd contacted Johnny in Belize to find out when and where he could load 900 pounds for us. He got back to me a few days later.

"Hey Gringo! The party will be in three to four days. How many kegs you need?"

Three kegs of beer meant three 55-gallon drums of fuel, though Johnny would've been happy to be planning a real party as well, one with his family, his friends, and more than one of the ladies he kept company with.

Doc was of course looking forward to working the night shift again and we went over the schedule together.

"Now, Billy, not to slow anything down, but about the vital role I and my hangar play in your operation …"

"Doc, Doc," I was already nodding agreement. "I am so aware of what a valuable player you are."

"Thank you, Billy. You're a real friend to me."

"And, Doc, I'm so aware how you're being paid well above the normal rate in proportion to your exposure, and, yes, I am so aware of how you're putting your liberty at risk. These things I know."

The man looked down, like he'd been caught out unexpectedly.

"Doc, that's exactly why you're getting paid $15,000 for three or four days use of your hangar that normally rents for $200 a month. Now —" I raised my hand — "Now I also realize you're putting your medical license in jeopardy. Doc, if I could figure how your license would assist me in smuggling pot in any way, I'd be glad to compensate you for it."

"True, true," he mumbled, still looking down.

"As it stands, Doc, there won't be any extra compensation on the grounds of your medical license. And whether you continue to put it in jeopardy is your decision. I simply cannot decide that for you."

"Billy, Billy. No need to become excited. I worry about your health but I still want in. I was just considering how I should be paid more."

"Doctor Philpot, you are in the best position in the organization as far as safety is concerned. You're getting paid as much or more than the unloaders who sit hours waiting on the unloading airstrip, waiting for an airplane to fly in loaded with contraband — and that's an airplane that might be tailed by our government's task force, by customs, by the DEA, by who knows who else. But if you really are in such dire financial straits and you just have to have more money, I could — at your special request — make room for you on the unloading crew."

"It's just a discussion between friends, Billy."

"The news isn't good," Big B began our call. "The 206's just got back from the Bahamas and there was a problem clearing customs."

"Did it get through?"

"Well, yeah. It got through."

"So, where's it now?"

"Sitting on the ramp at Ft. Lauderdale airport. Robert's pilot's afraid to go near it."

"What?"

"I didn't think you'd want to use it now, when it's, like, hot maybe."

I thought for a moment.

"B tell Robert that Johnny has the pot ready. If the plane isn't literally on fire, I want it. Hire a legal pilot from a flying service to ferry the plane to the Leesburg airport."

I reckoned that if a law enforcement agency had the airplane staked out and they pounced on the pilot, he could only say he was hired to fly the airplane to Leesburg, routine in his business. About an hour before noon the next day I met Big B at Leesburg as planned. We went to a nearby restaurant to run over our unloading plans. I was describing the farm in the forest clearing when I saw the 206 taxiing up outside.

"Okay. There's our man. Have him fuel it up and tied down on the ramp with one night's tie-down fee paid, then drive him to the Orlando airport and purchase him a ticket to Ft. Lauderdale."

Big B stood up.

"What will you do, Billy?"

"I'll keep an eye on the 206 from my car."

We shook hands and B was gone. I went out to my car and sat watching but no one approached the plane or seemed to pay it any attention. Nonetheless, I delayed so that the Lake City airport would be closed at my arrival. Late in the afternoon I took off from Leesburg in the 206 and landed in Lake City around twilight. Only Doc was waiting for me, perspiring in the heat of a July night. We pushed the plane into his hangar and closed the doors. We drove to a pay phone and I called the local Best Western.

"Freddie, my man, you okay?"

"Yeah, sure."

"Glad you made it. Get a good night's sleep, guy. Your ride is here. I'll pick you up around midnight."

Doc drove me home. The girls were outside watching the skateboarders do their tricks in front of our house. When I went in by the kitchen door, Kay was standing at the island chopping a head of lettuce.

"Hi," I said.

"Hi."

I glanced at the wall clock. I had about two hours and realized I really wanted to get close before I left.

"Baby Love," I said. "You're lookin' so good right now."

"Uh-huh."

She didn't look up but I sidled up to her anyway.

"Baby Love, you want to meet me in our room real quick?"

She smacked the knife hard against the cutting board and met my eyes with hers. My girl had many looks and they all conveyed exactly what she was thinking and feeling, a trait I both adored and hated. I knew she liked me home, safe, and out of mischief and she was always on edge when she knew I was about to do a load. I knew I'd have to wait until this job was done before my smooth-talking would have any traction.

I ate supper and tried to relax.

Doc and I went to one of his vacant rental houses where we'd stored the fuel bladder and other smuggling tools, then headed for the airport just after dark. Travelling east on highway US 90 the traffic was light but Doc drove right on by the turn-in to the airport. I raised my hands.

"Oh, come on, Doc. You don't have a stolen airplane in your hangar."

He ignored me.

"Doc, no one even knows what's in your hangar. Just drive on in and park the car like you always do."

He took a deep breath.

"Billy, you need to know something, son. I'm not getting enough money for my part in this. You on the other hand are making a lot of money."

"What are you saying, Doc?"

"I'm saying I'm going to have to have at least $30,000 if you are going to use my hangar."

I sat in stunned silence for a minute as the airport disappeared in the rearview.

"Let me see if I understand you, Doc. For me to use your hangar tonight the price has just doubled — and that's 'at least'?"

"I think just $30,000 is more than fair, Billy, considering all the money you're making."

It takes quite a bit to rile me, but it had reached that point.

"You fat sorry son of a bitch, Doc. You greedy lazy piece of shit." I took a breath. "Whatever caused me to trust you, you fuckin' disloyal scumbag?"

The man must have been expecting this because he took

a smuggler and his wife

the cursing well. When I stopped, he actually grinned. I realized he was relishing a moment of triumph.

"So," he said, stretching out the word, "What are you going to do if you can't use my hangar?"

He looked back at the road and I could see his smug little smile out of the corner of my eye. I thought a minute.

"Okay, Doc. Right. I get it. This is what I'm going to do. I'm not going to pay you one penny over $15,000. No. No, wrong. On second thought, I'm not going to pay you anything. I'm going to pull my airplane just far enough out of your hangar for the doors to close. Then I'm going to go to work installing the bladder right there in front of your hangar."

"Billy!" He turned to me but the smile was gone.

"Watch the road, Doc."

"Billy, you can't do that. That's crazy!"

"Doc, listen to me. Whether I can pull it off or not remains to be seen, but that's exactly what I'm going to do."

I was calming down now because I'd fixed my mind on one thing: I was not going to cancel that run.

There was a long silence, Doc pulled the car off to the side. He looked over at me and made a little laugh.

"Now, Billy, son. Before we let a little joke go too far and I let you do something crazy, let's get serious. You can use my hangar at the regular price, of course you can."

"You're sure, Doc?"

"My word, Billy."

With that, he turned around and headed back to the airport. In all probability, the man had just taken what he believed to be his best shot at getting more money. Back at the hangar, as we pressed on through the heat of that summer night, installing the bladder and fueling the 206, there were no more discussions of money.

At about midnight, Doc drove me to the house and I drove

from there to the Best Western and woke Freddie. I gave him a little pre-flight briefing while he washed his face and brushed his teeth. We covered the weather and the location of the loading strip, the strip where we'd landed the stolen Cessna 210 a month earlier. He buttoned his shirt and gathered his few belongings while I explained that the cylinder head temperature gauge of the 206 was inoperative.

"Apparently, the head temps were staying within limits because it flew from Ft. Lauderdale to Lake City with no cylinder head melt down. But just make sure you've got your cowl flaps open and your speed up during your climb out."

"Got it." Freddie picked up his duffle bag and nodded, grinned. "Let's go then."

We left his car parked in the airport lot and walked to Doc's hangar, opened the door and pulled out the 206. A last check to make sure he had all the maps, drinking water and survival equipment, then he gave me a quick thumbs-up, shut the door of the 206, cranked the engine, taxied out to the runway, and flew off under a beautiful night sky.

I went home, caught a couple hours sleep, and then drove to the Holiday Inn on the I-10 and Crestview exit, arriving at eight while most motel guests were still eating breakfast. Big B was there with his pal Wolfman, the same Wolfman who'd supplied the truck whose flat tire had caused the earlier catastrophe. I could tell Wolfman had not been up very long from his tousled hair and swollen eyes. He was about my size, 5'8, 190 pounds and stocky. With his full head of reddish-brown hair and even longer beard, his nickname may well have been a reference to Lon Chaney in the movie of that name.

Wolf told me previously that he had taken some flying lessons. He wasn't all that experienced but he volunteered his help in that area if we needed him. He seemed to want to smuggle but wasn't sure he had the heart. His real work was carpentry when he wasn't helping with our unloading.

We fueled up our truck and cars, checked our tires, and began the two-hour drive to the unloading strip. An hour and twenty minutes outside Crestview, we turned north and drove another thirty minutes on dirt roads through a forest.

I'd been to Joe's farm and its 300-acre clearing, miles from any major highway, about three months earlier. I knew it would be easy to spot from the air, but from the ground was another matter. We drove up and down dirt road after dirt road as time ticked away. Freddie's earliest possible arrival time was still two hours off, but we couldn't afford to be wandering when he arrived. I noticed we passed an old country house at least three times. Several people were sitting on the front porch, rocking away the day. Each time we passed they waved at us. We had to be the most traffic that road had seen since hunting season.

Just as my frustration was peaking, the orange clay road opened into a large field. We were there. Now we would just wait for Freddie's radio call.

At 3:00 the two-meter radio crackled.

"Mobile one, check, check?"

"Loud and clear, mobile one. Where are you?"

"About 25 miles out."

"Fly over. We'll check your tail."

We heard the comforting roar of his engine and a minute later Freddie flew over without visible company.

"Everything looks good. Please drop in for a visit, friend!"

He banked into one of his best crop dusters turns and was on the ground. We unloaded the pot and bladder, replaced the seats and ran the vacuum over the carpet. Wolfman jumped into the pilot's seat as planned and motioned for me to come over to him. He was looking at the throttle.

"What lift-off speed do I need for a 206?" he asked me.

"Jeez, I don't know the exact speed, Wolfman. Just pull her off when it feels like she's ready to fly."

He stared straight ahead, and it seemed like he would've preferred a different answer.

"Wolfman? Can you fly this thing?"

He jerked his shoulders back and adjusted himself in the cockpit seat.

"Ah, actually, like, I'm just a greenhorn at this. But I'll be okay, Billy. Like, I've got this."

"Alright, man, if you think you can fly a 206, then you go ahead and take off. But if you have any doubts, get on out and go with Freddie. I can take the plane."

"Nope, I'm good, Billy."

I patted his shoulder, closed the door, and ran over to the truck loaded with pot. Freddie was waiting.

"I think we ought to wait and make sure he gets off the ground."

Freddie's eyes widened as he must have seen something in mine. Wolfman taxied forward and was trying to position the plane for takeoff. There was some wobbling to the left and then to the right.

Freddie looked at me. "Are you sure he knows how to fly?"

"He said he could." I shrugged. "Guess we're about to find out."

The 206 was finally in position and Wolfman powered up and started his take-off roll. The plane gathered speed while it wandered a little to one side of the narrow runway, then to the other side.

"Shit!" Freddie yelled. "He's running out of road!"

That was just what I was thinking. The forest wall was only a hundred yards in front of him.

"Pull up!" Freddie yelled and as though Wolfman could hear him, he pulled steeply into the air.

I turned to Freddie.

"Let's get out of here before he tries something else."

July 19, 1987

I came home after practice and as I stepped on the porch something dangling from the top of the porch caught my eye. A green snake was so engorged from eating green frogs, he'd managed to get himself stuck in between the soffits. I'm lucky Mom's visiting from west Florida, She isn't afraid of anything. She heard me scream and opened the front door and grabbed the snake and pulled him ,,, into pieces. Ugh! But thank goodness she's here because with Billy gone, I'd never go in or out that door otherwise.

During the half-hour drive back to Freddie's, we celebrated by doing a couple of lines of cocaine, drinking a few beers, and smoking product. We drove the truck behind his house and into a five-car garage. We unloaded, weighed, and inventoried the bales at a total of just a few pounds over 900. This was going to be a good score. I went to a payphone and called Mark, who was my main buyer. He'd been standing by in Pensacola, only about an hour's drive south of Freddie's. Early the next morning we loaded about 250 pounds in each of Mark's cars and split the remaining 450 pounds between Freddie and Big B, who both had the necessary selling connections. Mark had paid for his pot within a couple of weeks and I paid Johnny in Belize and Doc in Lake City. The following week Big B and Freddie had paid for most of the pot I'd divided between them. They deducted their pay from the sales and gave me the remainder. Naturally, they increased their selling price to make a little extra for themselves.

"Freddie, listen, man. I'll be flying the next trip in the 206 and I want to use the same Black Water strip for the unloading site."

"I do something wrong, Billy?"

"Not at all. You've done a great job but now I want the two of us to split the flying duties and it's my turn."

"So —" He gave me a slightly puzzled little smile. "So, I'll handle the unloading and stash the pot?"

"And I'll pay you for your troubles."

I tended to worry a whole lot more when I was at the landing strip waiting for someone else to bring in a load. When I'm flying, I know exactly what's happening with our precious cargo.

It was almost August, and I was trying to do a load every month. I beeped Big B but he didn't answer. I called Dog because any day now I'd be ready to send him back to Belize to organize a new load. Dog didn't answer either. Then one afternoon Big B called. I couldn't disguise my relief.

"B! Where ya been man? I've been trying to reach you five days now. I thought you'd got caught up with the law or something. I gotta get Dog back south, man. We got to get back to work!"

I took a breath and realized I may have been a little over-zealous. A silence rang loud from the other end of the payphone.

"Big B?"

"Ah, Billy, there's been a few problems since we last spoke. We, ah, we can't use the 206 anymore."

Another long silence.

"Why can't we use the 206 anymore, B?"

Silence. Finally:

"Ah, so, Wolfman flew a load in the 206 and landed on a dirt road in west Florida."

"What?"

"So, after unloading they couldn't get the engine restarted and they had to, like, abandon it there ... on the dirt road."

a smuggler and his wife

"Why ... why wouldn't you just tell me you were working on your own, B?"

"Um."

"You know what, B? I don't like being left hanging in the dark."

"No. For sure."

"And know what else, B? I sure as shit don't like hearing that a plane I had such easy access to has joined everything else in a police compound!"

"I'm sorry, Billy."

"I'll see you later, B. I wish you luck, I really I do."

I slammed the phone onto the receiver with a clang.

July 21, 1987

We never seem to go out anymore. Billy has been gone so much and our old friends have quit calling to ask us to go out with them. I miss that interaction. Seems as if all I do is hang around the house and do mama things. Not that I don't love doing that, but I miss those adult moments and conversations. I guess I could go out with our friends by myself, but it just would not be the same.

Big B's side deal had lost the 206 and I was down to the Aztec alone. I was thinking again it was time to acquire my own plane. For better or worse, I wasn't associated with a drug cartel and didn't have lawyers, accountants, bankers on my payroll, or shell companies in my closet. As a freelance smuggler, what the oil business calls a wildcatter, buying an airplane presented a logistical challenge. First, I'd have to take possession without the seller or the government knowing the identity of the purchaser.

Second, I'd have to pay for the airplane without triggering the $10,000 cash transaction banking rule. In all likelihood the IRS and various government agencies would take some interest in an ex-con who suddenly shelled out a whopping pile of cash.

Trade-A-Plane was the popular trading publication at the time, and I combed through the current issue to assess every Cessna 206, Cessna 210, Aztec and Navajo. I decided on a Cessna 210 for sale in Arizona. The 210 was fast, could carry a decent size payload, and could operate out of short, improvised airstrips. As a single-engine airplane, she would require very little maintenance compared to a twin Navajo or Aztec.

I called Superstition Air Service in Arizona and nonchalantly inquired. The sales manager confirmed the plane was still on the market.

"Thank you, ma'am, I'm looking at several planes, but I just might be in touch."

I hung up; certain I was going to buy that airplane. I just didn't know how. Late that afternoon I phoned Art in Detroit, who I'd met in federal prison in Milan, Michigan in 1984. I explained I was willing to pay $5,000 for someone's name to register the airplane and for an address where the FAA could send the permanent registration. Art was always down to help with any idea I came up with, so I recruited him to call Superstition Air Service in Arizona and tell them he wanted to buy the Cessna and guarantee a $5,000 non-refundable deposit if they would fly the airplane to Detroit. He was a barber by trade and conversation came easy to him. I trusted him to inquire about the airplane without raising suspicion.

I got the confirmation that evening and the next morning, I stuffed $25,000 cash into my cowboy boots, drove to Jacksonville and boarded a plane for Detroit. Art met me at the airport, and we went to a bar named The Bottoms Up, where he introduced me to a man named Pete. We started drinking and shooting pool.

"Ya know, Billy," Art said at one point, "we ought to name

your new plane 'Pete.'" Art, short and stocky, was leaned against the bar watching as Pete and I squared off at the pool table. He was a jokester and I could tell by looking at his grin that he was poking fun at Pete.

"Why is that?" Pete wondered, chalking his cue.

"Because Billy here's buying a beautiful little plane and he's lookin' for someone who'd let him register it in their name."

"Oh yeah? Why's that?"

"Because the authorities are worried about Billy even though the man's got — how many, Billy? — like, the man's got twenty years of flying experience and never had an accident."

Pete lined up the number two ball. "Why is that?" he asked. The man was an exceptionally economic conversationalist.

"Because he's a goddam good pilot, Pete, and he's got $5,000 for anyone who'll let him register the plane to their name. The plane would be, like, yours in a way."

Pete banked the number two ball in.

"I'm solids," he said, and then he looked up. "$5000," he said. "I'd be interested."

I drew a bead on the number ten for the far corner.

"I don't know, Pete. Are you a pilot?"

Pete took a big swallow.

"Nope," he said, "Ain't never been in no airplane."

I sunk the number ten and the green number fourteen.

"Well, that's good, Pete, because I won't be offering any joy rides."

The pool game ended with Pete winning on my scratch.

I joined him at the high-top table.

"If it gets any heat, the DEA or other Law Enforcement agencies will probably get in touch with you and ask a lot of questions."

He nodded. Since he wasn't a pilot, he should probably disavow knowledge of any airplane or any smuggling operation.

"If the cops ask you about a plane, you...?"

He looked me straight in the eye.

"What plane? I don't own no damn airplane. I never been in one."

"Perfect. You'll get your part as soon as you go to a bank and get a cashier's check for $5,000 payable to Superstition Air Service."

We shook hands.

"Hey," Art suddenly chimed in. "Let's go and see if we can find a bank right now!"

Within less than an hour I had the cashier's check in the mail to cover the deposit on the Cessna 210 airplane, and I paid Pete $1,000 of the $5,000 that I had promised him.

We returned to Bottoms Up and finished the day's drinking and pool shooting.

August 1, 1987

Billy has gone to buy an airplane. He's meeting with someone he met in prison in Michigan to buy the plane. This is not a good idea. I told him so, but what does your ignorant wife know about the smuggling business? Nothing, But I know you can't be as trusting as Billy is and stay out of jail forever. Billy trusts everyone. He thinks these new partners are like Mike, Buddy and Tom but they're not the same. He doesn't really even know half of them except through other people. He tells me I'm just a negative thinker. Maybe I am, but I damn sure know that the people he's dealing with may not be as reputable as he thinks. I know trust has to be earned and so far, none of them have earned my trust. Not to mention Billy's on parole and so are many of the new people he's dealing with. Are they being watched like Frenchie was? Who knows?

I left $15,000 with Art so Pete could buy three more $5,000 cashier's checks. I was on Federal Parole and my legal travel was limited to the Middle District of Florida, so I had to travel carefully. I boarded an airliner to Jacksonville, Florida and drove back to Lake City. I let Doc know that I was in the process of buying a Cessna 210 and would need to use his hangar for a day or two to work on the airplane immediately. I could almost hear him salivating.

"So what'd you get, Billy? Tell me all."

"I found a highly modified Cessna 210, equipped with a Robinson short-take-off/landing kit and a custom balanced and blueprinted RAM engine. On top of that, it's equipped with a Q-Tip propeller."

"Whew!" Doc was breathing hard. These features were all desirable and expensive.

"What'd it set you back?"

"A round $75,000."

"Well done! You stole it, dear boy. You stole it."

"No, Doc. This one I actually paid for."

Art called Superstition Air Service every day until the check arrived in Arizona. They gave us a firm commitment to deliver to Gross Isle airport outside of Detroit in three days. I briefed Doc, who agreed to be standing by his hangar, and made an airline reservation to Detroit.

I was preparing to leave home in a few hours' time and was sitting on the edge of our freshly made bed, the $100 bills counted out and stacked in piles. Kay appeared in the doorway and leaned casually against the frame, her fierce eyes conflicting with her body language. I stuffed one of my cowboy boots with folded bills and tried to avoid her stare.

"I just want to know if you've thought this through all the way?" she asked me.

She wasn't privy to all the details because, as usual, I didn't want her to be liable for any of my actions. She nonetheless understood a lot without explanation.

"Don't worry, Baby Love." I gave her a little chuckle. "I've got my tracks covered. Anyway, I won't be gone long."

She exhaled and switched her lean to the other side of the door frame and then pointed one foot. God, I thought, that's a pretty foot. It drew my gaze like a magnet pulls a compass needle, up her body from ankle to belly and the soft curves hugged by her nightshirt. I finished stuffing my other boot and then sat motionless. She stepped suddenly to me and I reached for her hips and pulled her close. Her hands ran through my hair and I kissed the gray cotton that covered her belly and then was thinking about kicking off my boots and taking off that nightshirt. Instead, I stood, moving my hands up her legs to the small of her back and pulled her close into a tight hug. She looked up at me.

"Be careful," she said, then pressed her lips to mine, twisting our embrace into a goodbye kiss — a sexy, aggressive kiss meant to torture and last. That was her plan all along.

"I will."

Nothing more to be said. I left by the front door, my toes wriggling to get comfortable with $70,000.

Art met me at the Detroit airport. We picked up Pete and ran from bank to bank buying cashier's checks in $5,000 increments. Before the banks had closed for the day, we'd purchased enough checks to cover the balance due on the airplane. We returned to Bottoms Up and ordered drinks, then rolled a joint or two.

Noon the next day we called Arizona. Delivery of the plane was delayed due to bad weather. I called Doc and told him I wouldn't be in that night. I probably thought about calling Kay,

a smuggler and his wife

but I knew my home phone lines might be tapped and the less she knew, the better. I'd be home the next night. We returned to Bottoms Up.

The next day we were working our way through hangovers in a small restaurant within walking distance of the aircraft parking area at Gross Isle. I called Arizona. The 210 would be arriving shortly so we ordered a few beers while keeping an eye on the parking ramp. An hour and a half later a brownish gold-colored 210 appeared and descended. I sent Art and Pete out to meet the pilot with instructions for him to fill the tanks. Pete signed the papers, gave the pilot the checks and returned with the temporary registration and the keys to the airplane. I gave him the balance of his $5,000 and he met the wad with a big smile.

I left Detroit immediately and headed south in a well-maintained Cessna 210 in perfect shape. At a little airport in Tennessee, I bought some gas and returned to the sky well ahead of schedule. I was thinking that getting home at a decent hour was going to improve my luck with Kay. I arrived on time in Lake City and when I turned onto the taxiway, I could see Doc pacing in front of his hangar with the doors open. I pulled right in and we secured the plane. He drove me home and we exchanged satisfied compliments about this clever acquisition. But my mind was on that last kiss.

4

We're leaving for Sanibel tomorrow. Billy's answer for everything. If he spends enough money on us, we'll forgive him.

I slept in until 9:30, ate a late breakfast, joined Kay in the shower and left with my Crown Royal bag of quarters. I let Art know that I had a good flight back from Detroit and alerted Dog in Atlanta that I'd need him to make a trip to Belize.

The 210 would need a Loran C Navigational System and a pair of Flint Aero wing-tip tanks that would add 30 gallons of fuel to the 90 gallons that were standard capacity. These refinements would put the polish on an up-to-date smuggler's ability to fly with confidence from Belize to South Alabama. The tanks would have to be ordered and installed and I was in no mood to wait, so I decided to use a bladder tank for my first load. An avionic shop in Ocala had an R-Nav Loran, top of the line, with a two-day installation. That night I dropped my 210 off at the avionic shop in Ocala and Doc gave me a ride back to Lake City.

The next morning, I drove to Atlanta and met with Dog, gave him $20,000 cash — $15,000 for a down payment on the load of pot and $5,000 expense money. I called Johnny in Belize and advised him that Dog would be arriving in Cancun the next day and would need a driver to get him to Belize.

The next morning, I drove Dog to the airport and saw him off, then drove back to Lake City and on the way, gave Freddie a call because I needed him to get a couple of his friends together for the unload at Blackwater airstrip. I arrived back home in the evening before dark, had a shower, and crawled into bed with Kay. She was reading, propped against her pillows, seemingly engrossed, but after a short while she looked up.

"How was your day?"

I wiggled closer and rested my head on her shoulder.

"Pretty productive," I said. That didn't seem enough somehow. "Should be flying a load soon," I added.

She said nothing.

"How was your day?" I asked.

She turned to look at me with that mixture of exasperation and humor I knew well.

"I took the girls to buy some school clothes today. Kim and Amy got into an argument about a purse. They both wanted the same one. I finally had to settle the argument by saying neither one was getting it and told them to pick out a different one. Kim got mad and smarted off. Really, I wanted to slap that smart mouth of hers. I don't know where she gets her temper."

I laughed out loud. We both knew where Kim got her temper. Kay shot me a quick disapproving look but proceeded to fill me in on each event and some of the funnier discussions she had with our girls, who were quickly becoming strong-willed little women themselves. I listened intently, committing the important details to memory.

Our conversation waned, and we were asleep.

The next day, Wednesday, I hung around the house with the girls and that evening Doc came by for one of his frequent drop-ins. Kay tolerated him with her usual measured courtesy and as usual rolled her eyes at his questions, questions he already knew the answers to. He loved the anticipation but had no patience for the process, but like some old teacher of rhetoric, just delighted in debating the costs, the timeline, and any detail he thought might support his critical — indeed indispensable — role in our efforts. Kay left the room to pursue more important matters. I shook my head.

a smuggler and his wife

"Oh Doc," I chuckled. "Oh Doc."

By Sunday afternoon, I'd paid for the updates and notified all my crewmembers. The weather report was favorable. Freddie had assembled all the trucks, scanners, two-meter radios and other necessary equipment. He'd be waiting for me at the landing strip. Doc came by and we drove out to a large bank of pay telephones. Dog in Belize informed me that the loading crew would be ready for me Monday morning at the Pine Ridge strip. At one of Doc's vacant rental houses, we conducted a last-minute inventory of the fuel bladder, the pump fittings and other equipment, then Doc dropped me back off at my house for a shower and a nap.

He picked me up just before dark and we drove to the deserted Lake City airport, rolled out his airplane, and flew to Ocala. I flew the 210 behind Doc to Lake City. He landed first and opened his hangar doors, checked the area out to be sure no one was hanging around, then radioed me to come on in. We pushed the 210 in and went to work removing the seats and drilling a three-quarter-inch hole in the fuselage behind the pilot's seat for the fuel line. My plan was to be airborne for Belize no later than three that morning, but I needed some rest. I went home and Doc picked me up at midnight. The road traffic was almost non-existent, and Doc was feeling confident about our situation. Instead of his usual drive-by, he turned straight into the airport and parked just off the road on a lazy curve of US 90 from where we could see the headlight beams of any approaching car. We opened the trunk and struggled to pull out the bladder and other equipment. The fuel line was wrapped in a big circle, so I looped it around my neck and lifted the bladder with both hands. At that moment, I saw headlights on the main highway.

"Doc. Don't close the trunk. Someone's coming — maybe the police."

He slammed the trunk closed anyway in one of those perverse moments when a man contradicts his own character.

"Billy, my boy, chances of that being the police are like the chances of us winning the lottery."

"We're *trying* to win the goddam lottery, Doc. Open the damn trunk back up so I can put this stuff back in!"

As those words exited my mouth, a car with a big star on the door came around the corner.

"It's the county sheriff," I croaked.

Doc was vigorously digging in his pockets for the keys to the trunk. He owned a lot of properties and carried all of his keys on one chain. I stood in the dark in the airport parking lot, both hands gripping an illegal fuel bladder and a fuel hose wrapped around my neck. In the car was a fuel pump, aviation maps of Central America, police scanners, two-meter radios in the car, and in Doc's hangar was a Cessna 210 waiting with seats out. Except for the pot itself, we were caught with every piece of evidence needed for a full bust. The cruiser was approaching quickly and the clatter as Doc searched frantically through fifty keys sounded like a clatter of death tolls in the night. Sweat had been dripping down my back a moment before, but now a wave of chills came over me. I nudged him with my free elbow. He froze. The sheriff's car had driven past the airport turnoff and into a restaurant parking lot right across the highway. The restaurant had long closed for the night. They were doing their security check.

"I've got them," Doc gasped and held up the trunk keys in the streetlight. We stowed the equipment and climbed into the car. I gripped the dashboard.

"Shit, Doc," I whispered. "Shit."

"I know, I know." Doc was whispering too. "I'm sorry. I am sorry!"

The green and white car sat in the parking lot for ten long

minutes until the cops came out from behind the building. They shone their spotlight around sort of casually then headed back to town. It was now 12:45. We got out of the car and unloaded the trunk.

"Sure you've got enough keys on that chain, Doc?"

"I'll keep certain ones handy next time," he said, and his voice was still shaky.

It took about an hour to install the bladder and fill it with fuel. When we were done, we sat around in the hangar, reminiscing about that time we were almost caught … a few hours earlier. At 2:30 we opened the hangar doors, rolled out the 210, and said goodbye. I taxied out to the runway and took off into a brilliant star-filled sky, climbed to 12,500 feet, and set a course direct for Cancun. The weather was mild and calm, visibility unlimited.

August 16, 1987

Billy's left, headed to Belize. He promised that it would be the last load this month. Ha! Promises, promises. Another night of no sleep and worry. We leave for Captiva in three weeks so he better get his act together by then or he will have one mad Baby Love. I wish he'd let Freddie fly and stay home himself. At least I wouldn't worry about him ending up in the sea. Not that I didn't worry when he wasn't flying but at least I knew he wouldn't die at the bottom of the ocean. Lord, why do the minutes seem like hours? He should be home tomorrow.

I bought two new books, plenty of time to get them read, I guess.

Experienced pilots know that when you're flying a single-engine airplane at night over mountains or water there is an automatic "rough" built into the engine. In these situations, your senses became a little keener and you can detect your engine's every minute misfire and cough. Now Riley Aircraft earned my respect because the RAM engine never so much as hiccupped. I had never flown behind a smoother running engine. It was the first time I'd felt that good in years. I was back on my own two feet again. The good weather and my daydreams of the future held up until I reached Cancun, shortly before sunup. I could see, off to the south, lightning and dark clouds. As I flew past Tulum, I encountered the first rain. A few minutes later, my Loran C navigation system went out. The Loran C is adversely affected by the static charge that airplanes pick up when flying in and around thunderstorms so that just when you most need the precise navigation that a Loran C system provides, it malfunctions. Well, I was never accustomed to having a Loran C anyhow and none of my trips before prison were guided by one. My strategy with storms was to concentrate on flying a constant heading, keep the airplane under control, and trust my instincts — not all that different from the storms in life. Once I was out of weather the Loran C should come back on but if not, I'd just have to figure out where I was the old fashion way.

The rain intensified and the lightning put on a spectacular show. The ride wasn't all that bad, I told myself, if it didn't get any worse. And after about twenty minutes the rain started to slack, and daylight was breaking. On the horizon, it was clear that I'd already passed through the biggest part of the storm and what lay ahead was just smaller scattered thunderheads. The closer I got to Belize the more scattered they were. The Loran C kicked on and then back off again as I crossed the Belizean/Mexican border at Chetumal. I flew on south/southwest past the town of Orange Walk.

The Pine Ridge landing strip came in sight and there was standing water all up and down its length. I circled around for a closer look and decided that even though it was completely saturated, I could handle it. I lowered my undercarriage and entered a landing pattern. As I came down on a short final, I could see only short gaps of hardened mud between watery stretches. I aimed for the driest spot I could see and touched down as soft as possible on the main landing gear. But the dry stretch went only for a short distance until I hit water a couple of inches deep. It sprayed out in a giant fan formation. The airplane slowed but I gave it throttle, hoping the right amount of power would keep me from getting stuck. In this way I splashed my way to the drier east end of the strip, cut the engine, and got out.

"Hola!"

One of the crew leaders came over and shook my hand,

"Hola, Gringo Billy! Good to see you, man!"

"How long since the rain stopped, Juan?"

He took his straw hat off and wiped his brow with a big red kerchief.

"A half hour, maybe. Now is raining in my hat."

Clouds of steam rose off the puddles scattered along the runway. I walked up and down the strip and found it to be in even worse condition than it had appeared from the air, dry and firm in a few spots and deep with water in others, as if God himself had left his giant footprints in the mud.

When I returned to the airplane the crew had fueled it with over 120 gallons of 100 octane aviation fuel and loaded it with 900 pounds of marijuana. I was smiling but this was going to be an extremely challenging take-off. My throat was tightened, and my muscles clenched.

"Adios!" I called.

"Adios, Gringo!" they called back. All smiles. They wouldn't be in the plane.

I cranked up and throttled up. Nothing happened. The 210 didn't budge. I continued adding power until I reached 100% and still nothing. I cut power to idle, got out, and sloshed over to the crew.

"Stuck!" I explained. "Stuck in mud! Everybody help out and push!"

Friendly smiles.

Many of these men spoke a dialect of English or some creole, but the rest were likely fluent Spanish speakers.

"Ayuadame!" I repeated in Spanish. The group hustled over to the plane and Juan ran up to me and shouted over the engine noise.

"Señor Gringo, we take some load off, no? Not so heavy, the plane."

"Are you kidding, Juan? I flew all the way down here for this damn pot and it's all goin' back with me! You guys push here, behind the rear windows on the back of the damn fuselage so you don't hurt this damn plane and you don't hurt yourselves. Understand?"

"Si si. Push!"

I climbed back in and powered back up to full. The crew slipped and sweated in the mud and then the 210 broke loose and started rolling forward. I steered to the right side of the strip, the driest looking area. When I reached a semi-dry stretch, the plane accelerated considerably, and the knot of tension eased in my throat. If I could hop-scotch from dry spot to dry spot, I ought to get enough speed for lift off. In aviation, 'balance field length' is the length of runway needed to accelerate to rotation but then, if necessary, the length needed to abort the takeoff and stop. In my line of work, however, I rarely had the luxury of a balanced field length. On every takeoff out of the Pine Ridge strip, an airplane reaches takeoff speed well past the point of no return. It's all or nothing. Now I had full power on, the flaps set for soft field conditions, the elevator positioned to keep the nose wheel as light as possible in the hopes of preventing it from plowing through the mud. I could do nothing more.

I was gaining speed, gaining speed. The dry stretch ran out. A patch of water. Another, shorter dry stretch. Then water, nothing but water. My 210 bolted up a bit as if hitting a giant root growing from beneath the ground: another dry spot. I held the throttle full ahead. The dried mud mustn't give way to wet mud. A little more speed, we'd be off the ground, my hands sweaty on the throttle, time to pull up. Up!

A long puddle of red-brown water.

"Shit!" I yelled. "Shit! Shit!"

There wasn't room to clear the pine trees at the end of the road. I had 120 gallons of 100-octane aviation gas on board. I chopped the power, and the nose wheel came down hard, just before the smaller pines at the end of the strip. My dirty plane was stopped, her nose dug into the ground like a bird looking for worms, and I was stopped with her.

The prop was totaled, the nose gear and right main landing gear were buried. I put my head in my hands in defeat. Even after digging the nose and right main gear out of the mud, even if by some miracle, they were undamaged, I wouldn't be doing any flying that day. No time to fret. The only thing left to do now to get out of the bush, away from the plane. The crew unloaded the pot, and I drained and removed the bladder and the Loran C, climbed into a Land Rover, and rode passenger for the long drive to Orange Walk.

The road was near quicksand, almost impassable. We bumped along at a top speed of five mph under a morning sun that was glaring like a furnace. I stared out a muddy window as the scrubs jiggled slowly by. If I'd just had a little drier runway, I'd be well north of Chetumal at that moment. And while I was thinking those gloomy thoughts, I considered that I was in fact on parole, forbidden to travel outside of the middle district of Florida. Just the fact that I was in Central America would be valid reason to send me back to prison and if the prosecution could prove why I was in Central America, that would easily justify a whole new conspiracy indictment, new charges, and more prison time on top of the parole violation. I needed to get back to Florida before my parole officer discovered I was out of town — way out of town.

It took three hours to make our way to the main highway, one of the few hard-surfaced roads in Belize, running from Belize City to Orange Walk to the town of Corozal, across the border from Chetumal, Mexico. It was an hour and a half on the highway to Johnny's compound in Orange Walk, where the crewmembers started unloading the Land Rover and a shocked and puzzled Dog and Johnny greeted me at the door. I followed them into a backroom of the house, and it was obvious that they'd already started celebrating. Caribbean white rum, pot and cocaine were strung out across the table in the center of the room. I walked straight to it, poured a big glass of rum and took a gulp before I even spoke a word. They joined me because they knew they'd need it.

"Can we get in contact with a mechanic in Belize City — one who's got a prop?" I took another gulp. "With any luck we can patch things up and I can fly back to Florida in a day or so."

"Billy, you need some serious rum." Johnny got to his feet. "I'm on it, man. You guys enjoy the goods."

He went out. Dog poured us another drink and offered me some cocaine, which I declined. I'd done more than my share of cocaine before I went to prison and I guess you could say that I liked it, or more accurately, I liked it too much. While in prison I'd decided that I'd do my best to stay away from it. I'd known many people who used cocaine, but I could not cite a single success story. I was pro-choice, but for me and almost everyone I knew, the cocaine experience had been a disaster.

As the afternoon turned to early evening we drank, smoked pot, and made plans to repair the 210. We were generally feeling good and it had turned dark by the time Johnny's crew reported in.

"Hey boss!" Lead guy Ramon was smiling in the doorway. "We secured the pot back in a safe house."

"Gracias, Ramon." Johnny was rolling another spliff. "You checked the plane?"

"Si si. We burned it right out."

Johnny finished rolling then looked up puzzled.

"What you say?"

"We burned the plane. Si."

I felt momentarily lightheaded.

"You ... you burned my airplane?"

"Yes, sir."

Johnny leapt to his feet, his eyes wide, and launched a frightening barrage of obscenity that went far beyond my Spanish vocabulary. All I could make out, over and over was "Por qué? Por qué?" Ramon simply looked confounded. After all, they always burned crashed airplanes.

"Johnny, Johnny," I soothed him. "Calm down, man. No amount of hell raising is going to bring back the airplane. It's gone forever."

Johnny looked at me, still breathing hard.

"On second thought," I said, "Dog, pass the cocaine."

I considered calling Freddie, but it wouldn't be a good idea to call his house from Belize and it would just be a matter of time before he called to report my no-show. We continued to party until his call came through about 9:00 p.m. He tried to console me.

"Better than being hung up with the law, man."

"Can't rule that out yet. Ask Big B if they still have that old Aztec. If they do, tell them you need it to come get me."

"Right, Billy. You hang in there, man."

"Freddie, I need you to do something else for me. I'm gonna need you to call Kay for me and let her know it'll be a few days before I can get home."

I could just picture her face and with every day that passed she'd have more questions. I wasn't sure which I feared more — her wrath or the local police finding the remains of my airplane and bringing heat to the area. We devised a plan.

Late that night, we loaded a small boat onto a pickup truck and Johnny's men drove Dog and me and a small crew to the Rio Hondo River. We were greeted by the biggest and least friendly swarm of mosquitoes I'd ever encountered. We unloaded the boat in a terrible hurry and launched it and floated downriver, drinking beer, smoking pot, and snorting coke. I was pretty high. The moonlight and the river seemed perfect for a Hollywood jungle scene complete with spooky animal sounds and shining eyes along the banks. An hour passed and we put in at a small clearing on the Mexican side. Dog and I got out.

"Don't drop that booze, Dog, for God's sake."

"I got it, man, and the drugs."

We waved a silent goodbye to the boat crew, who immediately shoved off, leaving us with nothing to do except drink beer, kill mosquitoes, and wait for Johnny's man Ramon to arrive in the car that left Orange Walk at the same time we did.

Ramon had not gone to the boat-launching site with us. He'd driven straight to the legal border crossing, exited Belize and cleared Mexican immigration and customs. In Chetumal, he'd stopped by the house of a Mexican immigration official he knew personally, woke the guy up, and purchased two Mexican visas: one in Dog's name and one for me in the name of a James Johnson, obtained using the fake birth certificate I always carried with me along with some other falsified pieces of supporting identification handy for just this sort of occasion. Ramon showed up about four in the morning. We were exceptionally happy to see him.

A narrow trail not made for vehicular travel led out of the jungle. Mud below and a dreamscape of dripping vegetation above, all glistening in the lurid glare of our headlights. It seemed impossible that the little truck could hold us as we bumped and ground and slithered from left to right, yet Ramon's skill got us in the end to an actual road. We had planned to take a room in Chetumal but once we were there, Dog and I hatched the idea of pushing on to Cancun, another five hours' drive north, where we figured there'd be sights to see. The saintly Ramon consented and by midmorning we were checking into a room in the Plaza Caribe Motel, Cancun. It had been 48 hours since I'd had any meaningful sleep. We thanked Ramon for our delivery, though probably not enough. I took a shower, smoked a joint, crawled into bed, and slept for 24 hours straight.

August 18, 1987
It's 10:00 pm. No word, nothing. Where is he? Five hours overdue from when he said he should be back. My head is killing me. I can't even read. I've cried until I have no more tears.

I woke to blinding morning sunlight but found an open-air bar and grill beside the pool. Ordered a Bloody Mary and half a dozen tacos. The Bloody Mary down, I switched to cerveza and found the last taco to taste as good as the first. I was wiping the sweat from my brow and the taco residue from my face when Dog appeared like a bear returning from hibernation. I waved him over to my poolside table and saw him trying to stretch his face awake. He slumped down in the plastic chair.

"I'm ready for a drink," he explained.

I scooted my sweaty bottle of cerveza to his side of the table. "Try a few tacos and a swig of this."

August 20, 1987 8:35 am
Tom came by just after I took the girls to school. Freddie had told him to let me know it would be a few days before Billy would be back. A few days from when he left, a few days from today? He wasn't sure. Billy'd crashed the plane, he said. Crashed, what does that mean?
"Don't know," he said "Guess they didn't give Freddie details. Least Billy's not dead."
That's good to know, isn't it?

The Plaza Caribe is in the old part of Cancun's downtown section and is not one of the modern motels you still see advertised on Cancun's beach strip. It was clean and small, and all a person had to do is step out the front door to arrive in downtown Cancun. Recognizing a decent thing, we spent the rest of the week sightseeing. After we covered everything we could walk to, we rented a taxi and checked out the beach and strip. Dog was a decent travel partner, but I couldn't help but think about how Kay would enjoy the local charms. She was also easier on the eyes and the very best companion. I missed my home. Cancun's natural beauty was great, but I realized my favorite view of its beaches was from 10,000 feet.

We kept in touch with Johnny daily and Johnny kept in touch with Freddie. Johnny assured us that they were getting an airplane and it wouldn't take much longer. The heat from the crash was cooling and he'd send Ramon for us as soon as possible. Our last day, we took a ferry out to Isla Mujeres — the Island of Women — and checked out the bars.

> **August 24, 1987**
>
> *The girls are asking about their daddy. Where is he? When will he be home? How long can I keep saying soon, soon? I hate Billy! No, I don't, I love him. He must be injured in some way and just can't get back. What if he is in the hospital and they just don't want to tell me. Why does he put me through this? Why doesn't he call me and let me know something? Not one damn word from him or anyone since Tom came by four days ago.*

Ramon showed up the following morning and wanted to leave immediately. In the town of Bacalar I called Johnny, who informed me that we would be crossing the border into Belize the way we came, meeting up with Johnny's man Enrique and the boat at the little clearing on the river. It was to be another midnight jungle cruise. Dog and I looked at each other because we were thinking the same thing: mosquito repellant.

We killed eight hours in Chetumal, the coastal town on the border with Belize, and set off at midnight. Ramon's off-road driving skills once again got us through the jungle track and Enrique was waiting at the river. The 45-minute ride upstream brought us to the clearing along the river bend. Enrique drove the boat as far onto the shore as possible and we loaded the boat on the back of his pickup truck.

Johnny was waiting for us in Orange Walk with news. Freddie had finally contacted Big B and was in the process of picking up the Aztec.

"Few more days, we can load the pot again," said Johnny.

Dog and I looked at one another.

"What'll we do, Dog?"

"Better celebrate," said Dog.

As part of this plan, we ordered several bottles of Caribbean white rum, then laid out pot and cocaine. My reasoning was that if we threw a big enough party, time would fly and Freddie would arrive on time. We partied straight through until the next evening when Freddie did call.

"I just got back to west Florida with the Aztec," he told me. "Sorry about the delay. I'll be there between eight and nine tomorrow morning."

"Great, man. Use the Pine Ridge strip."

"Oh yeah? How's it looking?"

"Johnny sent one of his guys and it's all dry and in good shape. Be real happy to see you, man."

"What's all that noise?"

"What noise?"

"Laughing, like."

"It's a party, man. We're going at it hard now — waiting for you."

August 27, 1987

Billy's parole man called today. I told him he was working in Ft. Myers with his uncle. I know I must have sounded like an idiot. I told him I didn't have a number to reach him, but he would call soon, and I would tell him. God, please let him call. If I don't hear something soon, I'm going to call the law myself. The girls think I'm sick. I can't get out of bed today. I've slept most of the day. The nights are the worst. Sleep is impossi-

ble at night. I'm going to see Tom if I don't hear from someone by tomorrow.

August 28, 1987

Tom talked me off the cliff. He's right. If something was bad wrong, they would tell him to tell me. Wouldn't they? Tom is right, no one would just intentionally let someone worry. He promised to try to call if we don't hear something by tomorrow.

After I hung up, I knew I needed to be straight for the flight back. I stopped with the hard stuff and watched TV and smoked a few joints. Johnny got in touch with his crew and made all the preparations to move the pot and aviation fuel back out to the Pine Ridge strip.

I was up at four the next morning and downed a dozen tacos. I was beginning to really like those things. They are nothing like American tacos. They were rolled up tight as a fat cigar, so eating six was no problem. — breakfast, lunch or dinner. Still — I swallowed the last one — my wife's cooking was what I was hungering for, or was it just my wife?

I rode several hours with Enrique to the Pine Ridge strip, where the rest of the crew was waiting with the pot and fuel. Dog was to remain at the compound until he heard it was Miller Time, then head to Cancun to catch an airline flight back home. It was just breaking daylight. I walked the strip to check out its condition and at the end I discovered the sad remains of my 210. The only thing that hadn't melted was part of the tail and a foot or two of each of the wing tips. The propeller was mangled and charred, and that lovely RAM engine looked well done. A depressing sight.

'What if this' and 'what if that' was rolling through my mind until I snapped myself out of it. That path would accomplish nothing. I turned around and walked back to the other end of the strip and sat down in a big clump of grass to wait. At about 8:20 the radio crackled.

"Breaker, breaker, how do you read? I'm 10 minutes out."

"Freddie! Good to hear your voice. man. Come on in. All cool down here."

He skimmed the treetops at a high speed as he flew right over us. I radioed a reminder of our location because the strip was tough to see and as soon as he heard my transmission, he put the old Aztec into what looked from the ground like a 90-degree bank, his low wing appearing from our angle to cut the tops of the trees, then made a complete 360 circle of the strip.

"Breaker. I have you in sight! Stand by."

He leveled the wings and the landing gear extended from the wheel wells. The loading crew laughed and cheered at the man's low-level hot-dogging as he held a tight circling pattern, lowered his flaps, touched down lightly, and taxied back to our end of the strip. I motioned for him to turn around at the far end, so we'd have as much runway ahead of us as possible for takeoff. He shut the engines down and climbed out. I gave him a big hug.

"Welcome to Belize, brother. Mind if we burn your airplane?"

The crew sprang into action. I checked the oil while Freddie supervised the fueling. We were nearing the completion of the load when I heard a pop sound along with the hiss of air escaping. I saw a bubble of yellow swelling in the cabin. Someone had accidently activated the automatic inflation of our emergency life raft. We stood dumbfounded as a six-man raft inflated out of a package no bigger than a woman's purse. Rafts like that cost around a thousand dollars each and I had the idea I might someday need one. It was now just one more write-off.

We said goodbye to everyone and took our places in the cockpit. I took the left seat, the pilot's seat, and Freddie took the co-pilot's seat. My rule was: I made the takeoffs. In Colombia years before, I was doing a load in a Navajo and the co-pilot asked to fly the return trip. I had never flown with the guy before, but I'd known him for a while and he'd made a lot of trips. I must have scared him on landing when I'd come close to some donkeys and that's probably why he wanted to do the take-off. On take-off, at the critical stage right after adding full power, he took his right hand from the power quadrant and put it on the yoke. I immediately placed my left hand on the quadrant. Any multi-engine pilot know that you don't take your hand off the power quadrant during take-off. A power failure can result in a VMC roll and the power quadrant is where the action will be in that scenario. I vowed to never let it happen again.

I cranked both engines and gave them a thorough run-up, checking the magnetos and cycling the props. The memory was still fresh of that plane's popping and spitting right after takeoff on the previous trip. I ran both engines up to full power while holding the brakes. It all seemed as good as it could get.

"You happy, boss?" Freddie hollered.

"Let's get out of here!" I hollered back.

I released the brakes and started our takeoff roll. The Aztec was heavily loaded but she started a slow sway forward. The strip was dry, and the airspeed indicator inched toward liftoff speed. When we reached minimum flying speed, I pulled back on the yoke and we climbed out over the pine trees. The engine skipped a few times but there wasn't a pop.

The flight back to the Blackwater unloading strip was about as routine as a flight can be. We discussed the crash and Cancun and the Island of Women. As we left the Yucatan coast for the open Gulf waters, I asked Freddie about Kay.

"I had to let her know you crashed, man. But I told Tom to tell her you were okay, and you'd make it back in a few days."

Wow. This was not going to be good when I got home. Kay was a worrier and, yeah, I'd given her reason to worry, but the word "crash" would have sent her over the edge. It had been well over two weeks with no additional word from anyone and I am sure, in her mind, I was in the hospital with multiple fractures, cuts, and abrasions. What was I really doing? Partying it up and sightseeing in Cancun while she was imaging the worst I'm sure. I'd been an ass. It was not going to be pretty.

Freddie broke my train of thought.

"She really loves you," he chuckled. "I mean, your wife really loves you."

I nodded.

"I've tested her love, that's for sure. She's never wavered."

I looked over at him and he was smiling to himself.

"I think I'm in love with Sweet Pea," he said.

All Freddie and his girlfriend could do was battle and have sex in unending cycles. I cleared my throat.

"Freddie, I don't know if you love her or not, but I do know that being with the right one means a lot more than lovemaking and fighting. Still, I have to admit, in my book there's no better lover than Kay — and no better fighter either. She has a mean right hook for a female and I'm afraid I've, well, I've given her good reason to use it on me."

He laughed when I said this — though a little nervously, I thought.

"I got myself a winner, Freddie. But see, I didn't know it from the start, I didn't know I'd picked the best cook, the best mom and the best friend a person could find. I had to realize that through time and her devotion. And, far as I can tell, buddy, ya'll aren't quite there yet, you and your Sweet Pea."

"True," Freddie admitted. "True."

a smuggler and his wife

My thoughts turned to Kay and our first encounter. In December 1968, marriage was the farthest thing from the mind of the 19-year-old I was. I had plans to play the field all my life. I saw her as she pulled into Giebeig Amoco in a brand new 1969 gold Road Runner. I'd inquired about that very car when I saw it in the Plymouth showroom. The dealer told me a rich lady had already bought it for her daughter, who had just moved back to Lake City. The car looked good, but from what I could tell through the back windshield, I needed to check out the driver. The attendant was gassing the car up and washing the windows as I watched. When he was done, I figured if I was going to approach her, it better be right then. I circled the car as if I were admiring it and came up to her window. Yep, I'd been right. She was beautiful.

"What you got under the hood?" I was using my coolest of voices. I couldn't take my eyes off her legs in that miniskirt. She looked up, and her eyes locked me in.

"I think it's a 383. At least that's what it says on the hood."

I felt so stupid. Couldn't I have come up with something better than that? She signed her ticket and drove off without my even getting her name.

A few weeks later I saw her again at the local community college but by that time she had several guys interested in dating her. We dated a couple of times over the next year and a half, and I almost lost out completely when she got engaged. Luckily, the guy messed that up and I started dating her regularly in October of 1970. I don't know if you could call it love at first sight or not, but I knew from the first day that she was the girl of my dreams. Around Thanksgiving of that year, I did the unimaginable: I asked her to marry me and I've never regretted that choice. That fiery 18-year-old at the Amoco station had my heart for over twenty years and always would.

The unloading went well. Freddie rode back with the unloaders to the stash house and I flew the Aztec to DeFuniak Springs where I left it parked on the ramp. From there I called a taxi and rode back to Century where I had my driver drop me at a truck stop. I called Freddie to pick me up and then I called my wife.

She answered after the first ring.

"Hey Baby Love, how are you doing?"

Silence.

"Baby Love?"

"Your parole officer called and came by the house," she said. Her tone was cool.

"What did you tell him?"

"I said, you're in Fort Myers working and should be back soon."

Fort Myers was my cover location because it was about as far away from Lake City as I could be while still within my approved travel district.

"And he said?"

"He said you should get permission from him before you spent the night away from home."

I could also tell by the tone that I was going to have to do a lot of explaining, to Kay and to my parole officer. I'd rather have faced the parole officer.

"Anyway, Bill, he wants you to call him as soon as you hear from me."

Uh oh. She had used the dreaded "Bill". Only when she was really mad did she call me Bill. But apparently, she'd been convincing to the parole man, as usual.

I tried to sound reassuring and apologetic.

"Thanks for the message and I'll see you tomorrow."

I hung up. I didn't like hearing that my parole officer

was looking for me. I thought about calling him, but what if he pulled the old trick, asking for my phone number in order to call me back? Best if I waited until I got home.

August 30, 1987

Billy called this afternoon, 14 days after he left for an overnight trip. He'll be home tomorrow. My thoughts are: how many years would I get if I put a bullet between his eyes the minute, I lay eyes on him? He sounded perfectly fine, like he had just gone to the store and was checking in to see if I needed a loaf of bread. What person does that to someone else? I feel sick to my stomach. God give me strength.

I loaded the trunks of my buyers' cars until late that night and early the next morning Freddie drove me back to Lake City. The shit storm struck as expected and there was no flying over or around it. When Kay realized I didn't even have a scratch, her fears transformed into fury. I should have at least broken an arm or something. She stopped yelling after two hours, but it took the rest of the day before she'd let me touch her. When it looked like I might survive, I called my parole officer, who told me what he'd already told my wife.

"I … I didn't know I needed your approval to leave the house overnight. Tell you the truth, Officer Jackson, I thought if I was in the middle district, I was okay."

"No. You've got that wrong, Billy. You're making my job harder than it should be."

"I'm sorry."

"I want you to come into my office tomorrow."

"Your office?"

"Tomorrow at ten."

Thank God I hadn't called him from some distant outpost of business, but I put the phone down wondering if I should actually show up in his office. He seemed awful sore. Maybe he'd decide to violate my parole and have me locked back up.

"Hell," I thought, "just about everyone's mad at me."

Then a cheerful thought.

"Wait a minute. My pot buyers aren't mad at me."

August 31, 1987

He's home and sleeping in our bed. I'm writing in the living room. My fears have turned to rage. It's the first time since I came back home to him in 1980 that I question my decision. I'm questioning my sanity. That April day in 1979 when I made the decision to divorce Billy, I had reached a breaking point in my life. Either I was going to end my life or his. I had a plan on how to end my life, high speed north of town on 441, cruise control, close my eyes and let it happen, or I could just take the entire bottle of Xanax. I feared my anger at times would result in my shooting him. I would be so mad when he would come home at 1 or 2am smelling of liquor and whores that I could have easily pulled the trigger on him. What stopped me? Kim and Amy. They were 7 and 5. Who would take care of them? When I decided to leave it was like a ton of bricks had been lifted. I was happy again, I met someone new, fell in love again, married and started over. Why did I leave that life of happiness with a good man, a good father for my children to come back to this? What is it about this man that can make me the happiest and the saddest woman on earth?

"You know he hasn't changed. He'll hurt you again."

Those were the words of my then-husband as I was packing to come back to Billy.

"I know, but I have to give him the opportunity to try."

So, the situation I find myself in tonight, I went into with open eyes. Again, I have only myself to blame.

I slept most of the day until the evening, when as I'd hoped, Kay had cooled down and relented enough to make me dinner and let me kiss her. By the next morning I'd decided that rather than make a run for it, I'd see what the parole man wanted. I ate a big breakfast — no tacos — and kissed my girl goodbye and drove to Jacksonville.

I handed Jackson my monthly parole papers. He looked at them with disdain,

"Dekle," — He was really working hard at being tough; it worried me — "Dekle, I don't want you to be late with your report ever again. These reports are due on the fifth of the month. You do know today's date, don't you?"

"Sir, I'm terrible with calendars and stuff like that. I lost track of everything in prison, but I do know I'm very late with these papers. I mean I'm seriously late."

He pointed the papers at me aggressively.

"It's the thirtieth."

"Jeez, I'm sorry, Officer Jackson. I didn't mean to cause trouble."

He dropped the papers in a box on the end of his desk.

"The thirtieth," he repeated.

"Yes, sir," I said.

He fixed a stare on me. Truth is, I really had forgotten about the papers.

"Work?" he queried.

"Doing what I can, sir. Tires me out sometimes, that farm."

"But a regular job?"

"Still looking, sir. They say there might be one of them recessions coming, so I know it's important I get steady work."

"Hm. Home?"

"All good, sir. The family's glad to have me home."

He kept up the stare, which was disconcerting.

"I bet," he said.

I generally felt these meetings were going well when we'd get on the subject of my home life, my wife, my daughters. Jackson looked away a moment, then back at me.

"Dekle, I think you need to complete a drug test. I want to know if you've been staying clean."

I tried for a positive-type nod.

"Yes sir. Okay. I did just use the bathroom before coming in though. I might …"

I tried by my expression to suggest something a little painful. Jackson looked at his watch. He must have been hungry.

"Come back after lunch and give me a sample, Dekle."

"I sure will, sir."

I went over to Morrison's Cafeteria and drank more iced tea than a man is designed to hold. I sort of waddled back to the parole office an hour later and took the drug test.

On my way home, all the things I needed to do were running through my mind. Among the most pressing was the need to sell the remainder of the pot. Why had Mark, one of my main customers, not shown up for his share of the load? Where was I going to find another airplane? Logistics and heavier things were dancing a reel in my brain.

For the first time since coming out of prison, I realized that I was probably not going to make it on parole much longer and that didn't leave me many options. I could hang around until I was found in violation of my terms, whereupon I'd be immediately sent back to prison. They could deem a violation for almost anything ranging from the trivial — failing a drug test — to something as sinister as traveling out of my approved area without their permission.

The possibility of going back to prison was distasteful, indeed unacceptable. My other option was to just quit parole and go on the lam. This was also distasteful. Being away from my family would be bad but being away from my family and locked up would be really bad. I was approaching the turnoff to our road. All I could see ahead were two paths, both worse than a jungle trail in the rain.

September 3, 1987

The girls and I drove to Jacksonville today for some school shopping. They are all three excited about school. Kim and Amy Douberly at CHS as sophomores and Amy a big eighth grader. I am so blessed to have these girls in my life. I don't know what I would do without them to love and care for. Our first home football game and the Falconettes first performance will be this Thursday night. I have a really good team this year. A lot of talented and sweet-natured girls. This year is going to be great. I am so proud when they walk on the field to perform at halftime. Since the middle school doesn't have a band that performs, we are the halftime show. They make me so proud to be their coach.

September 4, 1987

It's the first CHS game of the year. Billy, Amy, and I went to watch Kim and Amy Doub. They are on the Tigerette dance team and they will be performing with the band this year. Don't know how that will play out. The performance was nice tonight, but they are so used to performing with contemporary music and not with a band that doesn't always have the same tempo. Nevertheless, they were excited, and they are performing on the same field that Billy played on in high school. Friday night under the lights! Maybe the rest of this year will go smooth for everyone.

September 6, 1987

We are leaving for Sanibel tomorrow. Billy's answer for everything. Buy your way out. If he spends enough money on us, we'll forgive him. That's how he thinks. He doesn't realize all we want is his love.

We should be here for a week. Going to do a little clothes shopping for the girls on the way back. The guy at the condo office told us about the Bubble Room Restaurant so we're planning on going there one night. The girls saw a lot of shops, so we'll go do a little island shopping tomorrow. The condo has a bedroom and loft, and it is right on the beach.

5

"Well, Billy. I understood you preferred death traps on account of the price. I was glad to supply you with one."

Some time off was in order. For a change I called my parole officer on schedule, but really just because I needed permission to travel — not to Central America for once — I didn't ask him for permission for those trips — but just to get away with my family. It had been years. Kay and I loaded up the kids with our beach cargo and suitcases and headed for a condo at the South Seas Plantation on Captiva Island, off the west coast of Florida near Ft. Myers.

September 7, 1987

We all went swimming today. The water is warm and beautiful and we have our own private beach. Our only problem is the stingrays — they're everywhere. You have to slide your feet in the sand to scare them away. The girls aren't much for that and neither am I. But the beach is beautiful.

September 8, 1987

Shopping Day and Bubble Room tonight.

I kept in touch with Freddie because I needed to know whether Mark had made it down yet to pick up his share of the pot. He hadn't. I started calling around because the man was so reliable. No one had heard anything. Everyone was afraid he was in jail. Finally, I phoned his friends down in Daytona Beach.

Mark had driven Freddie to get the Aztec so Freddie could fly down and pick me up after Johnny's guys had burned our airplane. The next day Mark was dead from a drug overdose. He'd been a good friend, a good person, a man of his word. He'd be missed by everyone who knew him. Another soldier not walking forward. I called Freddie. We'd sell Mark's share of the pot to our other customers.

Now I tried to soak up every moment with my girls: all the little laughs, affections, words in passing. So much depends on being present for what is real. Time, as has been said, waits for no one and our little vacation away from the logistical grind of organizing covert smuggling missions and parole regulations passed far too quickly. We returned home to Lake City.

Now to find another airplane, one of our own.

September 10, 1987

We're leaving tomorrow. A few days early. One of Billy's main distributors, Mark, was found dead. It appears he OD'd. I can see it has shaken Billy. I'm fearful that it might be him one day. What a waste of a life.

September 14, 1987

Debbie is going back to school to become an elementary teacher. She called and told me she starts next Monday. She has to finish her AA degree at the community college and then she's going to the University of North Florida in Jacksonville. I am so happy for her. I'm still substituting. Wish I could go back to school.

Well, I guess I could. I'm going to check into it for maybe next semester. It wouldn't hurt for me to take a class or two each semester. It would keep my mind on a positive track. Not elementary though. It would have to be secondary — maybe history. Yes, I am going to check this week to see how many courses I'd need. But 36 and going back to college? Is that even smart? Will my brain still work?

September 28, 1987

I finally heard back from the college and I need 6 classes to complete my AA. Debbie and I both had an AS in Business so the only drawback is I must take college algebra to finish. I'll take it last for sure. I hate math! Anyway, I'm so excited. I can start in January. Billy thinks it's funny that I'm going back to school. Why do you want to do that he says. I told him I was shopping for a new husband. He's such a shit.

December 25, 1987

We're at Mama's home for the holidays. Billy bought me a diamond heart necklace for my birthday. He even made me a card. It read, "I will always love you too muck!" When Amy was little, she wrote us from camp and said, "I miss you to muck" so Billy likes to joke about it. This is why I still love him despite his faults. I always will. We'll be here for a little over a week. Relaxing time before my new life begins, a college girl.

I began my search in the Keystone Heights area of North Florida. Paid a visit to my old friend Barney, just released from prison. He was rung up on drug charges prior to my stint in the pen, so, naturally, I was happy to learn that he was out and back in the aircraft maintenance business. I first met Barney when I was learning to fly at age 16 and he'd become my maintenance guy back when I was flying legally. He was a good, honest family man and, in my opinion, back where he belonged — out among airplane parts and working alongside his adult sons.

When I arrived, the hangar was filled with airplanes and Barney had most of the same old crew busy about the maintenance floor. I parked behind the building in a yard littered with dead plane parts. An Aztec up on jacks was the first thing I spotted in the hangar. I thought to myself, "There's some potential there."

Barney was in his office in his normal mechanic clothes: white shirt, blue pants with his name over the pocket. He was in his early sixties, stooped over, looking through a filing drawer. Even when he stood, he had a slight stoop. I knocked on the open door and hovered in the threshold. He looked up and shot me an expression of surprise.

"Oh my God," he said. "Oh my God. I *heard* you were out."

We shook hands and exchanged awkward shoulder pats. His eyes darted around.

"Yeah, Billy. Great to see ya. Ah, did any of the workers see you?"

His slight accent was ever so apparent when he spoke. I was never sure if it was German or French but it was definitely not American English.

"Yeah. Saw one of your old guys. We said hello."

"Great," Barney said. Then he lowered his voice. I leaned in.

"Billy," he said, "you know you are always welcome here, but you know, since we both had problems, I'd rather you not be actually *seen* here." He looked down and then straight at me. "I don't want no talk to get started that I'm back in, you know, the smuggling business."

Sweat had started to pop out on his balding head.

"I got you, man."

"My son Mick is down at the Model T Bar, Billy. You could both meet me here after closing."

"A drink always sounds good to me, Barney."

"Yeah, great, Billy. Just great."

Almost nobody wants to go back to prison. It's just that some of us want something more than we don't want to go back to prison. But I understood Barney and I sort of nonchalantly made my way out of the hangar and drove down to the Model T Bar.

Mick was sitting at a table and when he looked up, he recognized me just as his father had done earlier. It's a special feeling, seeing an old friend for the first time after you've been locked up for a while. It's like you've both returned from the same war but at different stages of the conflict, weathered into different versions of your past selves. Both Barney's sons had fought a few battles of their own and both had done some time. That's when the whiskey goes down like water, when the stories are good and the memories even better. For most of three hours Mick and I drank and compared notes. It was "old so-and-so got busted out in Alabama" and "I believe old so-and-so in Mississippi is getting out pretty soon, ain't he?" and on and on until we'd covered the highlights. Feeling full of good times past, we got in my car and drove south to the intersection on SR 21 and SR 100. The light was red. I drummed my thumb on the steering wheel. Mick noticed my cell phone, which at the time would have been a rare sight.

"How does this thing work?" he asked. I picked the phone receiver up from its base.

"Give me the number of anyone you want to talk to." The phone beeped out each digit as I thumbed it in. "See? It's easy," I explained.

"Look out, Billy!"

I'd relaxed my pressure on the brake and we were almost completely across the intersection, moments away from the plate glass window of a convenience store. I glimpsed the horrified expressions of on-lookers before I whipped the car around and shot west on SR 100. I picked up the phone from the console and used my calmest tone.

"What did you say that number was?" I asked. Mick repeated it and I began to punch it in.

"Look out, Billy! Christ!"

We were in the oncoming lane. There was the ditch, the road, another car. I threw the phone to the floorboard, swerved back into our lane, both hands firmly on the wheel.

"Yeah. Listen, Mick, tell ya what. We better make that call later. Got my mind on other stuff."

"Right, Billy. Yeah. Good idea."

Barney was still in his office going over paperwork. We took seats in front of his desk.

"I like that Aztec, right there." I gestured behind me to the plane up on mechanical jacks. Barney squinted and nodded.

"Oh yeah, I flew out to Arizona and ferried that old girl back. She'd made a gear-up landing, been sitting at the accident site until a dealer out there bought it. I put two new props on and flew her back here for more repairs."

"How'd she do?"

Barney sort of raised his eyebrows and nodded his head.

"I'm here, ain't I?" he said.

We walked out into the hangar and I gave the Aztec a good going over.

"It looks okay to me," I said. "What do you think, Barney?"

"Just keep her in the air, Billy."

"I generally do. Let me know the dealer's asking price."

I woke up the next morning with a giant hangover and the headache pounded my brain the entire, wasted day. My adoring wife was not so adoring since I'd returned home for dinner three hours late the night before. I was at least thankful she didn't bang pots and march around the house. I gave Barney a call the next day. The Aztec's price was $80,000 so I called Art in Detroit to let him know that I was buying another airplane. He laughed.

"Dang! Already, Billy?"

Barney had planes just sitting around in need of a test flight and the next morning before daylight I met him at Keystone airport. He had an older model Cessna 210 gassed up and ready to go and the owner wouldn't be back for a few days. I made a before dawn take-off, saw a beautiful sunrise, enjoyed good weather all the way to Gross Ile, Detroit. As before, Art and I went from bank after bank until we had enough cashier's checks to warrant a celebration at the Bottom's Up Bar. I paid the Detroit boys $5,000 for their efforts and took off for Keystone the next day. I gave Barney the $80,000 worth of cashier's checks plus Pete's name and address for the registration.

The previous trip had convinced Freddie and he and I had decided to become 50-50 partners in this plane. On my way back to Lake City I called him.

"We're the owners of a new Aztec," I announced.

"Great!"

"Well, actually, we're the new owners of an old Aztec."

"Still good. And I'll do you one better — I got us a strip. My buddy Blaine's got a little crop duster strip north of Atmore, Alabama. We can base the Aztec there, get gas there and do our maintenance there."

"That's what we need. Okay, I'll call Dog and arrange for him to get down to Belize and make the arrangements."

"Right. And let's get the Aztec moved from Keystone to Blaine's place."

We were pumped.

January 4, 1988

Billy has a new plane, and he's excited. He's like a kid with a new toy when he gets a new plane. They're planning a load soon, but I don't have time to worry with that right now. School is starting back for the girls, and I'll be starting classes soon too. I registered at the college for three classes, Physical Science, Child Psychology and Religion. Hope I haven't bitten off too much. I start next Monday. I have two classes with Debbie, so I feel good about that. My classes are in the morning, so I have the afternoons off for practice and to be with the girls and Billy.

January 11, 1988

My first day of class, I have Physical Science and Religion with Debbie and then Child Psychology. Nothing really happened today except the overview of class and we were given the syllabus and a calendar of expected exams and reports due. It's different than back in 1970 when I was attending class but my attitude is different too, I want to do good. It's almost a competitive feeling. I'm older than most of these students and I want to do better than them.

Dog flew down to Tampa from Atlanta a few days later. I met him at the airport and gave him a down payment for the 900-pound load of pot and some expense money. The next day before dawn I flew to Alabama and met Freddie at Blaine's little grass airstrip. We drove around most of the day making phone calls and drinking beer until Freddie flew me back to Keystone.

Dog called from Belize a few days later. All was ready. We'd be using a cow pasture on a Mennonite cattle ranch.

I drove to Freddie's place in west Florida. Apparently, his buddy Blaine, who owned the little duster strip there, was also a pretty good mechanic. He ran his repair business from the strip and unlike Barney had never been mixed up with the law.

"So what's Blaine's opinion of our Aztec?" I asked.

"You mean from a professional mechanic's point of view?"

"That's the only view he could have since he's not in the smuggling business."

"Right. Well, in Blaine's opinion, it's a piece of junk. Technically speaking."

Really?" I frowned. "It flew from Arizona to Keystone and from Keystone to here okay."

Freddie shrugged. "I'm just telling you what Blaine told me."

Blaine was a good guy from what I could tell. I knew he was just trying to look out for our wellbeing. But negative thoughts were not what I wanted to hear.

"Right, Freddie. Good to know, because if it's junk, it's our junk and in a few hours, it's going to pick up our next load of pot."

About three in the morning, I took off and headed across the Gulf to Belize. I had no problem finding the Mennonite's cow pasture and Dog met me there with the Mennonite himself, a gentleman named Poncho, and a small crew of workers who loaded and fueled my ride. I flew back to Northwest Florida and unloaded at our strip. It was a routine pot run, if there could ever be such a thing.

We kept the Aztec busy the rest of the month with two more runs, which I made alone. While we were prepping for the third run, Freddie approached me with an uneasy, almost distressed expression. If he'd been Doc, this would be a demand for more money in one form or another. But Freddie wasn't Doc.

"Um, Billy. I need to talk."

"Okay, Freddie."

"We're partners, right?"

"Right."

"Fifty-fifty."

"Right."

"But Billy, all I've done is unload."

I looked at the man and he looked back and I understood. He was a pilot.

"Freddie, you need to do some flying too, huh?"

"I do."

So Freddie and I flew down together and picked up the load. Freddie met Dog on the Mennonite pasture field and after the standard greetings, we all set to work. When we turned back toward the plane Freddie sort of whispered.

"What's with him?" He gestured towards Dog. I'd grown pretty accustomed to Dog at this point and hardly noticed that the man was extremely drunk. But in fairness, it was hard to find a time when Dog wasn't drinking.

"Guess there's something about success he can't handle," I suggested.

Meanwhile Dog for some reason had become involved in the fueling of the Aztec. Aviation fuel pumps work at a much faster rate than gasoline station pumps and the nozzle doesn't cut off automatically when the tank is full. When fuel began to overflow the tank and flood the top of the wing, we watched while Dog panicked, snatched the spout from the tank and sprayed fuel like he was a fireman overpowered by his water hose. He staggered a little and clamped his free hand over the spurting nozzle, which turned into a giant sprinkler soaking everything in a 50-foot radius. Dog cursed. He was determined to stop that flow of fuel with his hand and he pressed even harder. The harder he pressed, the bigger the area he saturated with aviation fuel. A quick-thinking worker shut the pump off. Dog stood like a disheveled kid who had fallen in a puddle but was actually a human torch ready to ignite. Later he reported that he had suffered for days afterwards from a medical condition known as balls o' fire.

January 20, 1988

They are keeping the new plane busy, but for some reason they aren't happy with it, so Billy is shopping again. He has made several trips to Detroit in the last year. I'm starting to have suspicions as to why he keeps going there. If he goes again, by gosh, I'm going. I know he still has a wandering eye because I see him lookin. Men are such jerks. Billy is easily influenced by the friends he keeps, and the new ones I fear are — I'm sorry to be writing this — pieces of shit.

January 25, 1988

School is going great. I feel more confident than I've ever felt. I guess I was like most kids in their teens going to college after high school: education was not what we were there for basically.

On the smuggling front, something is bothering Billy. He isn't his usual easy going self. I know he's worried about the plane and making sure the loads go off as planned but it's more than that.

February 1988. We decided to take some time off because our supply was running ahead of our sales and Blaine was getting more and more concerned about the condition of the Aztec. He threatened to terminate our arrangement because we were going to get killed and that wouldn't look good for him. I flew our poor Aztec back to Keystone and told Barney I was looking to trade for something different.

"Different how?"

"Different like in not being a death trap."

Barney rubbed his chin.

"Well, Billy. I understood you preferred death traps on account of the price. I was glad to supply you with one."

"Thanks, Barney. Maybe just not such an obvious death trap?"

"Well, you're, hmm, you're awful particular, Billy, but I'm here to serve ya."

6

I'd look out over the vastness of the ocean and think about how Kay was out on the other side of the horizon.

As good as his word, Barney came through with a Cessna 210 that flew like a bird. He'd arranged a direct swap if I paid another $5,000. The entire transaction went smoothly, very smoothly. That may have been when I started to experience — and ignore — a nagging voice. I was an easygoing man who liked to punctuate his thoughts about work routine with thoughts about his family but somehow the routine felt off and the little voice nagged on. Instead of trying to identify it, I swallowed it with a swig or two of beer.

I met Freddie about 8:30 one morning at Blaine's airport in Atmore, Alabama, threw the car keys at him, climbed into the passenger's seat, and rolled a joint. We rode around for hours discussing Glen and Frenchie's bad luck, the so-called war on drugs, the political mess. I recall displaying no emotion other than nonchalant benevolence and Freddie probably wouldn't have recognized it if I'd shown anything else. We were parked on the outer edge of Blaine's farm staring out at the cow field and we'd run out of opinions. A cool breeze moved through the open windows and an awkward silence settled over us both. Suddenly my buzz gave way to a sickening feeling sensation that washed over my whole body. I shook as if I had a chill and I could feel Freddie making an effort not to turn his head, not look at me. We each cleared our throats.

"We're out of beer," I said.

"Yeah, we need to get to work and bring in another load," Freddie said.

I pushed the dread under and the moment passed and

whatever message it might have carried would have to arrive by another channel. I put the dread back in its place.

I called Dog and made arrangements to meet and give him the down payment and expense money just as I had done so many times before. The next day I stayed around the house with Kay. She sensed my worry but when I couldn't come up with any solid responses to her questions, she suggested that we go for a walk. That evening after dinner we walked down to Alligator Lake and trails around our neighborhood. We didn't discuss work, but instead fell easily into a conversation about how we first found one another, how we came to be a couple, how young we were and what we might be like when we got old and gray.

"You thought you were so smooth when you told me that time that …"

"That what?"

"When you walked up to me and asked what I had under my hood at Giebeig's Amoco station in December of '68. Was that the best line you could come up with?"

"You had me mesmerized. I was scared stiff. I swear I had never just walked over to a girl I didn't know hoping she'd give me the time of day. But you, I had to try."

She rolled her eyes.

"There you go again with that BS, Billy."

"I could tell you were beautiful, the most beautiful girl I'd ever seen. I couldn't let you get away without trying. Once I got to your window and saw those legs and the rest of your body, I lost all thoughts on how to be smooth."

"So, you asked what was under my hood when 383 was printed on the hood in three-inch numbers that both of us could see?"

"I didn't have a chance to be smooth," I laughed. "You could read me like a book."

"I still can."

She flashed me a knowing smile, put her hand in mine, and turned our steps toward home.

The next day I met up with a reassuringly sober Dog in Tampa and saw him off, money in tow for the pot purchase. He was to fly to Cancun to meet one of Johnny's drivers, who in turn would escort him by car to Orange Walk, Belize.

I focused on Kay for the next four days and those days were great. The nights were unforgettable as she spent them intoxicating me with her calm reassurance and loving hands.

Freddie meanwhile was getting his unloading crew ready and organizing the landing strip, the meeting times, the phone calls. We met the day of the job.

"Freddie," I told him, "I feel I should be flying the first load in our new airplane, okay?"

He looked at me with startled amazement. "Why would that be?" he asked.

"Because I was the one who had found it. That's all."

He shook his head in disbelief.

"Billy, you flew the two loads in the Aztec without me and the last 210 we had, you managed to tear it up before I even got to see it."

I looked at him steady and kept a straight face.

"Freddie," I said, "I just left my wife but even she didn't nag on me like you're doing right now."

He set down the rachet wrench he was holding. I was surprised to see the expression in his eyes.

"I'm not the one who got our plane thrown into a fire pit, am I, Billy?"

I chuckled but not too hard. "Okay, Freddie. How about I'll fly this first load and then we'll alternate."

"Fine," he said and turned away from me to address one of the crew. 'Know what?' I thought. 'I'm going to be looking for another airplane. You and me could fly two loads at once without having a bitch-fit about it."

In all the years I worked with Freddie, that was the closest we came to a business disagreement. Just two flyboys who loved to fly.

We phoned Dog to tell him that we were ready. He'd be waiting for me on the Cane Patch Road, which runs north and south just west of the Orange Walk airport. I already knew exactly where he was, and the run. I took off in the Cessna. I flew, I landed, I loaded, I took off, I flew, I landed. It went like clockwork. It was almost too easy. It was almost boring.

We unloaded the Cessna, loaded up the trunks of several cars with pot, stored the remainder in Freddie's uncle's spare bedroom. I drove back to Lake City and exhaled a deep breath of easy-going air. I decided it was time to relish how good things were finally going.

I opened the front door to my home and saw the expression on my wife's face.

"What's wrong?" I asked.

She nodded towards our youngest daughter, Amy, sitting at the table with her book, some pretzels, and a fruit cup.

"Nothing," she said. There was that twinge between her eyebrows. She nodded. "Happy to have you home, hon," she lied.

"Heeeeyyyy daddy!" My daughter uprooted herself from her reading spot and gave me a hug. She was smiling ear to ear and I met that expression with my own. I asked her about her book and school. I kissed my wife.

"Okay, honey," she said. Your daddy just got home and he's probably tired."

When we were alone, Kay looked at me and it was a baleful look.

"Billy, there was a message from your Uncle J.E. He wants you to go to his girlfriend's house tonight and wait for his call."

Calling Uncle J.E. wasn't a simple pick-up-the-phone-and-dial procedure because Uncle J.E. was at that time a resident at the Tallahassee Federal Correctional Institution, doing time for marijuana smuggling. So around seven that evening, after our family dinner, I went to J.E.'s girlfriend's house to wait for his call. We exchanged the usual greetings and then got down to business. My uncle was aware of the last load I'd run from Colombia just before I went to prison. He also knew that most of the people involved in that load were also now in prison. Through the prison grapevine, which is probably as accurate a source of information as you can find for these things, my uncle confirmed that some of my old friends and business associates were presently being subpoenaed to a Federal Grand Jury. An investigation was underway concerning a sizeable load that, I and the young men I affectionately called "the beach boys" had completed back in 1984. The beach boys were the quintessential surfer-dudes. They spent their days in the Daytona Beach sun on long boards and only stopped riding waves to do a job. Four of those beach boys were now in prison and most of the others were at points apparently unknown to the Feds. Glen was the most recent of the four to be arrested.

"Billy." My uncle spoke slowly. "Billy, I, ah — listen, Billy I recommend that you take a vacation."

All of that worry, anticipation of some kind of fall, suspicion of the ease of things was now plowing through my abdomen like a sucker-punch to the gut. I should've seen this coming and, somehow maybe, I had, but it was still shocking. "Thanks, unc," I said. "Take care of yourself."

I hung up the phone. This conversation only confirmed what I had been quietly gnawing on for several days. Time is such a precious commodity; I thought, one that we have so little control over. It had occurred to me recently that now *my* time with Kay and my girls, as I knew it, was running out. So now, hearing those words from my uncle's mouth, made the ticks of the clock became deafening.

February 16, 1988,

Billy's uncle J E has called. His uncle is in prison and he hasn't spoken to Billy in well over a year. He said it was really important that he talk to Billy and soon. JE and Billy aren't what you call close and the only real tie they have is smuggling. I told Billy the time and place for him to be when he got home today. This worries me. What's up? Why the need to talk now? When Billy got back from the call, he said uncle's call was nothing—just his usual bullshit. Maybe so, but I can tell when he's not telling me everything.

Why, you may be wondering, was this news so devastating and serious? My association with the beach boys had taken place over three years earlier. I hadn't personally been caught. I can only explain what I've learned about the U.S. justice system — the hard way. I had every reason for anxiety.

Law enforcement authorities don't have to catch you; they don't have to act immediately or even have any actual knowledge that a particular something had been illegally smuggled into the country. They can instead play a wildcard. This wildcard is called "conspiracy." It's a term most have heard before. The term may be familiar but very few people know how it actually works and what it means in this context.

"Conspiracy" is a secret weapon with incalculable potential for destruction and even after being charged with it several different times, I'm still very far from having a complete and full understanding of it. It would probably take a library full of books and a law degree to adequately comprehend its incalculable potential for destruction. Experience alone has taught me the basics and the most important parts which can be covered in three points:

(#1) Hearsay is alive and well and an integral and large part of a conspiracy prosecution.

(#2) Most government witnesses have been caught in the act of committing a crime or are victims of a conspiracy charge themselves. The government pays them in the form of cash or freedom or both. This exchange — information in return for a lighter sentence or no sentence at all — is worth more than any amount of money.

Finally, the most important truth about a conspiracy charges:

(#3) The government almost always wins. Their conviction rate is well over 90 percent.

You may wonder still, how a person can get caught in a conspiracy. Well for Uncle Sam, that presents no problem at all. He has another secret weapon that he can spring on smugglers when they least expect it. That secret weapon is called, "The Grand Jury."

The Grand Jury consists of 16 to 18 regular citizens who have been randomly selected for jury duty. People just like you who work ordinary jobs for an honest pay and probably have zero time or desire for such things as civic duty. Who can blame them? Anyhow, one of these people is selected to be Foreman, whose main job is to sign the indictment. They usually meet two or three days a month at a Federal building, usually the Federal courthouse or a U.S. Post Office. There, they have their own private room with a big table and chairs. One chair at the end of the table is reserved for the witness. This seat is what I call, "the hot seat" when it is occupied by a witness who is not a law enforcement person. The other end of the table is reserved for the government's lawyer or prosecutor, who usually stands behind a small, official looking podium.

The government lawyer will confidently open the Grand Jury by calling a list of U.S. Customs agents, DEA agents, and FBI professionals. These men and women of the law are asked a series of leading questions as to why they believe that the person being investigated, who is referred to as the "target", is a smuggler. The agents often explain to the Grand Jury that their investigation began innocently with a tip from a confidential source. The identity of this person, this helpful source of information, cannot be disclosed or produced, since their safety may be at risk. The agents further explain to the Grand Jury how they were contacted by the source, this magical "Good Samaritan" appearing out of thin air, who related to them that he/she would like to report some criminal activity. The source explains that he/she doesn't want to get involved but feels that they need to "do the right thing" and report this activity to the proper law enforcement agency.

Of course, in reality, this person who is the "source" is hardly ever of such high moral character. Most of the time the source has been involved with the accused in some integral way and is either unhappy with how a previous deal turned out and so seeking revenge or is trying to save their own sorry butt from more time in the slammer.

One of Frenchie's friends, for example, had relayed the real reason the investigation on Frenchie was launched in the first place. The informant (or in less technical terms "snitch") was retaliating because Frenchie was fooling around with his wife.

Anyway, the legal proceedings continue with the agent explaining the process of their investigation. The noble informant reveals that the target is/was smuggling drugs and then names all people involved with the target. The agents, only doing their job, spring into action and place all those named by the source under surveillance. This is done, unquestioned by any other authority, even though the agents have gathered no physical evidence nor caught any of the named in the act of or behaving suspiciously with the intention to sell, smuggle, or deal drugs.

The agent conveys to the Grand Jury that after such necessary surveillance, the "target" — a well-chosen word — now appears to be "of reasonable interest." The target's behaviors that may confirm this notion are the agent's witnessing the target using pay phones or beepers, the target paying for everything in cash, and/or the target rarely demonstrating a routine consistent with having a steady job.

The agents now zero in on all who appear to be involved with the target. These associates are watched for weaknesses. Upon identifying a possible weak link, the agents subpoena him/her or pick him/her up for questioning. The agents intimidate and threaten him/her with astronomical amounts of prison time. All the while emphasizing to him/her the horrors of prison life.

When the agents feel that they have the person scared properly shitless, they cast a final net to seal the deal. "You are so lucky," they announce. "You are not who we really want. There's a way you can avoid spending the rest of your life in prison. ..., you can choose the road of righteousness and become a government witness! Just tell us everything you know about the target and testify before the Grand Jury." In other words, the more the old target knows and talks about the new target, the better deal the old target gets. As a precaution, however, the agents generally leave out these little tidbits of their process when explaining to the members of the jury just how the incriminating information was gathered.

The former smuggler — the old target but now a persuaded and motivated "government witness" — is understandably motivated. He communicates every detail he's ever heard about the new target and when necessary, embellishes the story in front of the Grand Jury to please the agents who are so in control of his fate.

This smuggler, now dressed in citizenship-award clothing, scared half to death, is now fighting for his freedom. He will say anything in the hopes of making his role in the prosecution's case as vital as possible, thereby increasing his odds of not going to prison. Integrity, honesty, friendship, partnership be damned along with all thoughts of perjury. All of those mean very little to a person who just sold his colleague down the river for a better bed in the pen, for fewer years inside and more years closer to home. And if he does go to prison, at worst he will at least have earned himself a meager stay in one of Uncle Sam's better accommodations, known as Club Feds. It's critically important to a snitch where he does his time because there are different levels of prisons. They range in security from the Club Feds, which don't even have a security fence, to low and medium security level F.C.I. At the top, with the highest security level, is the U.S.P. the United States Penitentiaries, which usually have walls 20 feet high with three rows of fencing decorated with razor sharp wire and flanked by manned gun towers. At the U.S.Ps, rapes, assaults, and homicides await him as part of everyday life.

After all the witnesses have testified to the Grand Jury, the prosecutor asks the members to vote. The prosecutor reassures the members that they are not voting on whether anyone is innocent or guilty. They may say something like, "you will not vote the accused's fate today, nor do you vote to decide guilt or innocence. You are merely deciding if there is probable cause that a crime may have been committed." For the average person, this seems too simple and straightforward. Since all testimony has come from an agent of the law or a government witness, voting to have the accused tried properly only seems fair and necessary. The prosecutor again reassures jury members that a vote "yes" only means that the target will be given a fair trial as guaranteed to him by the constitution of the United States. Most jurors probably think they're doing the target a favor by indicting him and giving him a chance to clear his name.

By these means, the target and most of his associates are indicted. In most cases these proceedings are followed by police storming a quiet yard in the wee hours of the morning. SWAT teams armed with automatic assault weapons will break down the big, bad (and non-violent) pot-loving smuggler's front door before he pours his milk into his cereal, throw him to the floor in his pajamas, and cuff him. As a bonus, these arrests usually produce more witnesses for the prosecution. After being arrested, "targets" want to cut deals too. The target learns quickly that he is headed to prison for sure, unless he is willing to hand over someone who the Feds are even more interested in.

I smuggled drugs into the country. I smoked pot, did drugs, but I was never violent, would never kill for money, and I would never sell out for less time on a crime I did commit. If I was caught, I was caught. I wasn't going to pull someone else down with me. And, at any rate, I was a little fish in the pond of pot smugglers so there would be few persons of interest I could use as bargaining chips.

With Uncle J.E.'s call, I had only two options: I could sit around until my inevitable indictment or I could haul ass. It really wasn't much of a choice, but one option was better than the other. Being on the lam isn't much fun unless it's compared to being in prison. My worst day on the lam was in fact far better than my best day in prison. On the lam, I wouldn't often be able to hold Kay, kiss her temple, share in her joys and struggles. Behind bars, I would never be able to. While on the lam, I wouldn't be able to do this as I always had, but being free meant at least some life with her was possible.

I had been preparing for this in case it ever came up. I

didn't want to be caught flat-footed. A few months before J.E.'s call I had ordered several books from Eden press and Loompanics. They were entitled: *The Paper Trip, How to Change Your ID* and *How to Vanish and Stay Gone Forever*. I read them and followed the author's instructions.

First, I obtained a birth certificate of a deceased man who would have been about my age had he lived. The man's name was Jim Lang. I took his birth certificate and went to Nashville, Tennessee to rent a mailbox from a small mail service on Murfreesboro Road. This gave me a legal street address. I then visited a sporting goods store and told them I'd just moved to Tennessee and I wanted to go fishing. They gladly sold me a fishing license. Big B then drove me out to the highway patrol station where I got into a long line of people waiting to take their driver's test. In less than an hour, I was legally licensed to drive in the state of Tennessee. A real driver's license and birth certificate can be a tremendous help for a man on the lam.

I got in touch with Freddie. I wanted to keep things going while I was out of the country and I was hoping we could achieve one more run before I had to go. After this last run, I would operate from Belize. Dog was on board as well. And in fact, all of my friends agreed that the new working arrangement was better than me not working from prison.

Things were tense though. I could now feel the heat from the flat tire bust as several members of that crew had been arrested. It was just a matter of time.

We pulled off one more run and when it was done, I knew the hour of decision had arrived. Now came breaking it to Kay.

This would be the hardest decision I ever made in my life. I didn't want to leave my family, but I didn't want to go back to prison either. If I stayed at the house, I would surely be arrested and face Lord knows what charges. If I ran, I could only run for so long. It would be just a matter of time before I got caught. I rationalized my decision: I could at least make money for Kay and the girls while on the lam. I would somehow arrange to see them. That was something I could not do in prison.

I would run.

February 18, 1988

Billy and I are going to Crescent Beach for our anniversary. Well, we have made it 17 years. It has been and up and down path, but we do love each other regardless of all our faults and I have as many as he does. Good to get away this weekend just the two of us. I am so glad he insisted we go. I have exams in two of my classes so studying is in my future when we get home.

February 21, 1988

Just when I think I'm out of the pin ball machine, Billy drops another quarter in and I start hitting the sides and ricocheting back and forth. He's leaving, going on the run. This is why we went away, not for our anniversary but for him to break the news to me. He and his partners decided it was the best thing for him to do. He and his partners decided! The ones that I don't trust, the ones that don't have wives and families! Those partners!! He didn't even have the decency to discuss it with me first. We have argued continuously since last night. What an anniversary. I haven't spoken to him all morning and we're almost home. He's leaving Wednesday, going out of the country until things calm down. He doesn't know for how long — maybe just a few months then he'll come home, and we can start meeting in secret. Please God help me see how this is going to work and how our marriage will ever survive it.

February 24, 1988

We got the girls off to school and my first class is at 9:00 am. Billy packed last night, and he kissed the girls bye and told them he would see them soon. They waved bye like they would see him in a couple of days, like they had done so many times before. That is so far from the truth. We won't see him for months — he's already told me that. He plans to go somewhere in Belize, but he doesn't give me any definite town or location. All I know is I have a location of payphones in Lake City that he will call me at when it is time. He said Tom will contact me if anything goes wrong. I'm thinking about what could go wrong. My God, I can't do this, but I can't go with him, I have the girls to raise. How have I allowed so many lives to get this screwed up? He gives me those same non-consoling words, "Everything will be okay, Baby Love, you'll see. I love you."

I watch as he drives away. I guess I stood there for maybe five minutes before I looked at my watch and went inside to get my keys to drive to class. I hoped I would see his car come back but that's a dream for another day.

I drove to Orlando and met up with Dog at J.D.'s son's house. We partied well into the night and planned what we would do once we were out of the country.

I got up the next morning and decided to call Tom before we left for the airport, just to make sure he knew who to contact in Belize should he need to reach me. Tom had been one of my first partners in the business, and he was the one person I knew I could trust if I needed to get in touch with Kay. I didn't want Kay to know because, as always, she had to be kept out of the loop. I knew Tom would be at his bar, Tom's Place, and I could easily speak to him before catching my flight.

"Hey, Tom, it's me. I'm about to take off and just wanted to make sure you had all my contact information if you need it. I'll try to stay out of trouble."

"Billy, you need to come back. Kay needs you."

"What's wrong? Is she okay?"

"They're at the hospital. It's her dad."

February 25, 1988

I was struggling getting the girls ready for school and thinking about Billy, has he left the country yet, when my stepmother called. They had rushed my daddy to the ER with a massive heart attack. I called Debbie and then Anne, Billy's mom. I'm not sure what I even told her and then grabbed the girls and out the door. It must have been several hours later as I was sitting in the hallway that I looked up and Billy was walking down the hall. I ran to him. "How did you know?" We talked briefly and then it was my turn to go in again to see daddy. I knew he was weak; his soft eyes were tired and looked so weary hooked up to the machines. I rubbed his rough, hardworking hands and told him I loved him. I was crying and Billy had his arm around me. We stayed for a few minutes and then left so Debbie could go in. The last thing I remember before I left was looking through the small window in the door and seeing my stepmother and Raleigh, my younger half-brother, kissing daddy.

Then he was gone. How can two days be so devastating and then we go on with life like nothing was the matter?

February 26, 1988

I lay in Billy's arms a long time before going to sleep last night. I had resigned myself to the inevitable, that he was gone for a long while. Now I'll be faced with watching him drive away again.

I'm trying not to think about that part of my life and to stay focused on what I need to do to face today. We're meeting Debbie and Carol, my stepmother, at the funeral home this morning to make the arrangements. It would be my daddy's and my mama's birthday on Sunday. He would have been 65.

February 28, 1988

My daddy's birthday. We buried him today. The service was short, and the burial was with Masonic rites at the family gravesite. We ate with the family and were back home before dark. I guess all this will set in but right now it doesn't seem real. What does seem real right now is that Billy told me he has to be out of here before sunrise tomorrow. I feel numb, like I'm in a nightmare that I can't wake up from. 1 Corinthians 10:13. I am going to need you Lord more than ever to help me through this.

February 29, 1988

It's 5:00 am and Billy's left. He kissed me bye and said he will call when he thinks it's ok to see us again. I have no idea when that will be. My heart is breaking. I couldn't walk him out to the car like I did before, I don't have the strength to watch him drive away. I have a couple of hours to myself before I wake the girls for school. I need to concentrate on them and college. I know time will move slowly but I need to fill it with good things and not dwell on the negative. If I don't, I won't make it.

March 1, 1988

My first day alone, alone as a single, married woman. I have no idea how long our separation will be, but I need to stop feeling sorry for myself and get a grip on this thing. I have two — no, three — girls to take care of, college to focus on and two dance teams that could fill in the rest of my free time. If I don't allow myself to focus on Billy, I can do it. Except for the nights I'll be okay. The nights are the hardest, when everything is quiet, and I have only my thoughts to keep me company.

Dog and I boarded an airline flight for Cancun, me traveling as Mr. Jim Lang. After a day or two in Cancun we moved down to Orange Walk, Belize. For the next six months, there and in San Pedro Island, I settled into a relaxed if mundane life as a single man and a Belizean citizen. Freddie came down and picked up three loads with the 210 in the space of a couple of months but I spent most of my free time drinking, doing drugs, snorkeling on the reef, plus assorted disreputable activities that passed the time. I missed my wife and kids like crazy but maintaining an almost constant inebriation helped stifle that longing.

March 21, 1988
We are getting into a routine. Thank goodness Kim's boyfriend takes them to school. I only have to worry about driving Amy Dekle since she goes to a different school. I've caught up on most of my college work that I missed when my daddy passed and did fairly well on my first exams. If I can keep my head centered on school, the girls, and dance I'll be exhausted by the time I hit the bed. The weeks have gone by relatively quick. Things are well on all fronts so far. All fronts except for missing Billy. My mind wanders at times in class. I need to focus more. It's been 21 days since Billy left. Not that I'm counting. The girls want to go to mama's for spring break at the end of next week. They know she'll take them to Panama City. Of course, they are all into boys right now.

I guess I'll let them go. Our spring break time is not at the same time. Mine is this week, so I can't take them anywhere. I'll be home by myself during the day, but I can study without interruptions, I guess. I have a paper due on April 6 and Billy's mama, an English teacher, is going to help me with it on Sunday. At least I have that going for me. It has been a while since I've had to do reports — all that footnote crap and stuff blows my mind. I am so behind on cleaning and doing laundry. With all the schoolwork and mama duties it's hard to keep up. The girls are excited about going out to mamas. I hear them planning on getting mama to take them riding down the strip so they can see all the spring breakers. Lord, what am I going to do next year at this time when Kim is 16 and can drive? I don't even want to think about it. I'll give mama a call tomorrow and see if I can meet her in Tallahassee with the girls. I'm sure she would love to have them for a week. I hope being by myself when the girls are gone is not going to be hard on me.

I tried pretending I was on an independent vacation instead of what I was: an outcast out of touch with his friends and family. I chartered a little sailboat for a day cruise. The captain was a cool dude and we bonded while getting high and fishing. We "fished" with his Hawaiian sling, a crudely crafted homemade spear gun that took some practice but provided hours of entertainment. When we returned to San Pedro, my new amigo, Captain Roberto, informed me that I was welcome to come along with him as a member of his crew whenever I wanted to. I subsequently killed quite a few days at sea, or rather just off the coast, on Roberto's old wooden boat. There was a like spirit between the two of us, Roberto and me. We both enjoyed the beauty and adventure of being out on the open water. I'd look out over the vastness of the ocean and think about how Kay was just on the other side of the horizon and soon we'd be watching the sun go down together again — that at least was what I hoped for. The steady thump and bounce of the waves and the simple business of running a boat can help a person forget. Sometimes that's what I needed: to forget.

April 1, 1988

I've just racked up my first accomplishment as a single woman. I was able to relay to the mechanic in a somewhat intelligent manner exactly what problem my 84 Oldsmobile was having. Billy always handled the car maintenance but now that ball is in my court. If I have any more trouble, I've made up my mind to trade. I can't be on the road having to worry about whether a car can get me to where I need to be.

April 8, 1988

It's 11 PM, I wonder where he is. Is he in Belize? In the US? It's not knowing that is hard. When he was home, I at least knew when to worry. Now, I don't know what he's doing. Is he running a load? I guess if something bad happens to him someone will tell me. What am I thinking? They didn't let me know anything before, did they? Maybe he is just partying like before to pass the time? Which is worse? I need some kind of sleep aid to help me at least doze off at night. My mind goes a million miles a minute the second I turn off the light. I just leave the TV on all night; it helps to concentrate at times on whatever is on. I can at least doze a little. What a way to live.

I'll be picking the girls up in a couple of days. I'll be glad to see them and have something besides overwhelming silence in the house.

7

I need some time with him alone. I need to know what he's planned for our future. I need to be included in the planning.

May 28, 1988

I've dropped the algebra class I was taking during the summer semester. It isn't worth me worrying about Billy and math too. I'll start it again in the fall. I did well my first semester even though my dad had passed away and my husband took off to parts unknown. Got two As and a B. I have picked up some substitute teaching jobs when I'm not in school. Billy left me with $20,000 here at the house and I have about $50,000 more at mama's so money isn't a worry but the more down time I have, the more I think about him. Money doesn't make things better; it only makes survival easier. I would rather not be alone than have the money! I drove over to my mom's this weekend to buy Kim a car. The Chevrolet dealer in Bonifay is a friend of my stepfather. In the showroom they had a 1988 red Chevrolet Camaro. It is a 6-cylinder coupe but that is enough for her. She knew that it was the one as soon as we walked up. All three girls ran straight to it as soon as they got out of the car. We looked at a few other cars, but her eye kept going back to the red one. The deal was made and my stepfather wrote a check and out the door we went in just a few hours. I'll give him the money back in cash. The girls are excited to death. Kim's birthday is the 30th so it will be a big birthday for her. She and Amy Doub have been planning the first night of driving it around to show it off. To be young again —, how it must feel!

July 1, 1988

Didn't have time to write in June. Too busy. We went to mamas for a couple of days to relax before we started dance team summer practice. When we returned, I had a visit from the US Marshall Service. They introduced themselves, showed me their badges and asked if they could come in. I was scared. It had to be that Billy was dead. They'd found his body floating in the Gulf. I could hardly breath. Then they started asking me if I knew his whereabouts. I told them, no, we'd been separated for 4 months and I had no idea where he was. Has he called you? No. Have you gotten a letter from him? No. Do you have a number to reach him? No. Then the other man spoke up. You do know he has another woman and family, don't you? No, I don't. Yeah, he has a lady by the name of Karen Stapleton that he has another family with. I looked at them both and I said, "Well, Billy isn't going to be by himself long, so I don't doubt it." I did some calculations in my head while the conversation was going on and figured out Billy had only been out of prison for a little over a year and a half. It takes 9 months to have a baby, so he had to have been working fast to have gotten a woman and had babies that quick. And I doubt he's been away from us long enough for all that. Anyhow, I damn sure wasn't going to let them see me squirm. I acted like no big deal. I explained that they needed to be checking with this Karen on his whereabouts. They gave me a card and told me to contact them if he got in touch with me. I assured them I would. I locked the door as they left and leaned against it for several minutes to slow my heart rate. I was relieved that evidently Billy wasn't dead but mad as hell at the thought that he had another woman. I don't think it's true — but how the hell would I know. I can't ask him. I don't know where he is. Maybe he is with Karen Stapleton. I'd kill him, if I only knew where he was.

As a principal of the little Century Cartel, I'd enjoyed a string of successful pot runs and was adjusting to life as Jim Lang. But for the whole of my other life, to this point I'd always had a place to go. I'd always be home for suppertime or able at least to return to our family routine after a short trip. Now going anywhere near my family would be the same as surrendering to the law. The house and phone lines were almost certainly under heavy surveillance. I felt increasingly like a piece of driftwood. I'd lost my home, I'd lost my wife, I'd lost my little girls. I'd lost Billy Dekle.

August 1, 1988

I've been angry and easily upset since the visit from the Marshall's Service. I struggled through summer camp with the dance team in July and I've coped with raising my girls while hoping that no one could see that I was near a breakdown. I keep wondering, am I that much of fool not to have suspected that Billy was having an affair? No, I had suspected him of being unfaithful, one-night stands, whores; but never having another woman that he kept on the side. All I had was a name, no way to check it out. Who would I ask beside Billy? I have gone from "it couldn't possibly be true" to "that SOB is living in another country with someone named Karen". I'm making myself sick going back and forth. I pray that God will help me with this because I can't keep on like I am. My nerves are frazzled and I'm tired and lonely. It has been 6 months and not a word from Billy. Either he comes home, calls me or I'm done. I can't take it anymore. I know I'm tired, but a person should not have to live with this much stress.

Today I went by the bar and saw Tom. I told him how I felt. He told me to give him a couple of days and he'd try to contact someone to find Billy.

With every week that passed, I needed more desperately to be with my family. I needed to hear their voices and see their faces. I wondered what they were doing. I wondered if they felt the same void that I felt in my life. No responsibilities other than getting myself up in the morning and deciding whether to hang out with Roberto or seeing what was happening at Johnny's compound or just sitting on the beach and getting high — it was all getting old.

I had just roused myself out of bed and cooked a little breakfast in the apartment in San Pedro when I heard a knock at the door. I figured it was the girl who cleaned the place for Johnny. I opened the door and to my surprise it was Tommy, Johnny's man.

"Gringo," he said. "Johnny say you need to call home at 11:00 today."

My heart stopped.

"Why? Is my family okay? Are the girls okay?"

"I think so but I don't know anything."

I checked my watch. It was almost ten. I showered and dressed. Was it Kay? Did she need something? Who had called and why? I quickly walked the half mile to the nearest pay phone on the island, killing the final fifteen minutes pacing back and forth in front of the phone. She answered after two rings.

"Hello?"

My heart soared.

"Baby Love. It's me."

There was a silence and then I heard the soft sound of sobs.

"What's wrong?" I was nearly shouting. "Is somebody sick? Are the girls okay?"

Finally: "Billy, I need you. I miss you. I can't take it any longer."

"Kay? Is everyone okay?"

"Yes, yes. But I miss you."

There was already a lump in my throat.

"Kay. Baby Love. I miss you too."

"When will it end?"

I took a breath.

"I'm coming home," I said.

I called Freddie, who told me he needed a hand with sales because he was getting behind. I pretended to care.

"I understand, buddy. So when you pick up our next load, you're going to pick me up too."

"You ... you sure, Billy?"

"Never surer."

August 5, 1988

I could hardly speak when I heard his voice. Every emotion I have had in that 6 months welled up in my throat. All I could do was cry. It took me a good 5 minutes to gain my composure. Billy told me how much he missed me. I told him I was done with this. I needed him, and he needed to make it happen. He told me to give him about a week and he'd let me know when and where we could meet. We talked for a little longer. "Don't give up on me," he said. "We'll be together soon." I sat in the car after the call just staring at the phone. I'd just talked to my husband who I hadn't seen in 6 months and I hadn't even asked him where he was. I didn't care, I was going to see him in about a week. It didn't matter as long as I could hold him. I'm going to tell him I can't live like this. We're going to have to figure something else out.

Now if I can make it one more week.

A week later, we took off just before noon from the makeshift strip in the cane patch. I was at the controls all the way back to Florida. There was no argument this time from Freddie on the flying duty, though maybe there should've been. Somewhere out over the Gulf, I began to get sleepy. I'd been up most of the night with the crew, helping them bale pot and celebrate. I wouldn't have been able to sleep anyhow given my excitement at heading back to American soil but now my eyes were becoming increasingly heavy and I began to nod off into the edges of sleep. Freddie bumped my arm.

"Hey partner!" He made a nervous laugh. "Think you need a nap?"

I jolted awake, disoriented, and then took in my surroundings and remembered where I was.

"Thank you, my friend. I believe I will."

I leaned as far back in the seat as possible, laid my head against the window, crossed my arms, and went to dreaming about seeing my wife and girls. I'd been asleep at least thirty minutes when I was jarred awake by turbulence. Again, I struggled to gather my thoughts and remember where I was. I looked through the windshield and saw we'd flown straight into a large, dark cloud. I glanced over at Freddie and noticed that he too was just waking up.

Hey, buddy," I said. "Real nice of you to take over so I could take a nap."

Freddie looked around the cockpit with alarm.

"Shit, Billy," he said. "I'm sorry, partner, I don't know what happened."

"That's okay, buddy. Maybe we'll both stay awake, seeing as how we'll both be dead if we don't." I resumed control. "At least one of us needs to be awake."

The rest of the flight was routine. After we landed, we unloaded and stashed the pot in a building behind Freddie's house.

Freddie had said he was behind in sales, but and in fact this building looked more like a marijuana plant wholesaler had taken up permanent residence, with new bales arriving daily. Several hundred pounds were left over from the last load. We inventoried the pot as quickly as possible and then headed for his house. Inside, Freddie waved me toward the back room.,

"Come on. I've got a little something to show you."

On top of his dresser was a powdery mess scattered everywhere, and three freebase pipes. It was kind of like we were kids in an ice cream bar with just the right flavors. I helped myself.

"This will give us the jolt we need," I said.

We spent the rest of the day and night freebasing cocaine and took a whole day to recover. I'd been home for forty-eight hours and I was already a mess.

As usual, I put my immediate desires before responsibilities. I'd been aching to see my wife and yet the last several months away had created a distance within me. This distance was far worse and more destructive than the actual distance between my family and me. I didn't know how to just walk back into my old life because my old life didn't exist anymore. I'd become Jim Lang, a single man with no commitments. I was anxious to see Kay but scared at the same time. I loved her still, even when my actions did not imply it, and I would always love her. I knew her love for me wouldn't have wavered once in my absence. The intensity of our feelings for one another would force me to face how hard this time had been for her and how responsible I was for her pain and loneliness.

I did the only thing I knew how to do: work. I put one foot in front of the other. I drank about a gallon of water, loaded the trunk of our haul car with 220 pounds of pot, and drove to just south of Montgomery, Alabama. I needed to handle some of the work stuff and refocusing my brain on our overpopulated storage room was a good way to get my mind right. I met up with Randy, one of Freddie's friends who was also a buyer. He and his wife owned and ran a little convenience store. Randy was a good guy, a reliable business associate, and only a moderate drug user. Like most of us he had done a little time but now he tried to keep a low profile and stay under the radar. Running the small store helped him do this.

I was just starting to unload the pot when he hollered at me from the back door,

"Hey man! I need to know what your plans are!"

This was an unexpected question. I was confused. He waved me inside and we stood in the back room of his store.

"So, Billy, do ya'll want to stay in business or what?"

I laughed, still confused.

"Well, hell yeah, Randy. That's the plan. Why?"

"Why?"

He seemed to have an idea I wasn't in the know.

"Well, Billy. You know. I have been tryin' to get more pot from Freddie for over a month now."

"From us?"

"Yes sir. That's right. Freddie'd say he'd be up on such and such day and I'd hang around the house wait'n on him and he'd pull a no-show."

"You talk to him?"

"Well, yeah. I'd call him to find out what happened and get another date from him. Then the son of a gun would stand me up again. If ya'll don't want to sell me any pot that's okay with me." He went under the counter and stood up with a brown paper bag. "But hell, Billy, I sure would appreciate it if you would pick up your damn money."

He said this jokingly, but Randy wasn't the kind of man who wanted to hold onto money that wasn't his. I shook my head.

"I understand, Randy, and I'm so sorry, really. I'm sorry for the no-shows and for letting you run out of pot. I don't know what Freddie's problem is. Really, I …"

Halfway through my apology he tossed me the grocery bag.

"That's got $340,000 dollars in it.," he said.

I looked in the bag. It sure did look like a pile of money. "And Randy, I apologize for you having to hold onto this money for us."

We shook hands.

"I'll be in the States a lot more now," I said. "If I ever tell you I'll meet you somewhere, then I will." I think he took me at my word, and I hoped he had because I certainly meant it.

Falling asleep when you're the only man at the controls of an aircraft is one thing but messing up a good deal with a good man is something else. Nonetheless, that would have to wait. It was time, past time really, to see Kay.

I called Buddy in Lake City and asked him to pay Kay a visit. She needed to know I was home and we needed to agree on a safe place to meet. I knew she would have worked this out in her head already and was just waiting on the word. She had and she was.

Her mother lived in west Florida in a pristine block house on forty acres of mature pines. The perfect place to get together. It existed happily in the middle of some pinewoods with plenty of country roads zigzagging their way through even more woods and countryside. My mother-in-law's house sat at the end of a long, dirt path for a driveway winding through rows of adult pine trees and ending at their home just off the Choctawhatchee River. There was no way any intruder could see who was at the house unless they trespassed by climbing the fence and walking a quarter mile through rough undergrowth. If anyone followed Kay, she'd know. If anyone was waiting there or showed up there, I'd have a means to get away. She and I both knew those woods like our own hands, and I'd enjoy a real advantage in making a break through the dense acreage should I need to. I just hoped this would not be necessary.

The weekend was still three days away, so I drove back to the town of Century and Freddie and I killed those three days partying all over Escambia County, Florida. We hit all the bars and strip clubs in Pensacola, and all the bars in and around Century. We even went into the woods with the unloading crew and built a big campfire. It was like being back in high school, standing around a makeshift pit and drinking beer. I meant to confront Freddie about his questionable mishandling of one of our most reliable buyers and the $340,000, but the subject never seemed to come up.

On the fourth day, I sobered. I took the car we'd purchased to haul pot and drove approximately two hours east to the vicinity of Vernon, Florida. I was eager but I was also very careful. I first checked up and down the surrounding country roads looking for anything that looked like it didn't belong. Once I was sure that there wasn't a trap, I pulled up to the property gate. The gate was unlocked. They were expecting me. I opened it quickly, pulled through, and latched it.

For the first time in over six months, I was seeing my family, one of my life's happiest evenings. I tried to take it all in, slow the clock, even for just a few seconds. It wasn't long before the girls caught me up on all their school activities. They were buzzing with excitement and their growth was undeniable.

There were two houses on my mother-in-law's property: the main house and a smaller home used for family and guests. Sometime around midnight Kay and I retired to the smaller of her mother's two houses, leaving the girls to stay within the care of their grandmother.

August 19, 1988

Billy's one week has ended up being two weeks — nothing new. But what's different is Billy. It's hard to describe how I felt when I saw him yesterday. It was Billy but it wasn't. He looked the same, although his beard had grown out more, but it was the way he acted — almost standoffish, like he was afraid to let loose, like we'd only just met. It was odd. When the girls had talked his ear off and mama had made sure all our bellies were full, it was after midnight. Billy and I went over to the guest house for the night. I took a shower and waited for him in the bed. I was nervous. What was making us like this? We've been married for over 17 years. As he crawled into bed and we snuggled up, the curtain began to come down. We didn't talk, we just enjoyed being able to touch each other and feel each other's warmth. His smell overcame me, and I lost all my questioning doubts as we lay in each other's arms. Tomorrow I will get my answers; not tonight.

August 20, 1988

"Who the hell is Karen Stapleton?"

That's how I started this morning as I handed him a cup of coffee on the little back porch of the guest house. He was sitting there, looking out at the pond when I asked. The visit from the Marshalls had been playing in my head as I made the coffee in the kitchen so by the time I confronted him I was in full blown crazy Kay mode.

"And where the hell's your other family?"

I've confronted Billy many times for a multitude of sins over the years, sins where he was guilty as hell. I've gotten really good at spotting his usual song and dance and his attempts to use those baby blues to mask the truth. But his look this morning was confusion. Either her name wasn't Karen Stapleton, or he truly didn't have a clue what I was talking about. I told him about the visit I had received and the information I'd been given. He listened and I never saw guilt appear in his face even once.

"I've been guilty of many things over our years together, Baby Love, but this ain't one of them."

If he was lying, he was lying convincingly. I guess that was what kept me from choking him right there in that small wooden chair this morning.

A visit from the girls telling us breakfast was ready stopped the questioning. I let it ride for now. Our day has been simple. We just enjoyed each other and the girls. He was Billy again, easy going, throwing out those cute one-liners to aggravate the girls and me. He focused his attention on me — sneaking kisses and delivering the familiar slapping on the butt. I had missed him terribly and his smell — that Billy smell that fills my nose when he pulls me close — I don't want it to end.

August 21, 1988

When we left mama's this morning my heart broke. He waved bye to us and stood in the driveway until we were out of sight. I watched him in the rear-view mirror. Had he missed me as much as I had missed him? He told me about the life he had been living — going by an assumed name: Jim Lang. He said everyone — even people who know his name is Billy, people like Freddie and a couple of the others — have started calling him Jim. He said it's like being someone else. He was almost excited as he was telling me this, like he viewed Jim as a character in an action movie he was starring in. That's causing me some mixed emotions. How much of this Jim is taking over Billy? Maybe I'm taking too many psychology classes and I'm reading more into this than what I should. He seems to enjoy the new life a little more than I'm enjoying my life of being a separated woman — the character I'm playing for other people. I'm just picking up bits and pieces, but Jim does seem to have a different agenda in life than Billy. Not sure that I like Jim. We agreed to meet in Jacksonville in about 2 weeks. Kim was to have a minor surgical procedure done and he planned on being there. We figured that in a big city hopefully we won't run into anyone. I told him I would book a couple of rooms at the Residence Inn in Bay Meadows and they would be under my name. I would see him there. I'll have three nights with him then. I need some time with him alone. I need to know what he's planned for our future. I need to be included in the planning.

I was to meet my wife at the little house in the woods many times over the next few years. We would wind up staying there so often, I nicknamed it "The Love Shack". That first weekend passed much too quickly and the time to say goodbye came much too soon. My touchstone was and always would be Kay. I had glimpsed my old self again in her eyes and felt my strength replenished when I held her in my arms. When I'd decided to go on the lam, I had underestimated how tough it would be. Back in the presence of my girls I realized that I might have made the biggest mistake of my life. There was no going back now and I had to soak up as much of them as I could, memorize every line of every smile on their beautiful faces and tuck it away in my mind for those coming days when I couldn't remember who I was or where I came from.

8

I had to admit even to myself that I was shaken and I needed her, needed to lie in her arms, feel her close to me.

October 28, 1988

Billy's 39th birthday was a few days ago. He was working, he said, and couldn't be with me. He had a deal coming up. It's been a few weeks since we've seen each other. He said Thanksgiving for sure we'll be together. I wondered what he was doing, who he celebrated his birthday with. It's the days and weeks between our meetings that make me wonder and worry about his down time. Is he ok? Is he thinking about me and the girls? Is he on a load? Is Jim Lang making sure Billy Dekle is safe and still a part of his family's life? Or does Jim never think about Kay and the girls? Where does he stay? How does he do his laundry? Where does he eat and spend his free time and with who? He doesn't work all the time, I know, so what else does he do? This is what I tune into at night when I lie in bed and can't sleep.

Classes are easy this semester since I dropped the math. All A's so far. The Tigerettes are performing well and I love watching Amy doing so well on the middle school team. I'll be glad next year when they're on the same team again and I'm only going to one football game a week instead of two and trying to keep up with my schoolwork as well. The girls are doing well in their schoolwork. Amy's starting to take an interest in boys. Lord, give me strength to help raise these two without Billy. Their personalities are so different. Kim has a mouth on her and she and I get into some heated arguments. Amy, I know, gets just as mad at me when I tell her she can't do something or we disagree, but she doesn't verbalize it like Kim, so she stays out of the line of fire. I hope I'm raising them to be strong women. One thing this crazy life of mine has taught me is to be strong. You have to look out for yourself. You need to know how to do things on your own and above all don't let people see your weak side or push you around. Better yet, don't have a weak side.

San Pedro Island, Belize. November 1988. I was back to being Jim Lang full time and Jim Lang was tired of sitting around amusing himself with his familiar non-creative pastimes. He needed to fly a load to the U.S. and he watched the stormy Caribbean skies impatiently for a break in the weather. I'd flown down to Belize a little more than two weeks earlier and run into a series of delays. The unloading crew had called from Florida and put the trip on hold on account of bad weather. Two tropical storms moved through the Belize area back-to-back.

Finally, the weather broke.

I awoke around 5:30 a.m. It was 1988 and Thanksgiving would be on us before too long. My plan was to grab a quick breakfast and take off just before daylight from San Pedro's small unlit airport, fly thirty minutes to the airport just outside of Orange Walk on the Belize mainland, drop off Tommy, a friend and member of our Belize crew who'd been with me over in San Pedro. I'd pick up another crewmember who'd guide me to the clandestine Belize airstrip where I'd load 900 pounds of high-grade commercial Belizean marijuana and fly back to the U.S.A. where its value would increase seven-fold just for crossing the border. After leaving my hands, the cost would then keep snowballing until it reached the hands of mainstream America.

I was running a little late, so I decided to eat breakfast in the air. It was a short walk to the airport, so I grabbed a can of Vienna sausage from the little bachelor pad cabinet that Johnny kept in San Pedro. I gave my single-engine Cessna 210 aircraft a quick visual inspection, Tommy and I got in, and I made the necessary preparations to start the engine. I engaged the starter.

The propeller barely moved, then came to a complete stop. I heard the familiar click, click, click of a dead battery. I sat there with the yoke in my hands. The battery hadn't been weak on my last flight. It must have died while I was waiting for the tropical storms to clear out.

It was early morning and I hadn't even eaten breakfast. I sat in my airplane and considered my options: I could cancel the trip and spend the day hunting down a new battery or I could prop the airplane.

"Propping" a plane is cranking the aircraft's engine manually by spinning the propeller by hand. It sounds easy, but it takes technique. Without care, this process can turn a person into confetti in the blink of an eye. For all that, propping the plane was my better option.

I'd started flying airplanes when I was sixteen years old and I had quite a bit of experience propping planes. I knew that if appropriately primed, the fuel-injected Continental IO-520 engines should start quickly by hand, on the first few tries. On the other hand, after a fuel-injected engine gets hot, it's prone to vapor lock, making it very irritable to start even with a good battery. Thankfully, the engine would be cold this morning, and I wouldn't have to worry about vapor lock. If I had to prop it later, though, when it was hot, I'd need an experienced man in the cockpit to jockey the throttle for me. I didn't have the luxury of an experienced man but I did have one who spoke English fluently and that would be an advantage if I needed him. With any luck, we would soon get the plane in the sky and breakfast in our stomachs.

I had already primed the airplane with the boost pump before my earlier attempt. Now I set the throttle and mixture.

"Tommy, I need you to listen very carefully to my instructions. You're going to have one easy but critical job. When I pull the prop, you *must* be holding the brakes firmly, so the plane doesn't move. I don't want to be cut into little pieces on this strip today."

Tommy shook his head and listened intently as I went over the process again with him. I made sure to show him how to shut the engine down if there was a problem.

"Si, Jim, I got it."

I stressed the importance of the brakes again and then climbed out and went to the front of the plane. I pulled through a couple of revolutions with the magnetos off to get the feel of the compression stroke. I walked back to the cockpit and switched on the magnetos. I returned to the prop and started very carefully propping the plane pulling with both hands. On the third pull, the big Continental engine roared to life and Tommy did his job of holding the brakes flawlessly. I ran around and jumped in the pilot's seat, closed the door, and while I was strapping my seat belt on, I was thinking, "Well hell, at least the worst part of the day is behind me."

We took off from San Pedro just as the sun began to break over the eastern horizon. After about ten minutes we started to encounter some light rain and some low-lying clouds. I descended to stay under them as they turned into a solid overcast. I stayed under the building sky and dropped to treetop level. Visibility deteriorated further.

I don't mind flying low, and I probably fly as low as any pilot. This part of Belize was flat, with no mountains and few towers, but visibility was minimal and it only takes one tower to ruin your day. I'd never been suicidal, and I wasn't going to start that day, so I climbed back up through the clouds and got on top. Now I was concerned I might not be able to see the Orange Walk strip — a pilot's nightmare. Suddenly, the clouds under me began to break up and there was the ground peeking through holes of clear air. I picked up my two-meter handheld radio.,

"Johnny, how is the weather there?"

"Pretty miserable here," he came back.

At that moment, someone else broke in on the radio.

"Hey man! You just flew right over us!"

a smuggler and his wife

I looked down through a hole in the fog and saw some vehicles I recognized. They were parked at an intersection on a small narrow lime rock road running through a large sugar cane field. There also appeared to be some Belizean workers nearby working in the sugar cane.

"I have you in sight," I radioed back. "I'm on my way down.!"

As I descended, I radioed more instructions, "Okay, man. I'm going to leave the engine running. Let everyone know they need to be careful while they are loading and fueling. I had trouble cranking this morning and don't want the same problem."

"What a stroke of luck," I thought. Somehow, I'd flown right over the spot I needed to find in the fog when just a few minutes earlier, I was sweating out whether I'd even be able to see Orange Walk airport in order to land and pick up somebody who could guide me right here.

I didn't like having people guiding me unless they know how things look from the air. I've picked up people to guide me to airstrips before and the first turn after takeoff I could tell from the look on their faces that they were utterly lost. Cutting out the landing at Orange Walk was a real stress reliever and saved a considerable amount of time.

I circled and landed from north to south. I taxied up to the intersection and turned around where the truck with the marijuana and fuel were parked. The cars carrying the rest of the crew were all stationed at this location. After turning around, I throttled the engine back to an idle, I got out and had some of the men help me push the plane backward a few feet so that it would not block the intersection. The crew could now get around more comfortably while they loaded and fueled the aircraft.

The Belizean loading crew sprang into action. About the closest thing I can compare this operation to is a pit crew at the Daytona 500 race. An experienced team can turn a drug plane around and get him back in the air with a load of pot and fuel within a few minutes. Speed is essential. If the law is on the way, and the plane can take off before they reach the scene; the police are just out of luck. In America we operate on the "he said, she said" principle and no drugs are required to convict but in the courts of Belize, if you lay a drug charge on a man, you better have some drugs to show the judge and jury.

I was parked and men were on the move. Two hoisted themselves on top of each wing to pour gas from the buckets, five gallons at a time, into the four fuel tanks on top of the wings. I'd brought hand pumps and electric pumps down to make the fueling process less labor-intensive, but these guys declined them. They believed it was faster to pour the gas directly from the buckets into the tanks.

While the bucket brigade swung into action, the loaders, except for a couple of lookouts, grabbed the bales of the pot and ran them to each side of the plane for the packer-man inside the cabin. The packer-man, applying his skills, packs every nook and cranny of the airplane.

A Cessna 210 has two doors located below the wings, and we were utilizing both to speed the loading process along. Men were running in every direction. The truck parked in front of the plane was the hub of the operation. As I scanned the scene, I noticed a new loader I'd never seen before. My heart almost stopped. He was walking straight for the spinning propeller with a bale of pot in his hand.

"Hey! Look out!" I yelled at him.

He stopped and looked at me. I pointed towards the blur that was the huge blades cutting the air.

"You walk into that propeller," I yelled "you'll kill yourself! You need to be careful or you'll die!"

He smiled at me, dropped his bale of pot off and returned to the truck for another bundle.

"Good Lord," I thought. "If I hadn't been standing on the same side of the plane as that man, he'd have walked right into the prop. He'd have been killed instantly if I hadn't yelled at him."

This fresh in my mind, I did something I'd never done before. I called a halt to the loading and fueling operations and held a short safety meeting. I spoke slowly and used hand signaling to try and impress on everyone that the propeller was deadly. Before we resumed loading, I closed the pilot's side door, so there would only be one line of men to watch.

I positioned myself in front of the plane. I stood on the co-pilot's side, as close as I could comfortably, in front of and facing the propeller. By standing in front of the prop, the loaders would have to go around me to drop off their bale of pot. They would then take the same route back to the truck, thereby staying well clear of the prop.

Everyone conformed to the new, slower and safer loading procedure. The safety meeting had worked. I watched as the new man came around me with a bale of pot. He placed the bale in the plane. Then, suddenly, he turned in the direction of the prop. I can only imagine he was trying to take a short cut because when he spun around, he started back to the truck walking staunchly in the wrong direction. He continued toward the deadly prop. I was momentarily stunned in disbelief at what I was seeing.

"Stop!" I screamed. "No, No, No!" I yelled at him.

He looked at me. The expression on his face was one of utter confusion, as if to ask, "Why are you yelling at me again?" Then his expression went blank, neutral, almost vacant and in that instant his head was sucked into the propeller. I knew he was dead. It was a sound like that of putting a Kleenex into a bedside fan. A patch of his hair flew off in the prop wash and a life was sucked out of this world before my very eyes.

His body fell limp, his knees dropped straight to the ground, the propeller struck him again in the back, trying to pull the rest of him under the plane. There was not enough clearance for his body to pass between the prop and the ground, which caused the airplane propeller to come to an almost complete stop as the plane wedged itself up off the ground and fell backward a couple of feet to the alarm of the men on the wings. This freed the prop from the man's back, the engine caught and revved back up to normal idle speed. A mere hiccup for a big machine.

Nothing could be done to save him. The blow had killed him on impact before he hit the ground. The airplane lifting and falling back got everyone's attention. All work had stopped and we looked at each other with shock and disbelief on our faces.

Everything happened so fast. Like in a movie, everything slowed and blurred. Men were now moving about in a sort of frantic slow motion. I looked down at the young man lying dead on the ground with a gaping hole in his head. I could see a large portion of his brain before blood began to pour out. It was like a glass of red wine spilling out from behind his head.

A few of the crewmembers pulled the dead man clear of the spinning prop. I've never witnessed anything like it in my life. He'd simply walked over from the cane field in hopes of making a few extra dollars. I could see in the distance men still working the cane field. All I could do was stare at the scene. I was paralyzed. I wanted it to be a horrible dream.

Someone slammed the truck door shut and the sound jolted me to reality. Crewmen were getting into vehicles and deserting the site. I snapped my head up from its helpless stare in the direction of the body now emptied of life.

The truck was taking off, "Where are you all going?" I yelled but there was no one to answer. I needed to get the hell out of Dodge.

I tried to concentrate. First, I needed to check to see if the prop had sustained any damage. I went around to the pilot's side, climbed in and preceded to run up the engine and cycle the props. Amazingly, there was no detectable damage. The only other prop check I could do would require shutting the engine off. The battery would surely falter as it did that morning if I shut everything down. It was too much of a risk. As these procedures were running through my mind, I felt callous but there was no action to take. No person to call. No clock I could turn back to prevent what happened from happening.

I glanced at my fuel gauges and calculated I had around 75 gallons. I jumped outside and checked my four fuel caps to make sure they were secured, then I climbed back in, pushed the throttles forward and took off. At just over treetop level, I powered back to super economy cruise, then got back on the radio to notify the crew.

"Roberto, if you tell me a different spot, I'll land so we can finish… Tell me another road location and radio me."

His response was quick, "No man. You have all the pot and fuel."

"No, I don't!" I yelled into the radio.

"Yes, amigo, you do! We have no more to give you."

This was a pointless argument. They weren't going to load a plane they'd just witness killing an innocent human being. They had seen enough for one day. I didn't blame them. The real problem was, I didn't have enough gas to fly home.

It usually took between 78 and 95 gallons on my trip down and between 90 and 105 gallons on the loaded return trip. I needed to think this through. The route I took to the unloading strip breaks the coast at Apalachicola in the Panhandle. I would fly north/northwest until I am clear of Tyndall and Eglin Air Force Base's restricted areas. Once past the restricted area, I then turn more westerly and continue to our airstrip in the forest northwest of Crestview, Florida and just south of Brewton, Alabama.

The dogleg around the air force base restricted areas added quite a few miles to the trip. It was a lot smarter and safer to fly around Uncle Sam's air force bases as opposed to flying through them, even if the aircraft is not full of pot.

I wouldn't be able to make it to our strip on the Florida-Alabama line with the fuel I have onboard. But I also knew with what just happened, I needed to get myself and the airplane out of Belize — fast.

I was going to have to improvise in some fashion. If I could make it back to somewhere — anywhere — in Florida, I could find a dirt road, pasture, or even a little clearing out in the woods to land. I'd land the plane and walk away, abandon it and partial load of pot. I had a few thousand dollars in my pocket. If I could find a busy highway, I could hitchhike to a city and call for someone to come and get me. It was not a good scenario and getting caught was probable, but any way I looked at it, I was going to be shooting from the hip.

I remembered from previous runs that there was a secluded area with lots of roads just north of the coast of Apalachicola. It would be a stretch to make it that far, but if I could, it would be the ideal spot for me to ditch the plane and get away on foot.

A dead battery started my day, now with a dead body, that day had become a disaster. I still had a long and hard trip ahead and trying to clear my mind of the images of that young man would make it impossible to relax.

Aviation navigational aids have advanced by leaps and bounds in the past previous few years. Early 1989 was still pre-G.P.S. (Global Positioning System) era, but this Cessna did have a Loran C (Long range navigation system) and a Shaden fuel totalizer.

The Loran gave me an accurate fix on my position. The one in the 210 had features that would and could provide me with ground speed, heading, time, and distance to any waypoint that I programmed into it. The fuel totalizer would give me present fuel burn down to a 1/10one-tenth of a gallon per hour.

I quickly programmed Apalachicola into the waypoint function of the Loran and used the totalizer to calculate the fuel. I reached for the fuel totalizer knob and selected the time remaining fuel function and there it was, I had the answer. At my present ground speed, I could reach the Apalachicola area with almost ten minutes to spare.

Of course, this calculation was based on present conditions. If, along the trip, I should happen to encounter a headwind, the ten minutes to spare would turn into a deficit leaving me to swim the remainder of the way.

Under normal conditions, no one would set off on a flight of that distance with only a ten-minute fuel reserve. These weren't normal conditions. It was Apalachicola, here I come, with my life at stake.

I locked in on a direct heading to Apalachicola. It would take me over Mexico's Yucatan Peninsula. I'd been over the Yucatan many times, but I was always at a high altitude. Climbing to my normal altitude of 10,000 to 14,000 feet would consume too much fuel, so I would have to make this entire flight at a low-level. I didn't know the extent of damage to the propeller, so didn't want to make any power changes. Once I'd got to my desired altitude, I'd set the power to "super economy cruise" and keep it there, flying as smoothly as I knew how.

Treetop level flying limits forward visibility, and I didn't feel comfortable traversing the Yucatan at that low level. As smoothly as possible, I eased the plane into a shallow, slow climb until I reached an altitude of about 600 feet.

It wasn't much altitude for an airplane, but it did give me just enough forward ground visibility. The atmosphere cools off at a rate of about 2-two centigrade degrees per 1000 feet, so up at a cruising altitude of 10,000 feet on a 95-degree day, it feels like you've got air conditioning in the cockpit. In my situation, the low-level heat was just an inconvenience I would have to suffer through. At 600 feet, it was scorching. I tried to ignore it, but my mind kept filling with images of that poor man walking into the propeller. It kept replaying in my head. Also, I still had the issue of figuring out what in the hell I was going to do if I *did* reach Florida. No brilliant plans emerged.

I looked down at the scene below me. A low-level flight over the Yucatan was new for me. I saw things on the ground that was not visible on my previous high-altitude crossings. I could see the peaks, the church towers and cobbled roofs of several small

Mexican towns, and then there was a seemingly endless jungle that separated them. It was hard to imagine the ancient Maya and Aztec Indians living down there years ago. I scanned the green expanse beneath me. It was something I'd rather focus on besides the previous few hours.

Flying over the first stretch of the gigantic jungle, I could make out maybe a thousand acres here and there that were slashed and burned, with the odd huge tree standing alone. A few thatched-roof huts were visible, so someone apparently lived nearby. The cleared land had some form of cultivation going on because bushes were growing everywhere in the clearings. What, I wondered, could anyone be growing in the middle of a jungle at least thirty miles from the nearest road? Then it hit me. I was flying over what could be the world's largest marijuana fields. For the next hour and a half, I saw at least twenty more clearings ranging in size from 500 to 1,000 acres each. The people who lived in those huts and tended those fields below were in the same business as me. I felt a sense of comradery.

It was mind-boggling to think that a vast majority of their crops would show up in America. An incredible amount of labor would have to be expended to bring in supplies by burro to tend those fields. This agriculture, I thought, must have been as large and important part of the economy in Mexico as tobacco fields were in our economy, though tobacco probably cost American society far more than pot ever did.

Then, against my will, my thoughts wandered slowly back to the young man, his confused expression now etched in my memory. "Damn!!" I said out loud. "Damn! It happened so fast!" He was just going to get another bale, and in the next instant, he was dead. He was just trying to make a few extra dollars for his family. "Damn!" This sad notion played over and over again.

I crossed the northern Yucatan beaches after about three hours and then out over the Gulf of Mexico. I marveled at the beauty of the beaches. They seemed to go on forever. Undoubtedly, they must have been among the finest in the world.

I was nearing the halfway point now. My ground speed had steadily increased ever so slightly. I was encountering favorable winds, and my gross weight was decreasing with every gallon of fuel I burned. I was starting to think I could reach Apalachicola with a comfortable margin of fuel reserve but I'd need even more luck if I was to reach my intended destination and the unloading crew waiting in a forest south of Brewton, Alabama.

"If I have to land on a dirt road north of Apalachicola, I'll have to foot it out of a dense forest, won't I? Yes, I will." I was brainstorming out loud. "What will be my fastest way out of the area before the plane is found? A highway, obviously. How am I going to manage that? Of course, I'll check out the highways in that area as I fly over. Yeah, but that's going to draw attention to me, isn't it? Yes, it is. My chances of getting apprehended by the law will increase, won't they? Yes, they surely will. More than I like to think about. So what are my options? I can't think of any."

It was still hot in the cockpit, and I was continually wiping my face with a cloth. As I lay the cloth down on a bale, I noticed my fingernails were speckled. Alarmed, I examined myself closer. Dots of red are all over my arms and shirt. Red was everywhere. The death scene was all over me. I had been sprayed with a fine mist of blood and matter. The killer, my Cessna 210, was probably covered too.

Suddenly I realized that it wasn't a matter for rational consideration. It was desperation. I needed to get to my intended destination in that forest south of Brewton, Alabama. The only chance I had of reaching the strip was to cut out the dogleg. This meant my new route would take me right through the heart of Eglin Air Force Base's reservation.

"What are my chances of flying through an air force base and getting away with it?" I asked myself. "Who knows? I never attempted it. Never wanted to attempt it." I glanced down at the Gulf as it whizzed by. "I'm going to find out, right?" "That's right, buddy."

I set my course directly to my intended landing field. The fuel totalizer and the Loran indicated that I did not have quite enough fuel to reach the strip. But if my ground speed kept increasing, I *would* make it or at least I'd get close enough to reach my crew by radio. I could then have them pick me up. A forced landing somewhere other than the strip was possible.

My biggest and first concern however, was getting through Eglin's restricted area without the air force scrambling fighters to intercept me. I had never been so brazen or so desperate as to cut through an air force base's restricted area before. I hadn't heard of anyone else doing it either. I'd be traversing the entire base from south to north. Today was turning out to be a day full of nightmarish firsts.

I continue northward as my ground speed gradually increased. I knew the government had all the latest technology to spot aircraft coming in from the south and a vast arsenal of jets and helicopters to intercept them. About 130 miles from the coast, I began my descent to an altitude of between five and ten feet above the water in an attempt to stay under the radar. I was so close to the water I got the full sensation of the speed I was traveling. The waves beneath me blurred by. I was only a split-second miscue away from death and all my senses were on full alert.

Usually, I fly low level for approximately five to ten miles inland before I climb up to a reasonable altitude. This penetration would have to be different this time because I would be traversing the base from south to north. I'd have to stay at treetop level until I was a considerable distance past the restricted area. Lower was better if I had any chance at all at getting through Eglin.

The coast was coming into view at last. The feeling I'd get

when I'd see land after a long overwater passage is hard to explain. It is, without a doubt, a euphoric sensation. Gratitude, excitement, relief, the immense understanding of how small we all are in this great big world and yet still a critical part of its workings. All of this and so much more overwhelmed me at the sight of the American coastline.

I was riding along the beach in a few short minutes. It was like no other Florida beach: no condos or motels, just sand and trees like Mexico's deserted shores. I held five to ten feet of altitude between myself and the beach. When I saw trees ahead, I'd pull up at the last second, just enough to clear the tops.

My fuel situation was critical. A short distance north and I started coming across a lot of clear spots in the wooded areas. I dipped down below the treetops; then as I got to the end of each clearing, up I'd go.

I spotted some large bunkers or bomb shelters, manicured grass roads systematically connecting them. There was no doubt about it: I was trespassing on one of Uncle Sam's most prized military bases and breaking all kinds of F.A.A. regulations. The only reason I was feeling good about this intrusion was that, if my engine quit, I might be able to land comfortably on the roads without killing myself in the process.

And then I flew over the northern boundary. I was no longer a possible enemy alien and I was getting closer to my destination but the gauges showed two fuel tanks out of the four had almost no fuel remaining and the other two tanks were completely dry. A few minutes later, all fuel indicator needles were showing empty. It was still too close to call. It was coming down to how far the plane can could fly with gauges showing zero.

Every scenario I could think of is running through my head. On reflection, I preferred to avoid running entirely out of fuel at a low altitude and having no choice of terrain for a forced landing. I would, at least, need a few seconds with power to decide where to put her down. I'd already witnessed one person lose his life that day and I didn't want the second one to be me. This plane was going to be on the ground very soon, and I planned to land under power.

I decided to run on the one fuel tank that the engine was feeding on until I made it to the landing strip, or it ran out, whichever came first. If it ran out, I'd quickly change tanks to whatever fuel remained in the last tank. The engine would do an air start and I'll pick out a suitable nearby clearing to land in while I still have power. This was a better option than running entirely out of fuel a few feet over the tree tops.

I could see Crestview on the horizon and was on the final leg when to my shock a thunderstorm bubbled up directly ahead, right over our unloading strip.

"Yes, this is the sort of day it is," I thought. "I've flown through fog, rain, jungle pot fields, across the Gulf of Mexico and Eglin Air Force base and if my fuel holds out, I'm going to have to come down in a full-blown thunderstorm."

I'd need to make the landing on my first pass because there was no way I'd have enough fuel for another approach. I picked up the two-meter handheld and called Freddie.

"Base, this is Mobile One. Do you read me?"

"Read you, Mobile One." Freddie's voice.

"You got a storm there, right?"

"Weather's good here, buddy. The storm looks to be about a half-mile to the southeast of us."

"Oh man. That's the best news I've had all day. But keep your eye on that storm, my friend, because I'm going to go right through the middle of it and … ah, I'm a bit short on fuel and don't have enough to go around."

"Short on fuel? How did that happen?"

"It's a story, Freddie, but I am a little busy with that storm right now."

"Sure. Looks like a big one, man. Be careful."

The rain was dense and visibility nil, with what we call "moderate turbulence." My patience with that day was starting to wear thin when I suddenly popped out on the backside of the thunderheads. The field was about a half-mile right in front of me — a beautiful sight. The fuel tank I was flying on registered past empty, so I changed tanks. I didn't want to take a chance on the engine quitting while I was maneuvering to land. Maybe I *was* going to make it.

I did a close, tight approach and landing, with a roll out to the far end of the short runway. The crew was waiting. I set the brakes and jumped out.

"Guys! Get me some gas quick!"

The crew scrambled. I left the engines running in case I needed to make a quick getaway for any reason.

"See that propeller?" I shouted at everyone. "No! You can't, because it's still spinning! Stay way clear of it!"

We unloaded the small cargo of pot and put in ten gallons of aviation fuel. If this had been a normal load, I would have quickly replaced the seats and flown to a nearby airport, landed, called a taxi, and gone to the closest town to hang out in a quiet bar or restaurant until somebody could retrieve me. Not this time. Freddie came up to me and stood looking at my sweat-stained, blood-spattered clothes.

"Um, listen, man. Maybe you'd like me to fly this old girl to some airport instead of you."

"That's a very good idea, Freddie." I give him a quick rundown on what happened that morning. I tried to keep my anxiety and stress to a minimum.

"Even though the plane seemed to fly okay, the prop did take a pretty good hit. It would probably be smart for us to shut her down and do a quick visual for damage. The battery should be charged back up from the trip and it shouldn't be a problem." There was no sign of the law so we shut the engine off and looked at the propeller and then looked at each one another. I shook my head.

The Cessna 210 has a three-blade propeller. Two of the blades looked normal but the third blade was so twisted. it was bent forward on an angle of approximately forty degrees.

Freddie shook his head in disbelief. My guess was it twisted and bent forward when the airplane lifted and then sat back down again. If I had known that the propeller had anywhere near that kind of damage ...

"No pilot in his right mind would fly a plane with a prop looking like this," Freddie said — and he clearly included himself. Even if I could make it to a regular airport, it would be obvious from the damage to the prop that the plane was involved in one hell of an accident. I was suddenly tired.

"Looks like what I didn't know didn't hurt me," I said.

"So, what'll we do?"

"Let's get this pot to the stash house and leave the plane on the strip. We can have someone in the crew get the seats back in the plane and clean out all the residue. You and I can go see if we can come up with another prop."

Our strip, being in a small cotton field in the middle of the Blackwater Forest on the Florida/Alabama state line, was pretty secluded. It was only accessible by traveling down approximately six miles of a narrow two-lane secondary state highway then three miles of dirt road that led to the cotton field. As we left the area, we stopped and placed a mark on the dirt road as a precaution. If anyone had traveled on that road in our absence, we'd know.

We needed to get that plane out of there. We didn't want to lose it to law enforcement and if they did find the aircraft, it would be the end for this unloading site. Farmer Joe would feel the pressure too and no one wanted that. Keeping the heat off the members of our organization was a primary concern. Would the day never end?

After unloading the pot at Freddie's uncle's house, the crew went to Timbo's house to stay on standby in case they were needed. Timbo was a permanent member of our small cartel and served as a lookout or unloader, whatever was needed. We used his house, outbuildings and horse barn in Century to stash our load from time to time. His father, a prominent citizen in Escambia county, owned a concrete plant and sand quarry. Timbo worked for his dad when he wasn't smuggling or partying but, unlike his father, he had a few wild bones in his body. He liked fast cars, fast motorcycles and fast women. Drugs was a hang-up for this barely 30-year-old.

Freddie called Blaine, our aircraft mechanic, in hopes of a prop.

"No, Freddie, I don't have one and I won't be able to get one on such short notice."

Freddie hung up and looked at me.

"Well now, what are we going to do, partner?"

I'd already resigned myself to not getting the part we needed. That was just how things were adding up.

"We're going to do what we gotta do. We can't leave the airplane in the cotton field. Come daylight tomorrow morning that plane will be out even if we have to chop the wings off and drag it down the road behind a pickup truck." I thought for a moment. "Wait. Why chop them off? Nuts and bolts are the only things holding them on. We'll just get some tools and remove the wings."

We called Blaine back and told him that we were on the way and needed to see him. At Freddie's house we picked up some cocaine, dropped by the store and bought some beer, then headed up the road to see Blaine at his airport.

November 24, 1988

We left when the girls got out of school yesterday for mamas. I told Anne, Billy's mom, that we would not be having dinner with them because I wanted to get out to west Florida early. She understood. Billy was supposed to meet me here last night, I waited up until midnight and fell asleep on the couch hoping he would be here by morning. We waited Thanksgiving dinner on Billy until the late afternoon but he didn't show. The girls and mama know I'm upset but I try not to show it. I do not get why Billy or Jim, whoever or whatever he is calling himself today, doesn't know what it is like — like someone is reaching into your chest and jerking your heart out. You're still alive, but you want to be dead. You just want to stop the pain you're feeling. I'm happy I'm in the guest house, the Love Shack, tonight by myself. I don't want to talk to anyone or act like I'm not hurting. I just want to lie here and wish the choices I've made in my life were different ones.

It was a short drive to Blaine's shop.

"Do you think you can help us remove the wings?"

He was reluctant. "Guys, I don't want to get that involved in your line of work. I don't mind working on your planes, but this is too close and makes me fully involved."

"Well," I said, "how about loaning us the tools for the job?" He agreed, and we were off, back to Century to gather up the rest of the crew.

By the time we got to the cotton field, it was dark. We checked the marks on the road, and no one had been in the area. We felt safe to approach the plane. Timbo positioned himself as a lookout about one-half mile away on the dirt road leading to the cotton field. The plane was just like we left it. We got the tools out and started to work.

We first took the sump drains out, draining the gas put in after I landed. We then removed the wings starting with the wing root fillets. They came off easy with a Phillips head screwdriver. Once the wing root fillet was off, it exposed the real work.

We clipped the control cables and electric wires running to the wingtip position lights and fuel transfer pump. The fuel lines that ran from the wing tanks to the engine needed to be disconnected. To detach the wings from the fuselage, I picked up a hefty punch and small sledgehammer.

When I hit the punch with the sledgehammer, it sounded like someone firing a high-powered rifle. It was nighttime, way out in the forest, but sound travels for a long distance. The thought crossed my mind that there may be a game warden in the area and he would surely come to investigate the source of the noise. Game warden or not, we had to continue because the wings had to come off for us to be able to haul the aircraft down the highway. In just under an hour, we had the pins out and the wings lying on the ground beside the plane.

"Let's pull the plane down the road backward until we find a hiding place," I suggested. "At least until we get the plane a safe distance from our cotton field."

Joe, being a farmer with farming equipment, had a better idea.

"Hey, I got a small two-wheel trailer that hooks up to my pickup truck. We can load the plane on it."

He made a quick trip to town and returned with the trailer and some 2x6s we could use as skids for a makeshift loading ramp.

Loading the plane was easy with Joe's electric winch mounted on his pickup. We rolled the aircraft up on the 2x6 ramp and right onto the trailer. We secured the fuselage of the plane to the trailer.

It was between 2:00 and 3:00 in the morning, I was hoping that everyone on our route would be fast asleep. With the plane mobile, we needed to decide what to do with it. Joe offered another suggestion. Joe was becoming a valuable asset to the small organization.

"I've got a friend. He's out of town working offshore on an oil rig and he happens to have a barn. We can stash the airplane there for now and get it out before he gets back."

This would buy us about three days to come up with an alternate plan. Timbo led the way with a radio about one and a half miles out front. Joe and I followed with the plane in tow and Earl and another unloader. Freddie brought up the rear a mile and a half behind so that nothing or no one could slip up on us.

We traveled dirt roads, back roads, and state highways for 30 miles. The horizontal stabilizer on the tail section of the plane was over width, which would necessitate pulling off the road if we passed another vehicle. If anyone were to see us, they'd be sure to remember an airplane traveling down any of these roads. But our luck held and we didn't pass a single car on the way to the barn.

The doors had a chain and a padlock securing them. Joe had a pair of three-foot bolt cutters, which he put to use. We pulled the trailer inside the barn, parked it, and unhooked it. Joe reattached the chain and attached our new padlock.

The next morning, I awoke thinking about my old airplane mechanic friend, Barney. All around and back of his hangar he had airplanes scattered in all states of disassembly. He had crashed planes, planes with no wings, planes with no tails and about everything you could think of. He had an aircraft junk yard.

I called him and explained my situation. The plane, I told him, was already loaded onto a trailer. I gave him the ball size needed to hook up to the trailer.

"Okay. I'll send Mick to pick it up as soon as he can get

a smuggler and his wife

a truck with the necessary hookup." It was about a seven-hour drive from Keystone to our location near Jay, Florida. I gave Barney directions for his son Mick.

Mick showed up a little after 1:00 in the morning. We took him to the barn, hooked his rig up to the trailer, then led him down back roads to Crestview. He got a room until the next morning and then drove back to Keystone. Before he left, I told Mick that in a day or two we'd bring the wings over and pick up the trailer.

It was November 25th, and I was to meet my family at my mother-in-law's house for the Thanksgiving holiday. I should have been there two days earlier. I'd not been able to call to let them know I'd be late, so I knew they'd be worried. I stopped at the gate going up the driveway to the house. It was unlocked and I knew they were expecting me. Once again, I'd come too close to never seeing my wife or our children again. I thanked God in case He was still listening to me.

November 25, 1988

Billy finally showed up this afternoon. I know the story he told me was true and I know he's shaken by the nightmare he experienced. I'm trying to console him and let him know he shouldn't blame himself.

But who should I blame for the way I feel, the hurt I feel, the hurt I feel every time I say goodbye or have to lie awake and worry? Who and what is causing this hurt inside my heart? It's him. And when will it stop? I feel as if I am being selfish, but I need this man to grow up and face life, help me face it. Love should not hurt this bad.

It was always hard for me to express my feelings or show my true emotions. The only person who has ever caught a glimpse of what lay's just beneath the surface is my Baby Love, Kay. So often, I wouldn't have to say or show anything for her to know and understand. This recent adventure had left its mark. Now, I had to admit even to myself that I was shaken and I needed her, needed to lie in her arms, feel her close to me. It's hard to describe what happened, but once I was with her, the words came. She was angry about the risks I'd taken, but I always knew her anger was out of love, and right then I needed that love.

November 26, 1988

As usual he wins. I can't stay mad at him for long. We walked around the property this afternoon and laughed with the girls and ate leftover Thanksgiving dinner. There's a fine line between love and hate and Billy knows how to walk that line with me better than anyone.

9

The heavy transfer case caught on the right main landing gear and tore the brake line off. I wouldn't be able to use the brakes to control direction.

The 210 was safely stashed in the Keystone area. Instead of rushing to put the wings back on, we decided to cool our heels for a while. In light of the terrible accident, a new plane would probably be our best bet. Freddie and I discussed our options while sharing a few spliffs.

"We could go back to a twin," I mused. "A Navajo would be nice or maybe another Aztec. I'd sure love to find a nice J-model twin Bonanza."

"Yeah." Freddie's eyes were half closed. "I've always thought the J was the perfect smuggling plane."

We dug out some paper and made a list, with careful consideration of the cost of each model as well as maintenance and upkeep. We finally decided for no other reason than plain simplicity to stay with a 210. We'd made quite a few trips in the old 210 with no maintenance. In fact, if it hadn't been for the accident, it would still have been in action. I got out a copy of trusty Trade-a-Plane and in no time found a Cessna 210 that was tailor-made for our operation — a late model with a ram engine mod, a Robertson STOL-Kit, a Q-tip prop, an excellent autopilot interfaced into a top Loran C. The only thing we'd want to add would be Flint tip tanks.

November 30, 1988

I left him standing in the driveway waving goodbye to us a few days ago. He promised to make everything up to me at Christ-

mas. We could spend more time together. He just needed to clear up a little business between now and then. I want to believe him, and I know he doesn't intentionally try to hurt us but ... he does hurt us. We decided before we parted that we would fly out to California with the three girls for two weeks on December 17th. We will catch a plane out of Pensacola and rent a car in California and see the sights. I have always been a stickler about Christmas. I wanted to be at home to open presents on Christmas morning and have family time, but now I just want to be with him, I don't care when, where or how. I will make the reservations tomorrow for the five of us. I can't wait.

I called Art, the guy in Detroit who'd helped me secure my previous 210 and introduced me to Pete, who let us register aircraft in his name. I had a great deal of trust in my relationship with Art. He recognized my drawl right off.

"Hey, buddy!" he said. "I know you. You ain't callin' about the weather, right?"

"You're so right, my friend. Can you get in touch with a certain broker in California to see if a certain plane is still on the market?"

"Give me the details and stay at the payphone you're callin' me from."

He called ten minutes later.

"Still available, buddy. Set you back $85,000."

"Right. Call him and let him know we'll take the plane. Tell him you'll send him a $5,000.00 non-refundable check as a binder."

Early the next morning we borrowed a Mooney airplane from Blaine and were airborne with $90,000.00 cash. I realized I could make this deal and be back in plenty of time to see Kay and the girls for our trip out west. My usual guys at Gross Isle airport met us and the first item of business was something to eat and a few beers. We bought a single $5,000 cashier's check and mailed it to California, then hurried over to Bottoms Up Bar to drink and shoot pool. Somewhere in the middle of the third game I noticed Pete seemed unusually quiet.

"Okay, amigo," I looked straight at him. "What is it?"

He was staring hard at the end of his pool stick.

"It's this new plane, Jim. I'm getting antsy about this new plane. I already got an Aztec and two 210s in my name."

"So what, Pete?"

"Man!" He set the pool stick down hard on the green felt. "Man, Jim! I don't even know how to *fly*!"

"No need to get upset, Pete."

"Listen, Jim. I have this friend who's just gotten out of prison. He needs some money. He'll be glad to put the airplane in his name and make the five thousand."

"I understand, Pete. That sounds good to me. Really. Everybody's got his own line to draw."

We spent half the next day going from bank to bank. When Freddie and I took off back to Florida, we had enough checks to cover the balance owing on the California 210. We decided to do like we did with the other 210 we'd bought from Superstition Air in Arizona — that is, ask them to deliver the plane to Gross Isle and make the exchange there.

I called Barney.

"Hey, buddy. I found a 210 out in the LA area, and it has everything on it except Flint tanks. Can you install them as soon as I get it to Florida?"

"Yeah, Billy. I'll do that for you. And don't know if this will help you out, but I'll be leaving tomorrow for Chino to fix an airplane in the LA area. If you're in a big hurry, I can install those tanks while I'm there. How'd that be?"

I drove to Keystone the next day and gave Barney $7,000.00 in cash to pay for the tanks. I also gave him the cashier's checks and the phone number of the broker who was handling the sale of the airplane. Barney could take possession of the 210 from the broker and put the tanks on, then I'd fly out and pick up the plane and fly it back to the east coast.

December 8, 1988

The girls and I have been planning our trip to California. They are excited, all three of them. I have to admit I am too. It will be nice to be away and not have to worry about school or really anything. We can just have fun. It will be a birthday/Christmas present for me. Nine more days! I can't wait. I'm taking final exams this next week and it's hard to concentrate.

I drove back to Century and brought Freddie up to date on the deal.

"Shit, Billy! You aren't going to fly coast to coast in our new airplane and not take me, are you? Man, I've always wanted to fly to California and I'm not going miss a trip to Vegas at my age. I mean, I'm overdue, man. We can have some fun there."

"As always, Freddie, you make a good point. What kind of a trip would it be without some crazy asshole to share the entertainment with?"

Vegas. I hadn't even thought about that.

We scheduled a non-stop flight leaving the next day from New Orleans and loaded up on enough cash for our stay in L.A. and a good time in Vegas. We also brought some pot and enough cocaine to ensure we wouldn't get sleepy and miss something.

a smuggler and his wife

By the time we arrived at LAX, we were worn out. We caught a cab from the terminal to the airport Hilton. We didn't know how long we'd be staying but we wanted to be comfortable, so we checked into a $500.00-a-night two-bedroom suite with a nice living room and a bar. We paid in advance for a couple of nights.

Freddie took a nap while I turned on the TV and mixed a couple of drinks. I managed to reach Barney at the Chino airport. He liked the look of the plane and had already met with the broker, given the guy the money, and picked up the paperwork for the plane. He expected delivery any minute.

I hung up feeling good. My man was on top of it. He'd take possession of our new airplane and get right to work. It would take a day or two to put the tanks on but Freddie and I could find something around to do in L.A. and leave for Vegas the day after that. I kicked back and relaxed in a comfortable chair in front of the TV, then fell asleep. It had been a long day.

The phone rang about an hour later. Barney was the only person who knew where I was.

"Hi Barney! How you doing man?"

There was a silence.

"Barney?"

"Billy." His voice was quiet, his tone stern. "Billy, you need to get out of town now."

I sat bolt upright.

"What's wrong?"

"Don't know. Just get out of town."

I hung up. My mind was racing. We had a foolproof plan to receive the plane. What had gone wrong? All I knew now was I had to get the hell out of that city.

"Freddie! Rouse your ass, man! We gotta go!"

He didn't budge. It never was easy to wake him.

"Damn it, Freddie! Get your bags! We're leaving town."

He opened his eyes and looked at me confused.

"Okay, okay," he said. He dropped his head back on the pillow. I gathered up my bag.

"I'm going!" I yelled on my way out. "If you're going with me, better come now!"

Freddie jumped up,

"What? What's happening?"

"Barney called and said get out of town. That's good enough for me."

We caught the elevator to the ground floor and walked straight out through the lobby to a taxicab waiting in front. We climbed in the cab and it pulled away.

"Where to?" the driver asked.

"Ah, actually, we hadn't made our minds up yet. Name some of the towns around this part of the state."

"What? I dunno. Ah, San Bernardino, Redlands, Palm Springs ..."

"Yeah. Yeah, Palm Springs. That's where we wanted to go. How much would that cost?"

We were only a block from the Hilton at that point. I wanted to put some miles between me and L.A.

"I'm sorry, sir. I'm not licensed to go that far."

"I understand. But if I could make it worth your while, think you could make it to Palm Springs?"

He thought about it for about three seconds, reached over, pushed the arm down on his meter, and turned his bubble light out on top of the cab.

"Cab 345 to base," he said. "I'm not feeling well. I'm going home for the rest of the day."

We were at the eastern outskirts of L.A. I leaned forward to the driver.

"Since I'm making this worth your while, do you think you could stop at the next store so we can buy some beer?"

"Sir?" He used his most professional voice. "Sir, that is against the law, drinking alcohol in a car."

"You're right," I said. "How about we buy some big cups to put the beer in so no one could tell what we were drinking, and I'd pay you a little extra for drinking privileges? How about that?"

We bought a case of beer and some big cups. After we got back on the highway, and after a few miles of chitchat, I felt comfortable enough with our driver to fire up a joint.

"Care for a hit, sir?"

I saw him eyeball me in the rear-view mirror. He seemed prepared to shrug off his hard outer shell.

"That pot smells awful good, sir. We're already breaking the rules. I may as well take a couple of hits too."

I passed the joint up to him along with a cup of beer.

In Palm Springs, our well-rewarded driver dropped us off in front of a little bar in the middle of town. We went in, had a drink, and then walked over to a motel. We were pretty worn out, so we hit the sack. Our day had started in Pensacola, Florida and went from there to New Orleans, and then to L.A. and finally settled in Palm Springs.

December 12, 1988

I've started to pack. I know we are going to have to pay more on the weight of this luggage. I managed to buy a few pieces of jewelry for the girls for Christmas that I'll pack for them to open in California. When I get there, I'm going to buy some things for them for Christmas morning too. Hope Billy has clothes for the trip. He lives out of his suitcase anyway. I guess I'll wash his clothes and pack them when he gets to mamas Friday night.

The next morning, I called Keystone Heights. One of Barney's sons answered the phone.

"Hey, this is Billy. You heard from your Dad?"

"Not today. He usually checks in around 8:00 p.m. every day."

"When he calls, give him my room and phone number and ask him to call me any time after 5:00 p.m. Pacific time"

We had a whole day to kill before Barney would call so Freddie and I checked everything out within walking distance of our motel, then we called a cab and had the driver give us a tour of the town. After we'd seen all the sights, the driver told us about a mountain resort nearby that had a cable car to the top. It sounded like something we needed to see and we made it back just in time to catch Barney's phone call.

"Okay, Billy. Listen to me." He was talking a mile a minute. "After I gave the checks to the broker, I went to the airport to wait for delivery of the plane. Instead of the broker, two carloads of Feds pulled up looking for me, and these guys were mad. They grabbed me and questioned me for about an hour. I told them that all I knew was a man from Detroit called me and asked me to pick up a plane for him. When they couldn't get any more from me, the boss agent gave me his phone number. He said that when I heard from the man in Detroit, I was to tell him that the Feds had the money *and* the plane and if he wanted either one, to give them a call. That's when I called you."

I could tell the ordeal had shaken him.

"Looks like we lost an $85,000 plane before we even got it," I said.

You might call that really bad luck, but it could have been worse if the FBI had not been so quick on the draw. They'd have stood a good chance of getting the plane — and when we had arrived to pick it up, making two arrests — Freddie and me, But they didn't wait quite long enough.

"I'm sorry, Billy," Barney's voice interrupted my thoughts. "I feel bad about what happened."

I knew he meant it.

We had no option now except to put the wings back on the old 210. Freddie was upset.

"You think Barney might be ripping us off?" he wondered. I looked at him coldly.

"One thing I know for sure," I said. "Barney is an honest man. What he said happened, happened."

I went to a payphone and called the agent's number Barney had given me. As soon as some guy answered, I started in loudly in my best sort of Spanish accent.

"Why you take my plane?" I yelled.

"Who is this?"

"That ees my damn plane! Why you take it?"

"What's your name, buddy?"

I hung up on him. I knew I wouldn't get the plane back, but I thought by calling them I might take a little heat off Barney.

The next order of business: What would be our safest way back to Florida? A bus was out: we'd both had enough bus experience riding prison buses. An airline was out because I didn't want to go back to L.A. We considered buying a used car and driving back, but somehow, we hit on a more antiquated mode of transportation: the train. I'd taken a train once in my life, on a class trip when I was in the 4th or 5th grade. The only thing I could remember was that it was fun.

The closest place we could board going east was Indio, California. They would be loading passengers for New Orleans early the next morning at around 2:00 am. I wanted a sleeper car, but you had to reserve a sleeper about 90 days in advance. All we had to do was to be at the station when the train stopped and simply get on.

It took us two days without a bed, but it was a sort of enjoyable two days with the help of beer and the dining car. The conductor announced places of interest such as the OK Corral and Freddie and I were happy to be tourists and not in jail. In New Orleans we picked up our car and drove back to Florida. I took several days to recover from the train ride.

December 17, 1988

7:00 AM Billy hasn't shown up yet, if he doesn't get here by 9:00 am I'm canceling the flight. I don't know what I am going to tell the girls. He was to meet us last night here at my mother's in Vernon. It makes me nervous, but I have learned to expect him to be late. We need to leave by noon to be in Pensacola by our departure time at 4:00pm.

December 18, 1988

8:00 a.m. No Billy, no call. It's my birthday today, I should have expected it from him. I didn't sleep last night, and I look like hell this morning. I always pray that something hasn't happened to him — it's always my first assumption that he's hurt in some way. I don't know what to think. I'm so afraid that he's mixing different drugs together and will OD like some of his friends. Then my mind goes to he's a sorry SOB who cares about no one but himself. I'm fearful that one day I'll be cussing him and then find out that he's dead. My mama told me not to worry — he'll call today and everything will be fine. I told her I need to go to Dothan to buy the girls some Christmas presents. She said she'll go with me tomorrow. The girls are disappointed but know not to say too much because they can tell how upset I am. I'm sure mama has told them not to bother me. I can only think the worst. Please Lord, let him be okay.

a smuggler and his wife

On Sunday afternoon I drove to Keystone and met Barney early Monday before his customers started to arrive. He described how he'd been waiting for delivery of the plane at the Chino airport. He and the broker had made the deal and the money had changed hands and then the broker had left and gone to another airport across town to pick up the plane. Along the way, he drove by his bank and decided to stop in and deposit the checks then left for the airport to deliver the plane. Meanwhile, back at the bank, the clerk deemed the transaction suspicions and notified the Feds about the numerous $5,000 cashier checks. The FBI guys tried to call the broker but instead get his wife, who told them the name of the airport where they could find her husband. They intercepted him and found out that he was delivering the plane to Barney at Chino airport. That was when the Feds swooped down on Barney.

My plan was in ashes. Barney and I had no option but to discuss the wingless 210.

"I got it stashed at a small grass strip owned by a friend. I didn't want it at the shop because people ask too many questions. I'm going to work my normal hours at the shop, then after work and on weekends I'll work on your plane. I should have it back to you in two to three weeks."

I gave him a few thousand dollars in cash to get a new prop and the needed parts. We shook hands.

"Hey Barney," I said. "I appreciate everything."

He didn't smile. "No problem, friend," he said.

While I was in Barney's shop, I noticed a Keystone paper and glanced at it as Barney took a phone call. The date on the paper hit me like a slap in the face: Friday, December 16, 1988. Kay and I were to leave for California on the 17th. It was already Monday, the 19th. After the close call in LA, my family commitments hadn't even crossed my mind.

December 19, 1988

Mama and I were getting ready to leave for Dothan this morning when Billy called. He said he'd explain when he gets here. He said he'd be here in 6 hours and we could make more reservations. I could say I hate him, but the word 'hate' is not strong enough for how I feel. He has no concept of what his actions do to me and the girls. He can have no excuse for this.

December 20, 1988

His excuse was too lame to even attempt to believe, something about a California trip to buy a plane and train ride to avoid the law that took days. His eyes told me he was lying. Truly this is not the Billy I married. He's like a kid who continually repeats "I'm sorry" but does the same thing over and over again that gets him into trouble. I want to throw my hands up and say "I'm done" but I feel like I'm the only person who can save him from his own destruction. We went to Dothan to buy presents today and he did his best to make up. He joked around, tried to hold hands and kiss me. Fine, but I'm drawing near to my breaking point again. I want a husband, a partner, a friend, someone I can count on and be there when I need them. He can't or he won't. I don't know which. He tells me he loves me more than anything. How can he do that and do the things he does?

December 26, 1988

In the end we booked no reservations to California, but Christmas was nice anyway. The girls loved the gifts they got. I've calmed down, like I usually do, and I am trying to enjoy the rest of our time together. I love him and he's my weakness. I would tell anyone else to leave a man like this, get out of the toxic relationship you're in, etc. Why can't I follow my head and not my heart?

Two weeks after Christmas I picked up the 210 and flew it back to Jay where we'd rented a little hangar on a grass strip. The aircraft didn't fly the same as it did before the accident. It flew what's called "out of rig", that is, just a little bit sideways. But what mattered to me at this point was that we were back in business.

In Belize I'd always depended on Johnny or a taxi to get around since good vehicles were hard to come by in that country. I decided to remedy that problem and bought a four-wheel drive Chevy Blazer in Florida that I could drive to Central America and leave at the compound. I asked my friend Buddy if he would be interested in a little road trip, return airfare included. My plan was to stay in Belize until Freddie flew down for our next load. Not only would I get my own set of wheels in Belize, but I'd get to drive through Mexico and see the sites along the way. It was early January of 1989 and the weather was still cool. A road trip through the southern part of the U.S. would be beautiful that time of year.

January 8, 1989

It's do or die this semester on college-level algebra. Debbie and a couple of our other friends are already taking classes at UNF and I want to be able to start in the fall, so I need to do this. I have one other class plus the algebra. I can do this! The barriers are all in my head. I have a tutor all lined up and I've prayed that the good Lord will give me a clear head to get this done but I'm already having problems. I just don't get this stuff. I made a 72 on the first test and would not have made that if the professor hadn't allowed extra credit. Lord, maybe I'm not supposed to be going back to school. I know I'm not stupid, but algebra does not compute in this brain. It's a good thing that Billy called Debbie and left word that he was out of the country and would see me the first weekend in February. I need all my brain power concentrated on math and not him.

Buddy and I left Pensacola with a small amount of pot, about a quarter ounce of crank and an ample quantity of beer. The Blazer was in Buddy's name, so he was driving. He had been mistaken in the past as Hispanic because of his Indian heritage. That might have been an asset while we were traveling as long as he didn't have to speak. There was no mistaking his slow country southern drawl.

We had several big boom box radios to give to friends and I had a little over $5,000 cash in my pocket for expenses. We stuffed the air-conditioning ducts with about $25,000 cash, the down payment for the next load. We would be driving through some remote spots in Mexico that could be a little sketchy, so I packed a small Colt 380 pistol just in case. Buddy and I figured, with our adequate drug supply, we should have no trouble driving straight through the night, stopping only for gas. Two, maybe three days, tops.

We were passing through the swamps of Louisiana on I-10 and it was late.

"Billy!" Buddy's voice jarred me. "Something's wrong with the transmission! It just suddenly jumped down into second gear!"

We were on a stretch of Interstate with nothing to see but miles of bayou. Buddy was an electrician by trade, a self-taught mechanic, and very skilled with his hands. I knew if this concerned him, it should concern me too.

"Keep going, Buddy. Nothing to do but try to make the next exit." I unfolded my road map of the greater southeast. "The map says it should be right on down the road."

"Shit, Billy. How far?"

"Not too far, Buddy. Just keep driving."

The thirty miles to Vinton, Louisiana, the engine sounded as if it would explode at any minute. We took the exit and, incredibly, the intersection had a little auto repair shop, restaurants, and a motel. The local mechanic filled us in.

a smuggler and his wife

"Y'all run this thing so hot, y'all busted both heads."

For two days the vehicle was in the shop. Nothing to do but eat, sleep and go to a little lounge down the road, where we stayed every night until closing. This was an unexpected expense, but now the vehicle had new heads and we were off again, crossing the border into Mexico at Brownsville.

Just out of Metamoros, Mexico, we decided it was safe to change the mood.

"Buddy, how about you and me enjoying a joint?"

"Well, I guess there ain't nothing but open road ahead, my friend."

I opened the glove box, used the insurance paperwork to roll a fat one, and began cleaning the pot, picking each stem from its bud with practiced precision. We rounded a curve and Buddy slammed on the brakes.

"Damn! Put that shit up!" he yelled.

I looked up from my work. We were mere yards away from flashing lights and police bumpers. Nearly sliding through the police roadblock, Buddy slammed on the breaks and I clutched the paper and buds in my lap hoping nothing went flying. I quickly put the pot back in the glovebox as the police checked around the Blazer. I roll down the window. The officer stuck his hand through,

"Papel! Papel!"

My Spanish was limited but I understood him to mean papers.

I dug my visa out from my pocket and handed it to him. He looked at it and then looked at me, scrutinizing.

"Mas papel el automovil." He wanted the automobile's paperwork. This was a problem since I'd just been cleaning the pot on it.

I opened the glovebox and, like a magician snatching a tablecloth from beneath a table of dishes, I pulled the papers out leaving the pot inside. I handed them to the officer and while they were inspecting the paperwork, I got out five twenty-dollar bills. One for each of the officers.

I stuck my arm out of the window and waved the bills at him.

"Para ti y tus amigos," I said. He smiled, gave me the papers back, allowed us to pass without any further inspection. Buddy and I breathed a sigh of relief once we were able to put some distance between us and the police. We agreed we needed to be more careful.

Not too careful, though. We drove on the rest of the day and into the night, drinking, cranking, smoking and enjoying our Mexican experience. A landscape of golds, oranges, and yellows spanned for miles until the head beams were necessary to see beyond the dusky blue hues of the sinking sun. Everything was a picturesque blur until we reached the little town of Tuxpan.

We were in need of a refuel. In Mexico, unlike the U.S., they don't have a gas station on every corner. Gas is sold by the government and in a small town like Tuxpan, they usually have only one location. At 1:00 in the morning we were driving up and down the dark, deserted streets of Tuxpan, looking for that one place to get gas and this aimless pursuit attracted the attention of the local police. A blue light flashed behind us. Buddy looked over at me.

"Billy, I hope you know more Spanish 'cause this may end up not being very good."

We pulled over and saw four officers emptying an unmarked police car. Three were armed with Uzis and the other with a handgun. One motioned for us to get out of the car with our hands up. We did what they asked. It was almost involuntary. Large guns pointing in your direction makes even a foreign language clear.

a smuggler and his wife

One cop covered us as the other three looked through the vehicle. It didn't take them long to find the pot, the crank, and the 380 Colt. This made them very happy and they began speaking among themselves excitedly, motioning, and peering in our direction with knowing grins. They spoke so fast I could only pick up on a few words.

They showed me what they found. I knew trying to negotiate a deal was our only real hope.

"Habla usted Ingles?"

Nada. I knew a little Spanish, and it was time I put my limited knowledge to use.

"Oye qué pasa amigo cuánto dinero?" I was attempting to say, "Listen, my friend, what's happening. How much money?" This brought another smile to their faces. From their demeanor I could tell they were not planning to kill us, at least not now, but they had plans for sure.

They placed Buddy and I in the back of the police car. One of the officers jumped in the Blazer and we followed him out of town and down a side road to what appeared to be a dump. Thoughts crossed my mind of digging my own shallow grave, of Kay never hearing from me again, of a life nixed for some stupid adventure and car stuffed with cash and drugs. When we were well out of the town's streetlighting, they ordered us out. I wondered how many skeletons of other people who'd been looking for gas late at night may be hidden around that dump.

I locked eyes with the one I assumed was the boss.

"Amigo, cuanto dinero, cuanto dinero?" He smiled again and walked over to the dust covered Blazer and wrote on the window, removing the dust with his finger with every number: 25,000,000 pesos. The figure took up the entire window. It equaled $10,000 — a small price to pay for our lives.

This was no problem, but then again it was. I only had $3,500 in my pocket. The rest was in the air conditioning ducts and I surely did not want to expose the 25-grand stuffed there. I knew if I pulled all the money out of my pocket, they would have wanted all of that as well.

I tried to get them to settle for just the $3,500.

"Señors, we are pobre blancos headed to Cancun for a little fun. We only have a little money."

This was not their first rodeo, not the first Blazer they had pulled over, not the first two "poor" white guys they took for every penny after scaring them half to death. And naturally it was not the first time they had stripped a vehicle. They were ripping apart our car, piece by piece.

It was obvious to me that it was only a matter of time before they would find the money hidden in the vents. "Mas denero manana?" More money tomorrow was what I was trying to convey to the men busy tearing apart my Blazer. "Tomorrow," was not what they wanted to hear, nor did they want to hear anything else from me. I was promptly handcuffed and placed in the backseat of the police car. Buddy, evidently, presented himself as a little more well-behaved. He was allowed to watch the dismantling of the car outside and without cuffs.

It wasn't long before they hit payday. They began fishing the five thousand-dollar bundles from the air conditioning ducts one at a time. Their mood became quite festive as they shouted proudly raising each bundle in the air like a trophy or bundle of lost treasure.

From my narrow view I counted the money bundles they were thrusting above their heads. I figured they had missed one bundle. I hope anyway. I knew we needed to somehow get away with a little money. I took a chance and got out of the car and walked over to the men.

"Bueno, Bueno." I stuck my joined hands out. "Amigos." They took my cuffs off.

They were in good spirits now. I made an attempt to show I was in charge. In my best Spanish and sign language I expressed that I wanted some of the money back, our drugs and my personal possessions. He readily gave me my watch and drugs but would not return the 380 Colt. "Dinero?" I asked purposefully but respectful.

About this time one of the men gave a yell from beyond the hood of our car. He had found the remaining bundle and we were flat broke. Then the head officer took the $3,500 he had taken from my pocket and counted out $2,000. He handed it to me.

"Amigo, como se llama?" I asked.

I figured I needed to, at the very least, know the name of the man who decided not to end our lives on a dirt road just outside this small Mexican town in the middle of nowhere.

He smiled, "Me llama es Jorge."

Jorge had decided to settle for the money, and I was grateful. We still had our lives and enough cash to get the hell out of there. By the time we reached Orange Walk, we'd probably be down to a few hundred. They escorted us to a fuel station where we gassed up and pulled out. I thought I saw Jorge wave.

Driving through the mountainous part of the region was unforgettable. The sights, yes, but also the narrowly missed buses and automobiles curving at a lean around every slim bend of the mountain. Once daylight descended on us, I concluded that if I were to ever enter a car in the Indianapolis 500 race I would come to Mexico and find a driver at one of the local bus depots. Those men are completely fearless and can handle a steering wheel flawlessly.

As we proceeded further into the country, we stopped several more times at different checkpoints. We were pulled over one more time by an unmarked police car. Each time they searched the car, but after our first round of this, we kept our drugs and money hidden on our person. We proceeded without serious complications.

We drove on through the day and into the night. Several hundred miles outside of Chetumal we started having car problems again. Something was slipping in the transfer case. It worked fine when we were up to speed, but if we had to accelerate from a stopped or slowed position it would take a while to regain speed.

This was no problem on the open road but bumping through small towns proved a real struggle. There was no cruising through either, because every town had huge speed bumps the government had installed for their own purposes. Signs would be posted about a thousand feet from the bump warning of the impending jolt your car would inevitably make. We were literally creeping through town slower than I could walk.

Finally, we arrived at Chetumal when the moon was full and high in the open sky. We were in need of some rest before calling Johnny, so we decided to get a room at the El Presidente Hotel.

January 17, 1989

I'm barely holding a C in the class. I go to tutoring twice a week as soon as I leave class to try to ingrain what I've learned that day. It's a hit and miss. I go from the high 60s to low 70s in the class and that is with extra credit every chance I get. One thing this life has taught me is to keep on, even when you feel like you can't. Thank goodness the girls aren't giving me too much trouble. Amy is a freshman and Kim is a junior. If I had to put up with trouble from those two, I don't know if I could do it.

The next morning, we tried to reset.

"Johnny, we're in Chetumal with the vehicle and need you to send your guy."

I didn't want any further experiences with Mexican police.

We returned to the motel and killed a few hours swimming and lounging around the pool. It was not long before Johnny's man arrived. We breezed through Belize customs and immigration and drove straight to Orange Walk with little problems other than the transfer case slipping with acceleration. The Blazer was about done when we finally put it in park at Johnny's compound. It was as tired and defeated as Buddy and me.

Johnny met with us the next morning and we went over the past few days' events analyzing our situation. We'd lost our down payment, $25,000; we had a slipping transfer case in the Blazer, and we were down to a little over a hundred dollars. I gave Johnny the title to the Blazer, so he could borrow some money on it but only a few thousand came of the darn thing. That was what we had for pot money.

Predictably, no one wanted to let go of good pot without a substantial down payment and this we did not have until we came across a stash from Guatemala.

I examined and assessed the product.

"Looks good and smokes good," I told Johnny. "Too bad it smells like dirt."

Johnny raised one side of his mouth in a half snicker at me getting suddenly picky.

"Really, Johnny. No buyer I have in the U.S. is gonna be hungry for this stuff."

He shrugged. "Right, Gringo. But the best thing about this pot is the seller. The guy said we could have the entire 5,000 pounds without any front money."

I considered this astounding offer a minute. Was I going to let a smell come between me and saving our bacon?

"Alright, Johnny. I'll take a load back to our customers and if they like it, I'll be back to pick up the rest." The men started baling the pot, I called Freddie and told him to be on his way and he arrived in the 210 the following morning. Our flight back to Florida was smooth and easy. Buddy meanwhile caught an airline flight as planned and everybody was happy to be back stateside.

We called our buyers. A buyer from Orlando sent a big down payment and two cars to be loaded, though they didn't inspect the pot until they returned to Orlando. Then the buyer called me.

"Hey, Billy?"

"What?"

"You know what, Billy. This shit smells like shit. I'm gonna send it back and I want a refund on the whole load."

I told him, reluctantly, that we'd have his money waiting. Our buyer in Montgomery took the same line. A week later we were full on "dirty-shitty pot" and low on cash to replace it.

We needed a product we could sell. I called Johnny.

"This barnyard weed isn't selling, just like I thought it wouldn't."

He understood though he made no apologies for pushing the stuff out the door.

"Put us together a load of good pot, Johnny, one we can sell, and then give me a call. I'll have a down payment for you as soon as you can get somebody up here."

"That's okay, Billy. Yeah, that's okay."

"And Johnny, relay a message to the Guatemalans for me. It's going to be a while before we can pay in full. We have to find a way to sell the stuff first. If not, we can return it to them on the way down to pick up a new load."

I didn't want to do this, and I'd never heard of smuggling pot backward but if they wanted it that's what we'd do. In hindsight, of course, I should have had Freddie send down more money to Belize after the Mexican fiasco instead of messing with this barnyard pot.

February 4, 1989,

I met Billy at our Bar-be-que place in Alachua. We spent a couple of nights together. He told me he had just made a trip to Belize and had to get back to west Florida to finish a business deal. I told him about my class and of course he told me not to worry about it. He still thinks I am going to school for the fun of it. Sometimes I do wonder how his brain works. He sees this crazy life we're living as an adventure. In his mind, my school, the dance team, raising the girls, — they're all things I like to do; they're my adventures, like flying, smuggling and partying are the things he likes to do. Sometimes my urge to land a solid right cross to his head is so strong I can almost not stop myself. I think the drugs are killing any live brain cells that Billy ever had!

A few days later Johnny's man arrived in Pensacola. I sent him back to Belize with the down payment and within a week I flew down myself, picked up the higher-grade pot, and delivered a transfer case for the Blazer. As we rolled the heavy transfer case out of the 210, it caught on the right main landing gear and tore the brake line off. When I flew back to the Blackwater strip, I only had brakes on the left side for the landing and wouldn't be able to use the brakes to control direction. I ran off the strip at a very slow speed and bent the prop. I flew it back to the Jay hangar with the bent prop but now we needed another prop, an $8,000 fix.

Still, a man had to look on the bright side in our business. We had no problem selling the new load and that helped pay for both the barnyard shit and all our additional expenses. Eventually, off-season provided a fresh demand for marijuana, even if it did smell a little like crap. The barnyard weed, as the buyers called it, was dispersed among them and we were free of it once and for all.

10

Maybe: they thought we'd eluded them and unloaded at an alternative site. We didn't know what they thought, and we weren't going to ask them.

April 23. 1989

Amy has decided to run for vice-president in student government. I'm so proud of her. Kim was voted in as captain of the dance team. I hope the girls will both be strong-willed women when they grow up and go out on their own — much stronger than I was at their age. Maybe I am doing something right in my life, at least as a mother. Amy Doub and Kim are helping Amy make posters to put up at school and listening to the speech she must make next Monday. We'll be there. Then the school votes on Tuesday and we'll have our fingers crossed. She doesn't seem nervous, but I'm nervous for her. Buddy brought me some money by today. He said he'd seen Billy and Billy had asked him to deliver it to me.

May 3, 1989

Amy is the new student vice-president of Columbia High School. She'll be inducted into office next week. Wow. I would have never had the confidence at her age to do that. We're leaving to go out to meet Billy at mama's house in 28 days. Our family trip will be for a little over a month. The Tigerettes go to camp in July and then Amy has student government camp at the end of July. It will be a full summer but one I'm looking forward to.

Kay and I had made plans for a family vacation the summer of '88, before I went on the run. We tried again in December of 1988 but that was when the FBI took our plane out in California. Finally, in June of 1989, I arranged with Kay to meet at my mother-in-law's house so I could give them and me a much-needed getaway — a thirty-day adventure, visiting sites from Florida to California to New York and back. Traveling was commonplace enough for me, but what I was really craving was some normalcy, some Billy life.

May 10, 1989

This month is crawling by. I talked with Billy on Sunday and reminded him of when we are arriving a mama's and that we would be leaving for the trip the day after. He laughed when I told him to have his clothes washed and ready so I would not have to do them. He told me he bought some new clothes for the trip at a store in the mall and had not even taken the tags off. I can't even imagine him clothes shopping, I hope they match.

May 20, 1989

I started packing for the trip again. I bought 3 big suitcases. We're taking mama's Lincoln Continental. Thank goodness it has a huge trunk. I thought packing for two weeks was a lot but for a month is ridiculous. My suitcase is almost full. I can't imagine what three teenage girls will want to take for a month-long trip. They are all about the same size so I told them we can wash clothes at a laundry in California so only pack for two weeks. They can switch off wearing the clothes. Plus, I know them, and they are going to shop too. This time together is what I need.

a smuggler and his wife

May 31, 1989

Finally, we got to mama's place today. I got the girls out of school early, so we got here around 5 PM. It is 8:00 and I told mama I'd sleep in the Love Shack. She tried to talk me into waiting till Billy got here but I feel like everyone is on edge when we're waiting on him over at the main house. I would rather lie here in the bed and try to read. Try is right — it's hard to concentrate when I hear every little thing outside, thinking it's him. I put the light on outside hoping he would know I was here. You can see car lights coming through the woods for quite a distance, so every time I hear something I jump up and check out the window. Hopefully, he arrives soon, and this torment will be over!

June 1, 1989

We're in New Orleans for our first night. Billy got to mama's house around 9:30 last night. We left just after lunch today. Of course, things must be crazy for us. The car looks like we are bottomed out in the back. With the three loaded suitcases and the three girls in the back it is a sight. We locked the keys in the car on arrival at the motel. When we went to use the code to get in the next morning the battery was dead so mama's entry code on the door would not work. Billy is taking care of all that. We're going to eat at the Court of Two Sister's tonight and then tomorrow we're going to do some sightseeing. We plan to stay two nights, but we are definitely going by the Café du Monde for beignets before we leave.

June 5, 1989

Texas is taking forever to drive through. We're staying in San Antonio tonight and Billy left $30,000 in cash on the floorboard of the car as the valet drove away. He searched the parking garage until he found the car and luckily the money was still right there under the seat.

The Alamo is small and in the middle of town — not what I'd pictured in my head when I was reading about the valiant battle fought there. It was nice to eat by the San Antonio River and see the shops lit up at night. The girls enjoyed looking at all the Southwestern things but they weren't interested in buying anything. I find myself counting down the days when I should be just enjoying them. We'll stay two days in Carlsbad and go through the cavern, but I want to see the bats fly out at dusk, so we're spending another night. The girls are not so excited, but I want to see it. Billy said, "Whatever Baby Love wants."

June 8, 1989. Albuquerque, N.M.

I'm sleeping alone in the other bed.

If I'd been by myself, I'd have left. — driven away, left him, never to see or speak to him again. At this point I want nothing more than to just be alone. To not have to face the sunlight that will eventually come tomorrow morning. I suppose it's alright to call yourself a fool, because that is what I have been all along. Thinking he would change but knowing in the back of my mind that would never happen. I knew when he left to go on the run that my life would not be the same, but I held on to the idiotic hope that somehow our love was strong enough to endure this. As I was straightening up Billy's suitcase, I found drugs of all kinds, pot, cocaine, pills, etc. in a side pocket of a duffel bag. Not that this wasn't bad enough and the fact that he had it with us, but I also found a small journal with a rubber band around it to hold everything together: phone numbers, addresses, and a variety of business cards, the numbers of different girls. Beside most of the names it had their occupations: stripper, cocktail waitress, bartender etc. He probably had five or six with names like Porsche, and Gin — their entertainment names! He had business cards with little notes written on the back like "call me anytime" with hearts drawn on them from a place called Solid Gold, a strip bar in Pensacola. I also found a card from a clothing store that had the name and phone number of a female manager. The note on the back said, "Thanks for lunch, call next time to make sure I am here." I guess this is where he bought all the clothes for the trip! He had gone to a store to buy us drinks and snacks for the next day's ride and when he returned, I confronted him. He denied it at first, saying they were just friends of friends, then eventually he played the "men aren't like women, Kay" defense. "Men, they do things to just have a good time, Kay. None of those girls mean anything. I love you and if I don't act like a normal guy, people will think I'm gay." That was his defense. If he'd pulled out a knife and stabbed me repeatedly it could not have been worse. He admitted to buying clothes from this salesgirl for 8 months. I had asked him in New Orleans where he had gotten his clothes because it wasn't like his normal clothes. He told me he was shopping with Freddie and Freddie was helping him pick out clothes. He said he started taking her out to lunch and bought her some clothes and had even gone to a Judd's concert with her. He said he was looking to have sex with her at first but now since she wouldn't do anything, it was just for company because she wasn't like the other cocktail waitresses and strip dancers, she had a brain and reminded him of me. I guess he was trying to justify why he was still talking to her — because she brought out memories of me! If I only had a gun, I'd have shot him right then for thinking I was that stupid.

June 9, 1989

We left Albuquerque this morning headed to Flagstaff. I slept in the other bed last night, what sleep I got, and will continue to do the same tonight. I could hear him snoring last night and I wanted to choke the life out of him. How could he sleep after the fight we had? If I had betrayed someone like he had me, my conscience would have never let me sleep. I tossed and turned all night thinking about his relationship with these other women *and what consequences those little affairs could have for me and our personal and sexual relationship. I guess he doesn't have a conscience. It's hard for me to even concentrate on the things around me and on the chit chat that the girls were doing in the back seat. I wanted to be somewhere else, not with him and not in the car, but I couldn't do that to the girls, I couldn't let them see how upset I am and ruin this trip for them. I'm doing much of the driving so if we do get pulled over, he will not have to show his license, so I have at least been able to focus on the road. The girls are not so easy to fool as they once were. They know something is up between us, but they won't question me — it would make them uncomfortable. So, we mostly drove in silence except for the music of Segar on the radio. Then I lost it when he wanted to stay at the Radisson when it came time to stop. He kept going on and on about how he stayed there and how nice it was. All I could think was, who were you with when you stayed there? I stood us all on our heads when I slammed on the brakes in the middle of the road, threw the car in park and yelled you drive the damn car to wherever you want us to go. The girls definitely knew then there was something up.*

June 10, 1989

Still sleeping separate. Billy hasn't said too much about the argument and I'm not speaking to him. His theory about his misdeeds has always been, no matter what they have been, if we don't talk about it, it will just miraculously go away. Or if he apologizes for something, it should be like it never happened. It doesn't work like that. We toured the Grand Canyon. It was beautiful and I was able to enjoy the scenery and utter wonder of this amazing creation. Billy paid for us to go on a plane ride over the canyon. I wasn't a fan of how it made me feel — weird, like the bottom dropped out as we flew over the canyon. Amy got sick from the rough ride.

June 11, 1989

We arrived in Vegas today and we're staying at Circus, Circus. It is just as crazy a town as I remember. Billy's dad and mom took me here in 1974 just after Amy was born. They had previously been to Tijuana and found a table and chairs they wanted to buy. His mom wanted to go to Vegas, and we had flown to San Diego for the night, bought the table and chairs and then went to Vegas. I remember Elvis was playing and I wanted to go to see him, Jim, Billy's dad, wouldn't have that, and we instead went to see Johnny Carson. We are taking the girls to see Rodney Dangerfield tonight. Couldn't get tickets for anything else.

June 12, 1989

Billy wanted to stay a couple more nights. He's gotten tickets for the Hearns/Leonard fight tonight. No telling how much he paid for that. We now are staying at the Imperial Palace. It is on the strip across from Caesar's Palace, so the girls are ready to see the sights. They aren't supposed to go into the casino, but all three girls look older than they are, so they are in and out hoping not to get caught. We have two suites; our suite has mirrors everywhere even above the circular bathtub. They all three piled in the tub, fully clothed and I took a picture of them. They even saw Tom Selleck in the elevator. I'm sure he is here for the big fight at the Palace tonight. I can see the front drive of the Palace from my window but can't really tell who's arriving — just a lot of limousines. Billy was excited when he left. He, his father and his brother have always enjoyed boxing. We had even gone to watch Muhammad Ali and Bonavena fight in Jacksonville on a live broadcast from NYC while we were dating in 1970. That was many years ago and many memories had come and gone since then, good and bad. I don't know if I can get over this latest hurt. The days together on our trip are counting down and I still cannot allow him to even touch me. It's too painful.

June 16, 1989

We're in LA. Life between Billy and me will go on. I made my choice almost 10 years ago to return to Billy. Even though I knew it was a 50/50 chance he would change, it didn't matter. Now, I will live with that choice for better or worse. He will never again hold that same place in my heart that he had once held. I will guard my love and my heart against him. I know what he is capable of and I know it will continue to happen. I am his wife and the mother of his children and I will not walk away from that commitment. But it will not be the same for me — it can't be.

June 21, 1989

The girls loved LA, Rodeo Drive and Hollywood. Billy rented a limo and we drove around Hollywood and shopped on Rodeo Drive in LA. The limo driver took us by many of the Hollywood stars' homes, and we ended up at Universal Studios. We sat in the limo for a little while for Billy to pay the driver. As we looked out of the car, we realized we'd attracted quite a crowd. The driver laughed. "They think there is somebody important in here," he said. The girls of course were decked out in new outfits and sunglasses and purses that we'd just bought on Rodeo Drive.

"Hey," the driver said. "You all put on your glasses and let me come around and open the door for you. Girls, you grab your dad's arm when you get out and watch what happens."

He got out, came around and opened the door, and the crowd closed in with cameras in hand. I waited while the girls got out, then Billy. People started taking pictures like crazy, asking the driver who it was. We had our best laugh for the day.

We went over to Palm Springs for a night. We stayed for several days in the LA area. We left there and went through the Sequoia Nat. Park and then up to San Francisco. I'm not sure how far we've traveled but between riding and eating in restaurants I think we have all gained 10 pounds. Billy wanted to see Alcatraz, but it was too foggy. We plan to stay here another night before moving on.

June 22, 1989

Reno was not very interesting but the scenery through the Lake Tahoe area was beautiful. Our plans are to cut across Nevada and Utah and then stay a few days in Wyoming. Time is slipping away but the hours of driving help me clear my head about my future. I have run every decision I've made in the last 20 years through my head — the good ones and the bad ones. Hindsight is always 20/20.

June 25, 1989

We're planning on going through the Dakotas and then on to Detroit. The girls are getting tired of riding and Kim is dying to see her boyfriend. Every stop she grabs Billy's bag of quarters and goes to the pay phone to call him. Oh, to be that young and that much in love again!

June 28, 1989

Billy told me I wasn't acting like myself, his sweet Baby Love. I told him, yeah, and you haven't been acting like too much of a married man either. Of course, that didn't go over well. His comeback was, "I told you I'm sorry and it won't happen again." I told him if he wanted a divorce, I'd give it to him.

"Divorce?" he said. "I don't want a divorce. I love you. You just don't understand."

"You're right," I told him. "I don't."

I guess he just wants to torment me. Maybe that's equally satisfying to him.

June 30, 1989

We are at Niagara Falls and it is amazing. I never dreamed it was that big. This trip across America has been unforgettable in more ways than one. We start south tomorrow. Billy has some business to attend to and I have practice that begins on the 5th of July. We should be back at mama's house by July 2.

July 2, 1989

Our last night together. I don't know if this trip was a good thing for our relationship or not. Billy is a different man than when he left us, this I do know. It's been 16 months since he's been on the run and apart from his family except for stolen weeks and weekends here and there. I know he loves me, and I can't imagine how hard it is moving around with really no one to talk to at times but my life has been torn apart as well. I'm living the life of a single woman with only my children and school to focus on. It was not a choice I was even consulted on before he chose this type of life for us. I'm only 38 years old; I get lonely too. I'll share our bed tonight and then go home to that same lonely lifestyle tomorrow. How long can we last?

July 3, 1989

Billy left my mother's house right after lunch. He kissed us bye and drove down the long drive and out of sight. He was already planning that next adventure in his head.

The girls and I set off around 3 p.m. for home. It's Amy's birthday tomorrow and they have something already planned. I made it to Madison, Florida but I could go no further. We were a mere 70 miles from home, but I could not face that house — my room, our room — alone. I told the girls we were staying the night in a motel along I-10. I got two rooms and they were furious with me. They wanted to be home with their friends. We had been gone a

> month. I could not do it. Here I sit in a motel room with no one to talk to or confide in wondering where and who my husband is with tonight. I had wanted to leave him two weeks ago, never see him again. Now I just want to be in his arms, feel his touch and put my head on his shoulder. I don't know if I can make it. I pray God gives me the strength to understand what I need to do with my life.

The month-long trip felt more like a week. It was over much too fast. My family returned home and again I was left with the loneliness that only they could fill.

The night in Albuquerque, Kay found my little black book. It had names and numbers of, well, a number of bar dancers and party girls. She was hurt, mad, and now she knew that trusting me was out of the question. I knew she had suspicioned that I was not being faithful again, but this destroyed any hopes she had. Her intuitions were never wrong and now she had proof. Deservedly, I caught hell for three or four days. We tried to not show our distress in front of the girls, but I'm sure they knew something was going on. I had hurt the only one I truly loved. I knew it and hated myself for it, promised to stop, explained that no name in that book meant anything to me — one-night stands at best. We both knew things would be different from now on. She would always question my word and my faithfulness. I'm not sure why she continued to love me through the misery I put her through other than God's grace. It defied all logic and I knew the pain of my infidelity would not be, and was not in the end, at all easy to overcome. I suppose in time she came to forgive me, but she hadn't forgotten. I didn't then and I don't even now deserve that kind of undying love.

I soon made a quick run to Belize to top up the wallet and after I got back, I decided to stay at Freddie's to help with distribution, which he seemed sometimes to find difficult. I'd lived with him and Sweet Pea in the past and knew their relationship well, consisting as it did of fighting, freebasing and screwing. Now I remembered why I'd left.

I woke the first morning to their standard yelling and screaming. This usually led to a shoving and slapping match with Freddie the victor. This morning was no different until Sweet Pea called the police to report domestic abuse and in no time three cop cars buffered the front of Freddie's house, lights flashing. The sirens went silent and six officers exited their vehicles. I watched from a bedroom window as the scene played out in awkward slow motion. For me, law enforcement on the front lawn cut the morning humidity like a gust of arctic wind. Shivers ran down my spine.

Right behind Sweet Pea, Freddie stormed out of the house in a hollering, cursing rage, not thinking straight at all. I moved to the back of the kitchen, behind an entryway wall, where I could see well enough through the open front door. The pair was putting on a show. Freddie was in a full rant.

"I ain't going to jail because of you! Ain't *nobody* going to jail but you, whore!"

Sweet Pea was yelling crazy shit, her skinny arms flailing the air, waving around like a lunatic.

"This is my house!" Freddie was shouting defiantly. "I live here! You don't!"

I closed my eyes. This was bad.

"Lord," I thought, "help me get out of this and I'll stay as far away from this craziness as I can."

The truth was — and I was ashamed to admit this to myself — I'd already witnessed firsthand how violent this couple could become. It was at Gulf Shores, Alabama in October of 1988. I'd been living with Freddie and Sweet Pea for about a month and the fighting was a regular occurrence. But for a little entertainment one day, we three decided to check out the seafood festival. We were partying on the ride over and an argument started as soon as the booze flushed their veins. The tempo steadily progressed and by the time we parked the car I had to physically pull Freddie off his woman. Punches were thrown and craziness ensued. I got Freddie and me out of the car and told Sweet Pea to beat it. She heeded the warning and tore off, tires squealing. I was pretty disheveled and left Freddie at the festival, called a friend for a ride back to Pensacola. Before I made it home, Sweet Pea and Freddie had already locked themselves in the bedroom for some make-up romance.

Now the police were loading Sweet Pea into one of the cars, probably hoping to defuse the mayhem. They drove down the driveway and off to the station. This was my cue. I grabbed my bag.

"See ya later, man!" I called to Freddie.

At the station, I was to learn, Sweet Pea unlocked her Pandora's box of smuggling intel.

"Freddie's got drugs everywhere!" she yelled. "He's got pot stashed over at Timbo's house!"

She was talking about my poor friend, Timbo. He'd allowed us to stash a load of pot over at his house. But Sweet Pea was just warming up, her eyes bulging.

"He's a lying bastard and you ought to see what he's done to *me*!"

And on and on. By a miracle, she was so clearly high at the time she made her statements, the cops chalked it up to the rantings of a love-scorned druggy, which was somewhat true. Maybe they didn't feel she was credible enough to help them obtain a search warrant. In either case, had they believed sweet little Sweet Pea, they would have found close to 900 pounds of marijuana stashed in Timbo's utility room. Also, as is often the case in a small town, someone knew someone else. One of the policemen was a former classmate of Timbo and his wife and this kind fellow decided loyalty to friendship ought to count for something. He found a payphone as soon as he could get away from the station. Timbo's wife answered.

"Hey, this is David. Sweet Pea is at the station and if you have what she says you have at your house; you need to tell Timbo to get rid of it — quick."

This little lover's dispute had now gotten everyone's attention. We put Earl to work relocating the stash because regardless of our efforts to undo the damage, the heat was on.

The fussing and fighting at the house, the festival incident, the police visit, and my knowledge of Sweet Pea's mouth made it well past time for me to go. The crew quickly called a meeting about the event.

"Freddie," I explained. "I'm not trying to get in your personal life, but I'm a fugitive and this seems like a good time for me to hit the road."

Freddie shook his head and looked at the floor.

"I know y'all say Sweet Pea ratted on us, but I don't believe it. David might've been lying about all that, probably trying to get information and seem like he's on our side."

"Freddie, buddy, I know you want to believe her, but some of us don't have that luxury."

In fact, no one shared Freddie's feelings. We all knew full well that Sweet Pea had snitched and would do it again the next time a fight ignited her need for revenge. If we'd been a real cartel of bad guys li'l ole Sweet Pea would have been left in a ditch somewhere. But we were just a bunch of guys having a good time and trying to make some money smuggling the herb into America, supplying the demand for a high that so many were fond of here in the States. We would never hurt anyone ever, but Sweet Pea was an issue and the only one who could really get her out of our hair was Freddie. Sadly, for his sake and ours, he wasn't going to do that.

I left instructions for everyone else to go about their business as usual and to watch out for any suspicious police activities. I was anxious to return to Belize and secure a load of pot for our next trip. I thought I might at last see the sights in Belize now that I had the Blazer to cruise around in. Hanging about to witness more relationship drama wasn't my idea of a good time.

I caught a ride with Earl and Timbo to New Orleans, partied all night in the French Quarter with the guys, caught a flight to Cancun the next morning and slept all the way. I checked into the Plaza Caribe and called Johnny. My ride arrived shortly before noon, and we headed south, reaching the border around 5 p.m. The Belize immigration officer was about to stamp my paperwork when he noticed it already had one entry stamp. He flipped my passport from front to back, raised his eyebrows and stared through me for several long seconds. There was no exit stamp for my previous trip when I'd entered the country with the Blazer. Now I was entering again without having evidence that I'd left. According to the paperwork, I was *in* Belize — on the other side of this border checkpoint. Red flags were flying.

I should've accounted for this in some way but with all the drama back home, I was focused on getting the hell out of Dodge. The customs official was surveying my person and stature and most likely his options. He had a man entering his country legally but who must have, at some point, exited *illegally*. It upset him. He folded my documents, moved them to the side, and sighed deeply.

"Well, Mr. Lang, I am placing you under arrest, and we are going to hold you here until you can see a judge at a hearing, which will be appointed to you." His English legal jargon was spot on.

"Look, Mr. Sanchez, thank you. But what would be the normal fine for such an offense?"

I figured I'd throw some charm out on the table. I needed to get some sort of nonchalant read on how much trouble I was actually in.

"Mr. Lang," — a little thoughtful this time — "You're the first case of illegal exit I've seen. The normal fine for illegal entry is $200."

I felt, since he responded to my inquiry, that he expected the exit fine would be the same. I decided a proposal would be worthwhile.

"Mr. Sanchez, how about I give you the $200 so I won't be delayed by going to jail. I suspect you can put that money to better use than the government."

In Belize the exchange rate was two Belizean dollars to one US dollar, so we were probably talking a month's salary for him. He thought about this, again staring right at me.

"You want to give me the money, Mr. Lang?"

"I do, sir." I smiled and laid two hundred U.S. dollars on the counter. "I certainly do."

He returned the smile and slid his hand over the bills in a practiced gesture, swiping the stack off the counter the way a blackjack dealer moves cards off the green felt. He unfolded my paperwork, stamped it with an exit and then an entry verification. I thanked him. He nodded and waved me through as if no discussion had ever occurred. We headed to Orange Walk.

I spent the next few weeks driving around Belize in the Blazer in search of the best possible pot. Then, at the end of my first week I put my search on hold when I came upon the Mayan ruins at Altun. How many other relics of ancient civilizations had I flown over without seeing or understanding? How many other monuments to wealth and power still stand in the forest to remind us that all the wealth in the world passes away? I gazed in wonder, then drove on.

August 7, 1989

I started my classes at University of North Florida in Jacksonville today. It's so different from junior college! I can finally take classes in education and I'm majoring in social science grades 6-12. This will give me a variety of subjects to teach like history, geography, economics, government, psychology, etc. I figure I will have a better chance of getting hired. I am still doing the dance team, so my mind stays busy. I didn't hear from Billy on Sunday. I was hoping he would call while I was at Debbie's. I have no idea why he didn't; my mind is left to wonder. This is why I need to keep my mind busy!

August 14, 1989

I've been riding back and forth to Jacksonville with Debbie and three other girls taking classes at UNF. It's an hour and fifteen minutes from my house to the parking lot at UNF. We have to leave at 6:30 a.m. three days a week in order to get through the rush hour traffic. My classes so far are not too bad. I enjoy the history class the most: The Stuarts and Tutors. I am so glad I decided to do this. I don't think I would have made it staying at home and wondering what Billy was doing and where he was. He didn't call again Sunday. I am sure he will have a reason; and it won't be his fault. It never is. It's hard for me to describe how I feel, — nervous, worried, scared, lonely, unsure of life in general. I knew when I left my life in Apollo Beach that life would change, but I never expected this. I'm totally lost about my family's future.

August 20, 1989

Billy called after church today. He was in Belize checking on a vehicle he'd taken down for him to drive while he's there. I didn't ask why he would need transportation as he was supposed to be working, flying in and back out, making money, not joyriding around Belize. I am tiring of this life. Evidently my husband is finding ways to enjoy his extended vacation away from his family. I have two children to raise and no social life and my man is running all over Pensacola, Cancun, Atlanta and Belize acting like a single man. The girls never ask me much about their father's profession, but Lake City is a small town and in small towns people love to talk. When Billy was arrested on our front porch in 1981, he was front page news. I still have the same neighbors, the neighbors that stand behind their curtains and stare at me when I leave the house. The girls still hear talk from time to time at school, and I try to shelter them as much as possible. I get so angry when I see people that I've known for years whispering as they see me when I enter the grocery store and then stop when they see me coming toward them. They turn and pretend like they don't see me. I purposely walk up to them and make them speak to me. I learned over the years to be tough. If I'm to survive in this world, I have to hold my own.

In the second week I came across a grower who had a much higher grade of pot than the usual. When I got back to the compound, I asked Johnny to check out his price.

"I contacted the guy for you," Johnny reported. "He wants more money than typical, but I convinced him to take a twenty-grand deposit."

Before I left for Belize, Freddie and I had decided he'd bring $15,000 to pay for a load. That amount had been sufficient to pack the 210.

"No problem. I'll get in touch with Freddie and tell him to grab an extra $5,000."

Johnny was pleased. "But Gringo, he wants the cash in hand before the pot leaves his site."

"Of course. He knows he's got some good stuff. I respect that. Make the deal, Johnny."

A couple of enjoyable weeks in Belize had me feeling good and maybe things had settled down back in the little town of Century.

"Yeah. Okay Billy, terrific." Freddie sounded cheerful when he called me back a few days later. Everything's cool here, I've been staying close to the house and me and Sweet Pea, we're really getting along great."

I rolled my eyes, but he couldn't see that.

"Good Freddie, Happy for you, really. But please remember what we talked about. When you leave the house, make sure no one's following you." I tried to sound paternal, stern even.

"Billy, don't worry, man. I know."

Problem was, he had this kid-like way about him sometimes when it came to the aftermath of self-inflicted pain. Deep down, he knew I had more reason to be upset with him than I'd decided to be.

"Freddie?" I waited for a response.

"Yeah?"

"Freddie, if you think you've got a tail, don't go near the airplane."

"I understand completely, Billy".

He wanted me to feel assured and I really wanted to believe him.

"I'll keep an eye open, Billy. Really. I'll call when I'm ready to come down."

The crew knew we had heat on us due to Sweet Pea's trip to the police station. Before I'd left, they'd got the same briefing I gave to Freddie.

"When you head to the strip, everyone needs to keep a sharp eye out. If any of you notice anything unusual when you get there, say, "red light" when I call on the radio. I'll divert the load to our airstrip to the south of Jay, Florida and secure the airplane and the load of pot in the hangar there.

I was 99% sure the police knew nothing about the Jay strip, where the 210 was resting since we put the wings back on. If they had known, they'd have seized it already.

I got the call from Freddie Friday.

"I'll be down to see you on Sunday afternoon partner."

August 26, 1989

Well, I guess I handled my current problem as a mother correctly. Kim and Amy Doub were out tonight and they came home unexpectedly about 9:30. Kim was scratched from right under her chin down to her chest with about three claw marks and bleeding. She had been in a fight! Of course, it was about the boyfriend. I saw red. Her neck looked horrible. I took her and Amy Doub to the girl's house to solve this disagreement. When I saw the other girl, I knew it must run in our blood. The other girl had a shiner, and her eye was completely blood shot. Kim had definitely got a good shot in. We left with the understanding that boys are not worth fighting over — especially when they're at fault!

On Sunday Johnny and I were sitting just west of Orange Walk on the cane patch road waiting on Freddie. The refueling crew was ready. Freddie and I would hop over to San Pedro for the night before returning the next morning to load the plane and take off for Florida.

I had one concern. The road ran north and south and there was a stiff wind kicking up out of the east. This meant Freddie would have to land on our narrow road with a 90-degree crosswind. It would be a challenge, but I had confidence in the man's abilities.

The two-meter radio crackled.

"I'm ten minutes out." Freddie's voice. He was right on time.

"You've got a stiff crosswind kicking up. We're ready to do our thing. I've got the Blazer parked on the approach end of the runway. Look for it."

We soon had a visual. Freddie flew over the strategically placed Blazer so he could land just in front of it to avoid the potholes.

I could see he was in a landing pattern and watched as he turned to make the final approach. I could tell he was fighting the crosswind as he crabbed into the wind to hold his alignment with the road, lowered his right-wing into the wind just as he flew over the Blazer, kicked the plane out of the crab, and performed a wing-low landing flair.

"Damn good job," I thought. "Just the way I would have done it."

He was on the ground and rolling out. I relaxed.

Suddenly, the plane made an abrupt 90-degree turn to the left and most of it disappeared into the cane field. Johnny and I looked at each other and jumped into the Blazer. We got there just as Freddie was climbing out of the cockpit.

"Damn, Freddie," I said. "You are kind of hard on our ride, aren't you, partner?"

He shook his head as he eased himself to the ground.

"Guess I had a little attention lapse, Billy. Didn't realize I was so far to the left; I caught that wing in the cane."

We tied a rope to the Blazer and pulled the plane back onto the road. It had some limited damage structurally, some crinkles in the wings and cowling, and a whole lot of mud and muck in the landing gear. But the real damage was to the propeller. Each blade was bent back 30 or 40 degrees with nicks where the blades had dug into the ground. We didn't have another prop or the tools to change one, even if we had. There was in fact no time to do any repairs at all. We were only a few miles out of Orange Walk and leaving the area quickly was top of our minds.

Nicks in a prop are something to be concerned about because props experience a lot of load and stress. A tear can start at the point of a nick and a piece of the prop can tear off in flight, upsetting the balance of the engine. A prop is a flywheel and losing any portion of it is usually catastrophic.

Nothing could be done about the nicks, but I could do something about the 30-plus-degree bend in the blades. I sat down on the ground in front of the propeller, placing one foot on the prop at the bend and grabbing the end with both hands, I pulled hard on the blade. I repeated this on all three prop-blades until I had reduced the bends to a 10- to 15-degree angle. They still didn't look good, but it was an improvement.

The crew had fueled the plane, so the next matter of business was the business itself.

"Freddie, you got the down payment?"

He reached into the airplane and pulled out a Crown Royal bag and threw it at me. As soon as I felt the purple cloth in my hands, I knew by the weight of it that we had a problem. There was no way this bag contained enough money.

"How much money is in here, Freddie?"

He looked confused. "There's the whole $5,000, just like you asked for."

"No, I said I needed the original $15,000 *plus* $5,000 more!"

Freddie shrugged his shoulders, incredulous.

I turned to Johnny.

"My friend, as you see, we only have $5,000 for a down payment."

Johnny laughed out loud. "No way is that guy going to let go of that load for $5,000."

"Right. Of course. So how's about you doing some more negotiating with him?"

"You serious, Billy?"

"Or maybe you could loan us an additional $15,000?"

Johnny shook his head.

"Billy, it's no on borrowing money because I don't have it. And I would lay big odds on you not getting the pot for $5,000."

I didn't know what my plan was, but I did know that we didn't need to be discussing business in the middle of the cane patch.

"Come on Freddie. Let's go to San Pedro. Johnny can meet us there after he talks with the grower."

We got in the plane and prepared for takeoff. I cycled the props several times until I was satisfied that the bent prop was functioning. We still had a strong 90-degree crosswind — not beyond the crosswind-component capabilities of the airplane, but enough to make a takeoff both exciting and a challenge. Hitting the cane patch would cause severe bodily harm to us and the aircraft.

I'm not sure when it started or what suppression of emotion fueled it, but my comfort with danger and flying had become an addiction. If things were running without a flaw, I wholeheartedly expected the worst to come down like lightning on a sunny day. Chaos and danger brought me solace.

I was traveling at close to 90 mph on lift-off when the wind gusted and long stalks of cane blew into our path and caught the left wing. I applied full right rudder to keep the plane from doing what it had done earlier with Freddie. We broke clear of the cane with half a dozen stalks wrapped around the leading edge of our left-wing tip like streamers on a new bike. We landed at San Pedro Island and I stopped as short as I could on the runway.

Freddie hopped out and removed the cane. We didn't need our plane looking unpresentable as we were about to taxi up to the transit parking area. Hopefully, no one would look close enough to notice the bent prop or the mud. The cane stalks, though, would have been hard to miss.

We parked the plane and headed to the far end of town to the Paradise Village Bar. We stayed there a couple of hours until Johnny showed up.

"Okay, amigos. Your only option is to buy 200 pounds of the high grade for the $5,000 down payment."

Freddie and I figured that a 200-pound load would only profit us enough to pay the grower and the off-loading crew. We would realize zero profit. I decided to take a stand.

"Johnny, I know it's our mistake, but I'm not going to leave with anything less than 800 pounds. You should be able to stand good for our load."

Johnny shook his head, and I could see he was wearing a bit of a smirk.

"Right," I said. "If I can't get the full load, I'll go home empty." His eyes widened at this notion. I wanted him to know whatever we order is what we expected to load. We had established a good working relationship with Johnny; he should know we were not going to stiff him. Before he could even respond, I hopped off my bar stool and walked away, Freddie not far behind.

As soon as we got out of earshot, Freddie spoke up.

"What the hell, Billy? We're going to go back empty?"

I knew the guy deserved an explanation, so I stopped walking.

"Look, Freddie. My reasoning is this: if we don't make a stand now, we run the risk of making an order for 800 pounds next time and Johnny telling us to come to get the load and maybe he only has 700 pounds or something less. We need to show we're not going to let them shortchange us on any future load."

Whether Freddie agreed or not, I wasn't giving in on this. I stopped again.

"I know this is business, Freddie, but my friendship with Johnny should also count for something. I'm sticking to my word one way or another and they ought to recognize why."

So much for my principled stand. We flew back to Florida the next morning empty. I said I'd do it and now I was following through. No need to risk landing at the Blackwater strip empty just to pick up the seats. The guys waiting at Blackwater would of course be dumbfounded that we were empty, but it was what it was.

Close to the Blackwater strip, we called my friend Timbo and the crew.

"Nothing happening today, boys. Not landing as scheduled. Meet you at the hangar at the Jay strip. Make sure the doors are open."

Some garbled talking in static. I thought it might be Timbo.

"Go ahead, Timbo."

Again, the garble.

"Go ahead, Timbo."

A strange static response.

"The radio must be messing up, Timbo. See you at the hangar."

It was about fifteen air miles to the Jay strip and close to thirty highway miles. If I flew straight to the hangar, I'd arrive quicker than the crew, so I decided to kill some time. The crew would call on the radio when they arrived, and the hangar would be open. I'd wait for their cue to land.

I flew west toward Jay but spotted a large thunderstorm ahead, maybe five miles north of us.

"Freddie, tighten your seat belt. We're going to take this plane through Mother Nature's carwash."

I abruptly banked 90-degrees to the right. Instantly, a turbine-powered Bell Helicopter flashed right in front of our windshield, its pilot doing his best to avoid a midair collision with us. I pulled out of my bank and dove. The chopper passed overhead, narrowly missing the top of our 210.

"Holy shit! What was that?" Freddie was freaked out and so was I.

"That was the law, man! Who else is going to follow us that close?"

My mind was racing. He couldn't have been behind us long. I'd been flying across the Gulf at normal cruising speed and a Bell couldn't have kept up with a 210. He probably hooked onto us after we started to kill time, when I reduced power and slowed to conserve fuel.

"Okay, that thunderstorm is about to serve us twice!" I gripped the controls. "We're going to wash the plane *and* get rid of that chopper."

We entered the mountain of cumulous cloud — big, dark, full of water and plenty of teeth. It took us on a ride, and I felt the high of fear and tension. Then, after just ten minutes of storm-riding, we popped out into a clear sky. The chopper was nowhere to be seen.

"Did we lose him?" Freddie shouted. He'd been gripping his armrests the entire time.

"Yeah, I think so, buddy. I think you can relax."

The storm was no issue for me. The helicopter was.

"You were a crazy man just now, Billy! I mean, you were, like, *crazy*!"

"Ha, ha. Now you know how I felt when you and Sweet Pea were chatting with the police on your front lawn."

"What do you mean? Like, *I* was crazy?"

"And *your* cops didn't even have a helicopter."

He made no response and I hoped he was giving some thought to his own carelessness. It looked like we were in the clear, but I wasn't taking any chances. There was a real possibility we were being tracked by ground-based radar.

"Hold on, Freddie. We're going to get on the deck."

I dropped down to just above the treetops and flew straight back to the Jay strip and landed. We tucked the airplane safely away in the hangar.

We took back roads in Timbo's truck and met the rest of the crew at an old dump just east of the Escambia River. I told the assembled crew about the close call with the helicopter. There were some sidelong glances between them.

"Man!" Timbo shook his head. "That sounds like the same helicopter that flew right over us a couple of times while we were waiting on you."

"Yeah, you're right, Timbo." Joe was scratching his beard. "That was after we saw those four guys riding by in a car a couple of times!"

I looked at them like they were aliens.

"Do y'all remember me telling you before I left to watch for anything unusual?"

They glanced at one another sheepishly.

"Didn't you think that was a little strange? Four guys riding in a vehicle in the middle of the woods and a helicopter flying overhead? Why didn't one of you signal 'red light' when I radioed in?"

Maybe we'd all become too complacent. Maybe we were doing too many drugs to understand what strange looked like. Whatever, we decided to go to Timbo's house in Century. Freddie and I jumped in Earl's truck, and Timbo and Joe followed in their vehicle. Century was on the west side of the river and there was only one bridge that crosses the river on the north end of the county, on the road that connects Jay to Century. We'd rolled up to the stop sign to make the left turn toward Century when a county deputy car sped past us. He glanced over and stopped short, slamming on his brakes.

"Oh shit!" Earl said. "Is he coming after us?"

We turned left, Century and the Escambia River bridge just ahead of us.

"He's coming back for us!" Freddie shouted.

We were right behind Timbo and the deputy's car was right behind us. The main bridge across the river was ahead of us but before the main bridge was a shorter span needed only when the river overflowed its banks. At the foot of both bridges were access roads leading down the bank and popular with the locals for weekend parties. As we approached the first bridge, I glanced down at the party area. There were ten police cars parked on the road. My heart was in a full race.

"This is it," I thought. Their plan would be to stop us between the bridges, trap us plain and simple with a truckload of pot — if we had unloaded one. They'd been tipped off no doubt, knew we were coming in with a load. How did they know that? We didn't have any pot, of course, but I was a fugitive. Would my fake ID hold up under their scrutiny?" I fleetingly wondered how deep the water was here. Could I survive a jump from the bridge?

We crossed the first span and then the second. Six police cars now joined our little convoy. There was law enforcement everywhere I looked, but no lights flashed and no sirens sounding. No one in our car spoke a word. We turned down the street to Timbo's house, then into his driveway. We pulled around behind the house and down to his horse barn. Police cars buzzed by but didn't stop. We sat there, silent.

What had just happened? The bleed-over that we heard on the radio while in the air was probably from the proximity of their police radio in the helicopter. No question the law had the perfect plan if we'd unloaded any pot at the Blackwater strip but they had no plan if the plane did not land and unload. They didn't want to stop us and find us clean. Maybe they thought we'd eluded them and unloaded at an alternative site. We didn't know what they thought, and we weren't going to ask them.

The hard truth we all needed to face was that they would have nailed us had Freddie followed my instructions and brought the $20,000 needed to secure the load.

As soon as the police traffic died down, I left with the intention of getting out of the area for a few days. An empty run had left us with empty pockets and needing another $8,000 prop and left the law with an empty arrest report. Nevertheless, I was starting to question how much longer I'd be able to keep this up. How much closer to being caught could I have gotten than today? More than an empty plane, I was also feeling empty. I was tired, I missed my family, and my bursts of adrenaline-seeking danger were starting to collide with the heat rising around me.

11

I'm going crazy with worry. Tom said they told him Billy was alive, but is he injured in some way? Who is taking care of him if he is? Would he risk going to a hospital?

A cold rainy morning in late November 1989. I had a 6 a.m. take off to Belize planned but I was still standing in a cold shower at 5:30. I felt like someone had run over me with the proverbial Mack truck. The night before I'd been drinking, doing cocaine, and partying with friends until 2 a.m. Everyone had left to go home but I was too high to sleep, so I'd decided to keep things rolling. I laid out another line or three of coke and listened to music until about 5 a.m., when I started to get the spins. My thoughts were foggy. The cold water numbed the parts of my skin that weren't already numb. "Is this what an addict does?" I wondered. "Make excuses to keep going when the party is long over?"

When I'd gone on the run, I'd left the world of normalcy for an alternate universe where all things were dangerous and crazy. In one world I was a husband and father and was madly in love with the best person I knew. In my other world, Jim Lang's world, I was the life of the party, with more than enough friends as long as the money and drugs held out. I was the one everyone wanted to be around as long as I was providing the good time. I was without caution when a job had to be done and I would do it several hundred feet in the air. I was spending many sleepless hours riding a wave of highs that always ended in a wipeout, sometimes several days in the dark of a makeshift night.

I was worthless as a husband and dad, and my decision-making skills were more like the flip of an unmarked coin. Since leaving home in March 1988, I'd slowly fallen into the deep abyss of a culture and climate unknown to the man I used to be. I had no insight as to how to pull myself out. Whatever free time Jim had, he used it to do nothing more creative than move from one party to the next. The fun wasn't real and so many other things were no longer real.

I was getting dressed to leave, my head pounding, when a voice started questioning my sanity. "What is wrong with you? Who are you? You love Kay. You've married her twice because you couldn't live without her. Why are you jeopardizing everything just for something to do? You must be crazy. She left you once, don't you believe she could do it again? You want to lose her again?"

It was an hour's drive to Jay to pick up the 210. I was still super high. I got into the car we used for hauling and headed to the airstrip south of town. This was not going to be an enjoyable trip. The miserable weather would only complicate the fact that I would be flying high and without sleep. I could hear my voice, back in the days when I was a flight instructor, warning my students of the dangers.

"Guys," I'd say, "It's the dumbest thing you can do, flying inebriated or tired. You can't just pull an airplane over on the side of the road to rest or sober up. You're alone up there."

I thought about calling Freddie and rescheduling the trip. I was, after all, one of the bosses of what we jokingly called the Century Cartel, so I could of course cancel.

"Freddie would understand. Freddie himself is hung up on drugs. He should know how I feel." Sure he would, but if I cancelled the run, the rest of the crew would question whether I was maybe out of control. I'd be as good as admitting it.

"Hey, anyway. I know I don't really have a problem. Not really. Just focus on the job, Billy."

I drove under an I-10 overpass in north Pensacola, where a Waffle House sat just beyond on the left. I wasn't hungry, but I knew when I started coming down, I would be. It was going to take me 6 hours to reach Belize, and the munchies would hit long before that. I'd get two egg sandwiches to go.

The Waffle House was packed, and so was the parking lot. I whipped into the entrance of the lot and past the only available parking space I could see. I hit the brakes and threw the car into reverse and hit the accelerator and bam! — the car jolted forward. A fellow in a compact pickup truck had been following close behind and I'd run smack into him.

"Shit, Billy, this is all you need right now."

I put my car in park, left it running, and got out.

The other driver was already at full tilt, out of his truck, waving his hands at me.

"Man, you just ran into us! You know that? You're driving like an idiot!"

Like I didn't know that. I swung into my best diplomatic posture, one more mask I'd put on to get from point A to point B.

"I'm so sorry, sir. I'll certainly pay for your car repair."

But the guy was not in a negotiating mood.

"I'm not getting stiffed when this was your fault!"

"We're calling the police!" his wife yelled from the passenger seat.

"Yeah. Right!" He was sort of inspired. "I'll need to have a report done for my insurance!"

I was still calm.

"Now sir," I reasoned. "Is that really necessary? I'm sure I can..."

"Joan!" He cut me off. "Go into the Waffle House and use their phone and call the cops."

The police were the last people I wanted to see that particular morning. I had a good Tennessee driver's license in the name of Jim Lang, and I felt it would pass police scrutiny. The car on the other hand was registered in a different fictitious name with an Alabama address and Alabama tag. If the police wanted to question that and search the car, they would find in the trunk an empty fuel bladder suitable for use in an airplane, two two-meter radios, police scanners, an emergency life raft, and aviation maps of South and Central America *and* the Caribbean. Also $40,000 cash to pay for the load, a couple of handguns, and an assortment of cocaine and pot paraphernalia. It was basically a smuggling operation on wheels, not to mention I was still as high as a Georgia Pine.

The guy was acting as if I'd totaled his car. He was creating a scene and people were starting to take notice. I zoned out for a moment, scanning the parking lot and taking in cars and faces. It took me a minute to realize that the guy was now standing only a few feet from me and asking questions.

"What's your name?" he was asking. "Have you got insurance?"

There was the break I was looking for. I snapped back into the situation,

"Yes sir! Yes, I do. Just let me get my paperwork out of my car. Take me just a minute to grab it."

The driver's side door was still ajar. The car was still running. I walked at a moderate pace and sat down in my driver's seat. I threw the car into drive, slammed the door shut, hit the gas and started to spin out on the wet pavement. The now very angry man realized what I was doing and had decided he was going to stop me. He started into a full sprint toward the front of the parking lot, aiming to jump in front of my car. I certainly did not want to run over this crazy person, but I had to get out of there. It was a life-size game of chicken. I, in a full-size car, against somebody who thought he was Superman.

My tires stopped spinning, took traction and I sprang forward as he jumped out of the way. I had just enough room to get around the other stopped cars. I bounced out a gas station exit next to the Waffle House. I didn't look back.

I drove to the airstrip, thinking how tasty those egg sandwiches would have been, but not at the expense of getting involved with the police. I knew that the guy or someone watching had probably gotten my tag number but at this point, I knew the car was history anyway. I'd have to buy another one. More important, I was now twenty minutes late.

The rain stopped just as I took off. South of the Pensacola area I moved out over the Gulf. The weather was starting to clear and my experience at the Waffle House had undoubtedly helped me to come down off my high. Nothing like a shot of true adrenaline to bring you back to reality. Maybe this trip wasn't going to be as bad as I thought. Maybe the worst was over. Maybe I'd enjoy the ride and clear my head.

By the time I got to Belize, I was way more than two egg sandwiches down. I landed on the cane patch road and refueled. I then flew over to San Pedro airport to secure the plane for the night. I planned to get up early the next morning, load and return to the U.S.

I tied down the plane and started walking in the direction of Paradise Village Bar. Soon the thatch-roofed cabanas came into view. I sat down at one of the dining tables and ordered the house specialty — a Paradise Freeze. It was a delicious frozen fruit drink made with rum and garnished with fresh cut mangos, pineapple, and strawberries. It was just what I needed after a hard night of partying followed by a hard day of flying.

I was relaxed and on to my second Freeze. The face of the angry man at the Waffle House popped into my head. I had wanted to do the right thing by paying for the damage I caused to his truck. I understood the usual procedure: call the police, exchange insurance information etc. The risk of doing the right thing would have potentially cost me far more than his fender bender. I could only hope my mistake didn't cost the man too much.

After a few more fruit drinks, I ordered a big plate of snapper and then retired to the apartment we used in San Pedro for short overnights. I slept until just before daylight and woke feeling refreshed, or at least better than the morning before. I took a shower and headed to the airport.

Over the Belize mainland, I started looking for the road that I was to use as the landing strip. This would be the first time for this particular strip. The refueling crew said it was only a few miles from Orange Walk, just off the main highway, easy to spot. Just look for the crew's cars.

I spotted the cars, but I couldn't see a suitable landing area. I radioed the crew.

"Where am I supposed to put her down? I don't see anything that looks like a strip."

"We have a visual on you," they came back. "You're on the right road."

I could see a road, but it appeared to be open on one end, covered by a canopy of trees in the middle, and then open on the far end. It was a tunnel of sorts.

"Here we go," I said to no one but myself and the plane. I was about to touch down between hard dirt and trees. "Shouldn't be a problem," I said to no one again. "Yeah. Right."

I landed and the roll-out was as if I was flying through a majestic passageway. The loading area was entirely covered by trees and not visible from the air — a perfect set up. We loaded, and I took off through the tunnel and out the other end. It had been no problem at all and was actually pretty cool. Me and my 210 must have looked a little like a rocket shooting out of a cannon of green.

As soon as I got back to the U.S., I knew I needed to deal with the car. I contacted a used car dealer and picked out an 88 Grand Marquis Mercury. I registered it in my assumed name of Jim Lang. I kept the Waffle House vehicle at the Jay hangar until I got rid of it through a fellow I knew in Ohio.

By now, I was just happy to be back, and I was counting down the days until I saw Kay again. I wouldn't have to think about flying, smuggling, drugs, or the problems associated with this lifestyle in my alternate universe. Somehow, Kay would cleanse my soul. She'd help me find my way back to myself just as she had done so many times before.

October 26, 1989

I didn't have classes today so it worked out I could meet Billy last night in Alachua and spent the night. It had been a month since we were last together.

I drove from Jacksonville to Alachua. I'd had a long day and was looking for some Tylenol in his bag as he was taking a shower. Instead, I found cocaine and a variety of other drugs which I threw in the toilet and flushed it. He hasn't changed his lifestyle with drugs or anything else. If anything, he's gotten worse. This caused an argument but I don't care. I don't know this man anymore. It's like he's someone else when he's away. I know drugs are just the tip of the iceberg. We argued for at least an hour until we finally just gave out. What kind of life is this, for him or me? We love each other — this I know — but he's a follower and if it's what the crowd is doing, it's what he does. He doesn't know how to control his desires and he's never going to travel down the road less traveled.

November 1, 1989

Billy surprised me today and showed up at the University of North Florida. He was parked by my car in the parking lot. I don't know how he found it on a campus this large, but there he was, leaned against my car with his arms crossed. He just stood there and watched me walk all the way to the car. When I got there, he took my books and placed them on the trunk and took me in his arms. "I always wanted the prettiest girl on campus," he said, "and you're still it." How can I not love him? We're spending the next three nights together in Jacksonville. Luckily today was a day I had to attend school by myself so no need to worry about getting my UNF group home.

November 14, 1989

I dreamed about Billy and me last night. I don't dream much and having a nice dream made me feel so good this morning. I dreamed we were on our ski boat going down the Suwannee River like we had done so many times in the past, before he left. We launched the boat at Sandy Point boat ramp on the Santa Fe River and took the Suwannee River all the way to the gulf. Just the two of us. Billy was at ease driving the boat and I was soaking up the sun. We picnicked in the boat, and neither of us worried about smuggling, the law, or other women.

In the year after Barney put the wings back on the 210, Freddie and I ran five or six successful loads in the old girl. Out of rig as she was, she did the job and as we decided, "don't fix what's working." I took off for Belize not long after New Year's, 1990.

We were flying a single-engine airplane on trips that were mostly over jungle and water, as a simple matter of logistics we stayed with the 210. In my career as a smuggler, I'd flown everything from four-engine DC-7s to twin-engine turbines down to single-engine aircraft. All have their advantages and disadvantages. The most significant advantage of the DC-7, for example, was that it had a large payload, upwards of 20,000 pounds. The problems were that it attracted attention and was a nightmare to maintain. The bigger the airplane, the bigger the team needed to support it, and the bigger the team, the more coordination, exposure, and expense required. Twin-engine planes also offered a pretty big payload, but an engine failure in an aircraft overloaded with fuel and pot would result in the plane going down anyway since it could not maintain altitude with one engine.

In the '70s and early '80s, bigger was better. But as police forces perfected their enforcement of conspiracy laws and prosecutors sharpened their use of the grand jury, one loose tongue was all it took to get a crew of ten or twenty people arrested and thrown in jail, with the entire lot of them looking at outrageous sentences.

The single-engine Cessna 210 could haul a payload nearly as big as some of the light twins. It was almost as fast and didn't attract nearly the same amount of heat from the law. Maintenance on such an aircraft was minimal and could be managed by a small crew — on a smaller payroll. Most of all, there were fewer wagging tongues.

I spent a few nights in Belize partying with friends in San Pedro, out on Ambergris Caye. The island was a hot spot for scuba diving and game fishing, so a lone smuggler and his airplane had plenty of tourists and air traffic to blend in with. I skipped breakfast and brought along a honey bun and some orange juice to eat on the trip north. I had a little more than a quarter ounce of cocaine in my pocket in case I got sleepy, which was sure to happen. Staying alert, as I rationalized it, was the main reason for the coke.

January 4, 1990

We got home a couple of days ago and I miss Billy terribly. We spent Christmas at my mother's house again — another ten days of normalcy but not enough to catch up on time lost. He bought me a matching gold link necklace and bracelet for Christmas. He told me about several of his trips that had caused me so much worry. He never seems to think anything about his close calls. He calls them adventures. I call them the things that make up my nightmares.

I went to Jacksonville today to register for classes. One class; Research, is going to be tough. There's a 30-page paper due at the end that will probably give me a fit. Maybe Billy's mom will help me out. I'll need to put in at least 20 hours in a classroom this semester as well. The principal at CHS has agreed to let me do them in Mr. Mont's class. He has been an American history teacher there for many years. He's fantastic and I can't wait to sit in his class. I have three other classes but I don't think they will give me any trouble. I will have to drive two days with the group this semester and two days by myself because it's too hard trying to coordinate our schedules.

I took off from a Belize cane patch airstrip about 6:00 a.m. the next morning, Sunday. My cargo was approximately 900 pounds of high-grade marijuana heading for our homemade runway carved out of the forest along the Florida/Alabama line. I flew over the jungles of Yucatan and by 9:00 a.m. was at 10,000 feet over the Gulf of Mexico, 40 miles north of the peninsula. Everything was running better than routine The weather was perfect, with 15 or so miles of visibility, a little haze and scattered cloud below. Up ahead looked good as far as the eye could see. My fuel transfer pumps were working correctly.

What a wonderful morning it was turning out to be. I felt fortunate to be where I was and doing what I was doing. I couldn't imagine doing anything else. I loved flying and I enjoyed smuggling. To be sure, the lifestyle had led to some imperfect results but what was my alternative? Running a roadside paving crew, piecing together flight lessons to make ends meet? Too mundane, too predictable, literally too grounded. One day would be no different than the one before but there would always be the pathetic hope that it would somehow be. With smuggling, I knew without a doubt that every day would be different. The unexpected was probable — not just a hope or a wish but almost predictable. I yearned for it and this job, flaws and all, I had become who I was because I had designed it that way with every choice I'd made, starting with the first time I piloted an airplane. Not that who and what I'd become was strategic or planned. But here I was — in the sky.

I had recently turned 40. I'd started piloting marijuana-laden airplanes into the States in 1978, so I'd never understood how marijuana could be illegal. I had no moral hang-ups with my profession; rather, I believed that I was performing a service for people who enjoyed pot — an herb far more organic and healing than the very legal and toxic tobacco sold and taxed freely in open markets across the country. If it wasn't a needed service, why was the demand for it so, well ... high?

My mind kept wandering back to how good a little eye-opener would go with this beautiful morning. I realized it had been quite a while since I'd eaten anything and if I started on the cocaine now, I never would eat the honey bun. I decided to eat my breakfast treat first and then have a little bump of coke for dessert. Just like enjoying a morning cup of coffee with a tasty muffin.

I bent forward to reach inside the sack containing the honey bun. I was fumbling through the contents of the bag when I caught a little waft of something burning. I checked the alternator gauge to see if it was indicating a short-circuit in the wiring, but it was showing normal. Must've spilled a little oil on the engine. In the early darkness I'd added a quart of oil and probably didn't notice spilling some. I kept searching for my honey bun. There it is. I pulled the top off the orange juice and took a first sip. A mouthful of the sweet doughnutty breakfast cake would be next. At about mid-swallow, the engine cut out — pop, pop, pow, pow ... POP! — then sputtered to a normal run again.

A rush of adrenaline hit my chest, then my stomach. I spilled most of my orange juice into my lap as I turned the airplane south, back toward land. I figured I was about 40 miles out over the Gulf. Oh God, I thought. Look at the oil pressure gauge. I should've checked it when I first detected the odor but I was too distracted by thoughts of the honeybun and cocaine. A rookie mistake. The gauge rested on zero and I knew the engine could not last much longer. My first trip to Colombia in '78 flashed through my mind. A violent thunderstorm, a rough running engine. All I could think was, "What if I go down out here? Kay and my children will never know what happened to me."

Now heavy guilt descended. I thought of the great pain it would cause them, finding out some random, normal, unexpected day that I was gone. And the even greater pain: not knowing, how, where, and what had happened. If I went down over water or the jungles of Central America, my body and aircraft would never be found.

Kay was always nervous before I left to run a load. She never knew any of the details or when I'd return. I always believed the less Kay knew, the better. If authorities ever questioned her, I wanted her to be able to tell them she knew nothing and not have to force a lie. I never really thought much about how it might affect *her* while I was gone. I knew I was fine so why should she worry? Now that I was on the run, she never knew where I was — ever. She never knew if I was in some bar just enjoying life or dodging lightning strikes over a vast expanse of ocean. The life I'd chosen caused her more sleepless nights than any person should have to endure. Suddenly, through a stupid oversight, her nightmare and mine were becoming a reality.

It had been years since I'd been to church.

"God, it's me, and you know I don't bother you with trivial things. You know I don't make you a bunch of promises I'm not going to keep, promises like, 'Please help me now and I'll quit smuggling.' But if you could see to my making it back to land — any land will do — I'd be so grateful. I'm not asking for a giant miracle, like restoring the oil pressure, but if you could just, you know, help me get to *dry land*, I'll appreciate it and my family will appreciate it. Amen."

The engine cut out again: pop, pop, bam, bam. Smoke filled the cockpit. It seemed I was on fire and an airplane at 10,000 feet is the last place you want to be if a fire is burning some part of it. I lowered the nose for a final splashdown in the Gulf.

Abruptly, the engine was running routinely again and the smoke cleared. I pulled back on the yoke at around 9,000 feet. I was going to need every bit of altitude for gliding when the engine did pack it in for good. Minutes later it cut out again, smoke billowed up, and then it ran smoothly. Minutes later it happened again. An eternity in ten minutes.

I saw land. "I'm going to get close enough to swim," I thought. "Thank you, God!" I shouted out because it was clear He was in full control.

A huge bang, a grand finale, and a blast of smoke filled the cockpit. I couldn't breathe. I kicked the rudder sideways, pushed open the windows and directed some air in with one hand. I was now a glider trying to stretch my drift to a Mexican beach. It was my first-ever total engine failure in a single-engine aircraft. The silence was deafening, spooky.

At 3,000 feet, what appeared to be a lighthouse was quite a distance down the beach to the west. Straight ahead were tall coconut trees and some small thatch-roof huts at the edge of the sand. Could I make it that far? I kept the landing gear retracted to extend my glide.

At 1,500 feet, I wondered if I might actually have a little altitude to spare. Maybe I could make a flyover and gain a visual assessment of the condition of the sand. In aviation terminology, maybe I could do an "abbreviated 360-degree overhead approach."

I glided over the beach and decided to keep the landing gear up. The sand looked soft. If I extended the gear, the plane might nose over onto its back. I'd never belly-landed an airplane before. I'd rely on instinct and luck.

In my flight instructor days, we taught students to over-fly unfamiliar landing areas in order to get an idea of surface conditions. I crossed over the beach and began my turn, then realized I'd made a serious mistake. I was well over maximum gross weight, heavy with fuel and marijuana and without any power. My altitude bled away during the low-level turn. The coconut treetops were just below me. I braced for an embarrassing and deadly head-on collision with one of them but in the few final seconds I threaded the plane between them. I cracked the door open and lined up on the beach heading west, holding off to get the slowest possible touch down speed. I clutched the yoke. How far would this baby slide on sand grains? I felt her belly touch ground, make a short skip and then, to my surprise, barely slide at all. She went straight up on her nose and balanced there for a moment. The right wing bent down and caught the soft, powdery sand. The rest of her fell flat with a clank.

I looked around the cockpit. I felt my chest, wiped my brow with my forearm, cold and wet to the touch. I had some superficial abrasions on my right hand from being thrown into the instrument panel on the sudden stop. But — a few moments went by while it sank in — I was alive. The plane wasn't in flames. Other than the waves' slow caress of the shore, there was no other sound.

I got out and perched myself on the wing to see if anyone was coming out to the beach. I thought maybe the huts I flew over were signs of local inhabitants. There was no one. I was alone. The huts were abandoned. The area was deserted.

My first impulse was to burn the airplane, but then I thought better of it. If no one witnessed the crash, then no one knew I was here. Smoke from a fire could attract attention and I didn't want to alert authorities to my whereabouts.

I wondered if I should unload the pot and hide it in the bush bordering the beach. I discarded this idea as well. Anyone who found the airplane would follow my tracks in the sand. It would also take a lot of energy, which would make me thirsty. I had only a single one-gallon plastic container full of water to last me until I could find another source. As things stood at that moment, water was a precious commodity.

I needed to get as far away from this loaded plane as possible. No one I knew would be looking for me even when I was overdue. Kay, had she any idea I was late or missing, would send someone to search for me. Unfortunately, her ideas about what I may be up to probably did not include my current situation. It was Sunday. She'd be at church and then home to prepare for her classes on Monday. She wouldn't even know I was missing unless a crewmember took it upon himself to let her know I hadn't shown up at the meeting site. I hoped they wouldn't tell her anyway.

Which way to go? The choice was a narrow one. I could go up or down the beach, that is, east or west. North was the Gulf of Mexico; south was bush that quickly turned into jungle so thick, Tarzan would find it rough going.

This would be an important decision. If I started walking the wrong way with only one gallon of water and a honey bun, I might never see civilization again. I remembered the lighthouse I'd seen to the west while I was gliding in. There would have to be power lines to it or at least a generator to keep the light burning. There should also be a road that the lighthouse keeper used for access. I could follow that road or power line to the nearest town. Once I reached civilization, I would somehow work my way to Cancun and blend in with the tourists.

I gathered up the water and my overnight bag. I broke open a bale of the pot and pulled out a couple of ounces and my cocaine and stuffed them into the pocket.

I told myself my luck wasn't all that bad after all. It could have been a lot worse. If the engine had run for another few minutes, I would have been too far out in the Gulf to make it back to the beach. If it had quit too early, I would have gone down in the jungles of the Yucatan. I'd often thought that if anything could be worse than going down at sea, it would be going down in the jungle. The engine quitting in the small window necessary for me to reach the beach could be considered an amazing blessing. From that perspective, my present dilemma was a relatively small one.

I walked west with the gallon jug of water in one hand and my bag over my opposite shoulder. I walked until I got thirsty. I put down my bag and got a drink of water. I did a bump of coke, quickly rolled a joint, took a few tokes, and walked on. The beach was beautiful white sand with blue-green waves rolling in. As I walked, I looked for any signs of other people. There were no footprints other than mine. I walked for two hours with the same routine of water, smoke, and coke occasionally thinking of how romantic it would be to stroll with Kay on this beautiful, lonely beach. She was an ocean away and somehow still with me. I thanked God for that small miracle too.

As I was approaching the lighthouse, I could see that it was maybe sixty-five feet high but old and probably abandoned for many years. There were no access roads, no power lines to follow, and still no footprints or any other signs of human presence. Perhaps I was walking in the wrong direction. I decided to climb the lighthouse to gain a better vantage point. The door was open a bit and it was evident that it was not structurally sound. The spiral stairs were deteriorating and I questioned if it would hold up under my weight. The concrete base to the steps had started crumbling away, leaving a couple of strands of re-bar that were in advanced stages of rusting away. I knew that if the steps gave way with me, I could easily break a leg or cause some other injury that would be considered minor back home but would probably prove fatal under these circumstances.

Still, this was my best hope of finding my way out. I started slowly, slowly up the steps. Pressing lightly on the middle of each stair to test the give, I would then cautiously put weight on the side closest to the frame where support would be the strongest. The climb took about ten minutes. From that considerable height I looked to the south out over the trees. As far as the eye could see, there was nothing but treetops. I looked up and down the beach, and all I could see was sand and waves forever in both directions. I looked again west, the direction I'd been walking, and I thought I could make out some sort of structure in the distance — something like a radio tower barely visible on a hazy horizon. That would be my new goal.

I very carefully and slowly descended the lighthouse steps. At the bottom I took another drink of water and a little taste of coke. As much as I liked smoking pot, I decided against it for now until I could get more water. It dried out my mouth too much, and I was trying to conserve as much as possible.

I walked steadily for three more hours with the same routine: stop, take a drink of water, take a charge of coke, change hands with the bag and water jug. Still no sign of human life. Where was I? No footprints. Not even a discarded pack of cigarettes or butt. No liter of any kind. Just a perfect, pristine beach.

I peered ahead to what looked like a flooded portion of the beach. As I got closer, I could see that there was a cut out of the beach forming a waterway flowing well into the jungle. The water ran inland as far as I could see. At first glance, it didn't look deep, and it seemed as if it was only between 150 to 200 yards across. I felt I could ford it easily. After surveying the situation, I waded in at what looked like the best spot to cross.

My bag above my head to keep it from getting wet I waded in. When I reached knee deep, I began to bog down: the bottom was too soft; I waded back to the eastern shore again. I tried two or three more times at what I thought were more promising spots with no better luck. I was wasting time and energy, so I decided to find the deepest spot and swim for it.

I waded out into a deep portion of the little river and found that I could cross without having to swim. The bottom was firm all the way across, and the water at the deepest point only reached my chest. I made it to the other side without getting anything other than my person wet. I considered it a successful crossing. After reaching the west side of the cut, I changed into a dry pair of shorts and t-shirt and continued westward again.

Another hour of walking and then, out of nowhere, I saw some movement at a distance down the beach. As I got closer, I could make out two figures walking with a dog running alongside. I fled to the bush, joining the beach. I was nervous about them seeing me. For six hours I had been alone on this beach, so I wasn't sure how to proceed. There would be no way they could know about the plane this far away. As I spotted them, they surely spotted me, and their dog would definitely give me away. I thought it best not to act suspicious. So, I pretended my appearance on this beach was as normal as theirs.

As we drew close, I waved,

"Habla usted Ingles?"

"No, senor, no hablo Ingles."

We smiled at each other. They seemed friendly enough. Seeing these two people and their dog was, at the very least, the first real indication that I was walking in the right direction. There must be a village within walking distance.

"Gracias," I said and carried on. An hour later I came to a fishing village. Looked like it might have been home to maybe a few hundred people. Lining the beach were twenty or thirty fiberglass boats maybe 18 feet long, and all with 45hp outboard Yamaha motors. The town was a bunch of small, thatched-roofed houses, a few concrete buildings, narrow dirt streets, and a working lighthouse. I calculated that I could most likely walk through the village in less than five minutes, and that was what I intended to do.

a smuggler and his wife

I smiled big at everyone I passed, asking, "Habla usted Ingles?" Approaching the center of town, I spotted a small open-air cantina. I wanted to stop for a drink but then decided to continue. In a short distance, I came to a small boat basin with a pier and several more of the same fiberglass motorboats.

I'd given up on finding anyone who could speak English when a man walked off the pier and pointed, motioning at me.

"You speak English?" I was hopeful.

"Si, senior."

Finally, someone I could communicate with. He spoke broken English, but it was better than no English.

"I'm Jim." I decided my alias was the way to go since that's who my ID said I was.

"How you like nuestra isla, Jim?"

I was surprised to find out it *was* an island.

"It is muy hermoso," I assured him.

It turned out to be a big island named Holbox. When I crashed, I'd assumed I'd made it back to the Mexican mainland because on my low approach, I couldn't tell them apart.

"I am Carlos."

He was small in stature but anyone speaking English was a giant in my book. We communicated well enough for him to convey helpful information. The ferry, for instance, had just left for the mainland and would not be back until the next morning.

"Hmmm." I needed somewhere to stay the night and get a shower. "Moteles por la noche?"

He pointed to one of the small concrete buildings just a short distance from the basin. We walked over to it and using Carlos as an interpreter, I rented a room for one night. The price was about two dollars. The small motel was mainly for visiting fishermen.

I checked into the room and then asked Carlos if he wanted a drink at the cantina. He smiled with great enthusiasm and we were off to the small open-air bar in the middle of town. We sat down at a table in the back and ordered a couple of beers. I hadn't done any cocaine since arriving in town, and my appetite was coming back.

"Carlos, are there any resturantes in town?"

"Si, senor,"

He pointed down the street and I invited him to eat dinner with me after we finished our drinks. We enjoyed a supper of tacos and then returned to the cantina for more drinks. Carlos turned out to be good company — easy-going with an optimistic outlook and several entertaining fisherman stories. He obviously liked practicing his English and asking about words he didn't know.

We ordered around and then Carlos excused himself for a moment and headed to a table occupied by three men. From my bar seat I could tell they were old friends. Their conversation was animated and affectionate with laughter and pats on the back. Carlos waved me over and the men insisted we join them. He introduced his friends and explained each one with a sort of epithet. The first man was the "muy importante" man on the island — the lighthouse keeper. None of the others spoke English, so Carlos did the interpreting, first in Spanish and then to me in English.

The lighthouse keeper asked how long I would be staying on the island. I smiled and said, "dos o tres dias." Once he figured out I could speak some Spanish he pressed for me to come over to his house the next day and teach his son English.

"Si senor," I responded jovially. "Sure, sure."

After all, I was just a tourist enjoying the sites and engaging with the locals at any chance offered. This seemed to make him happy.

Carlos introduced the next man.

"Es un hombre muy importante en la isla. Policia."

They were all in street clothes, so I had to contain my astonishment and an impulse to run, I kept it together.

"Respecto," I said and shook hands with him, exchanging big smiles.

The last man was a fisherman like Carlos.

"A man of the sea like me," Carlos proclaimed and patted the guy on the back.

We drank beer after beer, smiled a lot, and called one another amigos. We were all enjoying ourselves and I retreated to the restroom a few times to take a leak and do a small hit of cocaine. It was due to my high that the beer wasn't affecting me as much as it was affecting my new Mexican amigos. This was fine by me. I needed to keep my wits about me.

The sun was setting, and as dusk turned to dark a swarm of flying, biting insects attacked us. Carlos and his friends were ready. They quickly piled something like moss by our table and set it on fire. The fire caught. They piled more moss on the flame until it was producing more smoke than fire. We stood around the smoke, basking in its warmth, drinking our beers and within ten minutes the attack was over. The lighthouse keeper extinguished the fire as quickly as it was lit and then we all returned to our table. I was marveling at what I'd just witnessed, but everyone was acting as though nothing had happened. I thanked them for not allowing me to be eaten alive by a bug swarm and they laughed and nodded their heads at me.

The night wore on and on and the Mexicans were sloshed. I, however, was still in pretty good shape. Finally, they called it a night. As the party broke up and everyone swayed their drunken way, I leaned over to Carlos,

"I need to talk to you before you leave, amigo."

As I assessed it, my situation was serious. I was the only gringo on a Mexican island. An airplane loaded with marijuana was abandoned seven hours walking distance down the beach. Linking me to the plane wouldn't take rocket science. I had no

Mexican visa, was a federal fugitive and had been on the run for two and a half years.

I knew quite a bit about travel in Mexico, and I knew that if I got to a highway without a visa, my chances of making it any distance would not be good. There were checkpoints on all Mexican roads, and I would have to bribe my way through each of them. I had about five thousand dollars cash, which would go a good way toward bribes, but when Mexican authorities finally discovered the airplane, they would then be looking for the pilot. They'd connect the dots, and five thousand dollars would no longer be enough.

It looked like my best mode of travel to Cancun from the Island of Holbox would be in one of the fishing boats and Carlos was the only person I'd found who could speak English. After dinner and a night of drinking, I felt as if we truly were amigos. In fact, I genuinely liked the guy and I was hoping his eagerness to converse matched his eagerness to help me out of my jam.

"Carlos, we are amigos, right?"

He smiled and nodded a drunken gaze across his face.

"Carlos, I'm an airplane pilot. Today, I was flying to America in my airplane." I extended my arms like wings. "But …" I made a noise like an engine cutting out and mimicked a crash-landing. His eyes widened and he seemed to be trying to focus. "Carlos, I need to get to Cancun because when they find the airplane, I could be in mucho trouble."

He shook his head and chuckled a little.

"You are a bandito, amigo?"

I figured it best not to lie to my new friend.

"Yes. I'm a bandito, but I'm a good bandito."

"You have marijuana I like to smoke?"

Now I was chuckling. We were friends for sure.

"Yes, I do." I motioned to the motel, and we made our way.

In the room I rolled a joint and stepped outside under a brilliant canopy of stars. We toked and passed the blunt.

"Carlos, can you take me to Cancun in your fishing boat?"

He pressed his mouth into a hard line as if he was considering something.

"I will pay you a good price for the trip," I said, making the obvious more obvious.

"Amigo." He was rubbing his chin. "I am only first mate. Captain has to decide. Cancun, she far off and the boat motors, they are very tired."

I didn't want to push. He had not said no yet or taken off in a sprint toward the local law. I wanted him to think about the money he would make for this boat trip. There was no doubt that he was my best chance of getting off the island safely and undetected, so I was prepared to make it worth his while. I needed him to consider and accept my offer once the beer and drug haze faded.

I considered how desperate I really was. I didn't want to wind up in a Mexican jail for any amount of time. In 1979, I'd been busted with a load of pot at Boscobel airport in Jamaica and done thirty days in a couple of different Jamaican jails. The conditions were terrible to say the least and I didn't want firsthand experience of the Mexican versions.

"I think your marijuana is good," said Carlos.

I offered him more. We were bonding and I wanted to strengthen this new friendship.

"I have something else that you might like, Carlos."

I pulled out my bag of coke.

"Coca, I have never tasted," he said.

He was grinning wide with approval. I motioned for him to come back into the room.

On the small bedside table, I spread out four medium size lines and chopped them up with the blade on my pocketknife. I rolled up a bill and snorted two of them. Then I passed the bill to Carlos so he could follow suit. We both lay back in our chairs and talked about the fishing boats and his job as first mate. He was enjoying his first experience with coca. He pointed to the bag of coke. He was ready for some more, so I chopped us up two more lines apiece, a little larger than the first ones. We snorted them up and he continued his narrative. Mid-sentence Carlos snapped his mouth shut. He couldn't speak. I knew what was wrong. A little too much cocaine had locked up his voice. After a moment he shook himself out of it and stood to go.

"See you manana. Amigo, after I speak to my captain."

The next morning came quickly; things did not sound promising.

"Captain, he say the motors, they too tired to go to Cancun. The policia, they want to know why our boats are there."

I considered. His captain's biggest concern was the possibility of having to explain his actions to authorities.

"Tell the captain he can just drop me off in walking distance of Cancun. Or, even better, Carlos, he can drop me off at the pier in Isla Mujeres."

I could take the ferry from there and blend easily with other tourists.

"Si, si, amigo. I go speak to my captain again."

I waited for Carlos to return but after about an hour, I got antsy. I grabbed my belongings and headed toward the pier hoping to meet him along the way. The town was now alive, boats being loaded with supplies and engines roaring to life in preparation for fishing trips. I neared the pier just in time to see Carlos, the policeman, and another man get into two boats at the basin and speed off. Any person with half a brain could see what was happening.

A load of pot parked some ways down the beach represented a small fortune in Mexico. Clearly these men were putting first things first and were going after the marijuana before anyone else stumbled across it. They were traveling in boats, faster than footing it, but it would still take a couple of hours to locate the airplane. The last place I wanted to be when they returned was in this small town where I could be easily spotted and handed over to the law. What I needed to do was disappear and wait things out.

I walked uptown and bought a gallon of water and some food. I tracked out to the beach, looked up and down, trying to make up my mind which way to head. Anyone looking for me would assume I put distance between myself and the plane, so I decided to head towards it instead.

I walked at a normal pace for an hour until I came to an area of undergrowth where the forest extended out almost to the water's edge. This was where I would make camp and watch for developments up and down the beach. I crawled on my hands and knees burrowing my way toward the middle of the bushes. In the middle, I flattened out a comfortable spot to lie down. I broke enough branches off overhead so I could stick my head out and turn like a periscope.

I spent most of the day in and around my makeshift house. I smoked pot, did cocaine and contemplated what my next move was going to be. I watched the fishing boats speed to and from along the coast and considered how lucky I was to have flown the load on Sunday. Sunday was a day of rest in this part of the world. Judging from the boat traffic I was witnessing that morning. By night fall, shortly after dark, I was invaded by a large air wing of the flying, biting insects. I copied the fishermen, gathering dry seaweed and dry leaves in a pile, put a match to it and stood in the smoke. As if on cue, the invasion disappeared as fast as it had come.

The night was beautiful with a round moon, stars and a few scattered clouds to decorate the horizon. A gentle breeze blew, mixed with the sound of the surf rolling onto the shore. I stared up at the vast unfettered space above me and thought of Kay. I thought about what she'd say to me if she could see me here camping out in this jungle brush.

"Just look what you've gotten yourself into now, Billy."

Not long after night set in, I heard two boat motors moving closer. They slowed just beyond the beach and shone lights along the shoreline as if they were looking for something or someone. Were they cops looking for me? Was it Carlos maybe trying to find me? Should I jump out of the bush house, wave my arms, get their attention? Or would I be trading my nice bush house for a Mexican jail cell?

The part of me that said keep your periscope down and wait for them to leave, won. I needed to try and sleep. I was exhausted and sore and aching from all the walking the day before. I felt secure in my nest and drifted off to the soft sound of the sea.

Just before daybreak the next morning, I was awakened by a light rain shower that refreshed me just enough to jump-start my energy, but not enough to soak me. I checked my water supply. I'd need to make a trip to town for more. If I could get there early enough, I could slip in and out before anyone noticed. I still felt that my best chance off the island was Carlos and he would be back by now.

I set off at a brisk walk and I reached the village at first light. It was already abustle with its daily routine. Fishermen were going back and forth from dock to town, outfitting their boats. I popped into the small market and bought some water and food. Everything seemed cool. No one was paying me any attention. Everyone was preoccupied with their chores.

I decided to take a longer route back to my hiding spot and pass by the village lighthouse. Maybe I'd see Carlos. I sat down on the base of the lighthouse and munched my breakfast sandwich. Twenty minutes later, as the sun warmed the little street, along came Carlos. He walked straight to a boat with an armload of supplies. I hurried over to him.

"Carlos, I need to go to Isla Mujeres."

There was an urgency in my voice that surprised even me. He looked at me apologetically. I swallowed and cleared my throat.

"Lo siento amigo, I just really need your help."

He mumbled something unintelligible and I realized that he was part of a crew — five men and two boats. The captain was one of these: a short, slightly built man like Carlos. He did not appear to be the man in charge as he was as busy stocking the boat as the other men. Carlos relayed my message but the captain seemed determined not to go. I could see he was a man focused on his business — fishing. His dark black hair and sun-tanned face was glistening with sweat under the warmth of the sun. He was a "captain" of few words and Carlos was going to need help convincing this stubborn man. I reached into my pocket and pulled out five folded one-hundred-dollar bills. I flattened them out and held them up to the men.

"Tell them that they will all get one hundred dollars if they take me to Isla Mujeres."

Carlos smiled and explained to the crew why I was waving cash in the air. Now I had allies. They were all talking at once, urging the captain to comply. Obviously one shake of the man's head and I would be dead in the water. To my overwhelming relief, he reluctantly — and eyeing me suspiciously — finally agreed.

I passed out the bills hoping it would speed things along, but it had the opposite effect. All five men turned and broke into a jog back toward the village. I grabbed Carlos's arm to stop him, but he turned and smiled.

"They want to go put their money at home," he said.

I shook my head. "Please tell them to hurry!"

I felt the urgency in my throat and I suppose he heard it.

They were back in only a few minutes. We boarded the little fishing boats.

Each of the fishermen paused and did the Catholic sign of the cross as they moved into the small boats. I understood the sign and was thanking the Lord for my own reasons. We shoved off and out to sea and followed the coast. The fishing boats were packed with nets, gasoline containers, supplies and diving masks with long hoses running to a gasoline-powered air compressor. Carlos, his captain, and I were in one boat. The three others were in the second boat.

As we neared the point, I remembered my stuff in the bush house.

"I need to stop and get my bag from the beach!" I yelled over the roar of the motor.

They agreed to stop and when we arrived at the bush house, I jumped out, picked up my bag, laid it in the boat and hoisted myself back in.

"We stop at the ranch to eat before we go to Mujeres," Carlos said.

We traveled east about five hundred yards offshore and parallel to the coast. The weather was good, and the heavily loaded boats were taking the small waves with no problem. I felt a small surge of happiness.

"Why do you need all of this gear just to go fishing?" I yelled.

"We stay at ranch two weeks fishing then go back to Holbox."

I was thunderstruck by my good fortune. The little wakeup call of rain that morning had saved me. So many things were falling into place. I was feeling more and more like my timing was closer to a series of designed miracles.

The captain maneuvered the boat in and out of the waves and Carlos described the ranch operation, which consisted of fishing for two weeks, living at the ranch, and selling their catch to a big Japanese processing boat anchored offshore.

"Carlos? Carlos, policia at the ranch?"

"No, amigo. Nobody there until we there."

"But I saw you and the police leave to get the pot yesterday, right?"

"No amigo." Carlos shook his head. "We went to get no pot."

I didn't push the issue. It made no sense to put Carlos in a defensive posture of any kind. The ownership of the pot didn't matter anymore. It was history. What mattered was getting as far away from the scene of my crash as I could and then obtaining a Mexican visa.

An hour and a half of bouncing along the sunlit ocean and my airplane came into sight. She was still sitting motionless on the beach like a whale who had given up the urge to swim. I motioned to get Carlos's attention and pointed toward the shore.

"Airplane very, very tired," I said.

Carlos nodded in agreement.

"Carlos, why are the huts around the airplane deserted?"

"Es old coconut tree plantacion. The trees they die and plantacion es abandon."

One stop for refueling and several hours later we were docking our boat along a beach as pristine as the one I crash-landed on. The jungle was nearby. I looked at Carlos. He nodded.

"This is ranch, amigo."

The crew pressed through the thick, soft powder covering the short coastline and over to a row of huts. Along the way the men chased off families of iguanas that had taken up residence in the absence of the fishermen. The huts were constructed of sticks lashed together by dried vines. The only new part of each was a tarpaper roof. The main hut was L-shaped, about twelve feet long and eight feet wide, with the long part acting as the bedroom. The bottom part of the L, six by six, was the kitchen with many windows. Two openings served as doorways located at the back of the kitchen and the front of the main room. There was no electricity, no running water, or toilet and the floor was sand. The kitchen was an identifiable space because in the center was a fire pit for cooking. The windows were for ventilation.

It was a shelter in the most basic form. I observed Carlos stringing one of the hammocks up in the bedroom area. He pointed to the bed and then to me. I must have looked as tired as I felt. My legs and feet were as sore as I could ever remember them being. My cocaine was gone, and any numbing effect it had produced was also long gone. My body ached and I was very aware of this dull, full-body pain that reached through every muscle. I stretched out in the hammock and it felt wonderful.

After they unloaded all the supplies, Carlos came over to the hammock.

"They go to catch fish; I get fuego ready to cook tortillas."

I pulled myself out of the hammock and over to where Carlos was preparing the fire.

"I need agua from well," he said. He headed out of our hut toward the green forest just beyond the doorway.

"Hold up, Carlos. I want to go with you."

I was tired but I knew I would probably never see an operation like this again.

He picked up a plastic container that looked like it would hold about two and a half gallons of water and we walked down a narrow path into the jungle for about one-quarter mile. The trail widened out just a little, and there was the well. It was only maybe thirty-six inches in diameter and the water line was probably fifteen feet down. There was nothing to keep a person or animal from falling in. It was just a hole dug in the center of the trail with a rope tied to the handle of a pail. Carlos took the bucket and lowered it into the well. Just before the container reached the waterline, Carlos skillfully flipped his wrist, causing a wave to run down the rope tipping the pail over on its side so it would fill up with water. He had clearly honed his skills at this little trick.

He pulled out around fifteen buckets full of water before he felt it was clear enough to use. We filled our container and returned to the little ranch house. Carlos mixed the water with cornmeal and started making corn tortillas on a small table in the kitchen. He used dried coconut husks on the floor of the kitchen to build a fire. The crew returned from catching fish not long afterward.

"These people don't play around," I thought. "When they go fishing, they bring home fish!"

I napped in the hammock while the fishermen prepared lunch: delicious fish soup and corn tortillas, made with maybe a little tainted water. It was a new experience for me, looking at my soup and it looking back at me. Personally, I would have cut the heads off the fish, but the whole day had felt like a National Geographic TV show.

Carlos approached me.

"The captain, he ask you want go ahora to Isla Mujeres or manana?"

A night's rest at the ranch in the little hammock was so very tempting. My weariness and the sense of security from the Mexican Federales this ranch provided made it difficult to choose another boat ride. But the same voice that had warned me to stay in the bush house the night before was now reminding me that Isla Mujeres was where I needed to be. "Don't be stupid," it was saying. "Don't stay longer than you need." I was two days overdue at the landing site. I knew that back in the States, the crew would have assumed I'd crashed and died. I didn't want them calling my family and upsetting them. Getting word to one of the guys back home was of great importance.

"I'd love to spend time at the ranch, but I need to get to Isla Mujeres. Let's go ahora."

We loaded some extra gas containers in one of the skiffs. Carlos, the captain, and I shoved off.

Isla Mujeres is a small sport fishing and resort island off the northeast corner of the Yucatan Peninsula not far from Cancun, basically a rock formation sticking out of the water in the Yucatan channel. As we headed east, the sky started to grow dark and it began to drizzle. We were still parallel to the coast and the waves were beginning to get bigger as the wind began to kick up. Our ride was rougher, but the little boat seemed able to handle the weather.

We ran in and out of light rain for what seemed like three hours, then made a quick stop to gas up. I looked ahead. The sky was getting darker and the waves were significant. After about another hour, the light rain had turned into a full-fledged storm. On the dark horizon I could make out Isla Mujeres.

I didn't know much about seamanship but I could tell it was going to be a rough ride. In order to get to the island, we had to leave the protection of the coastline and make a run across open water for maybe four miles. I could see plenty of giant whitecaps breaking just ahead. The swells were getting outrageously big and the boat began to take a severe beating. In a matter of minutes heavy rain and big waves gave way to violence. We were down in a hole surrounded by a wall of water and a few moments later we were on top of a giant swell, looking down into a valley of churning surf. In twenty-five years of flying, I'd never experienced anything as remotely terrifying. The ocean, when it meets a darkened sky, is a force like no other. Compared to the magnitude of the sea, we were nothing more than a leaf in a waterfall.

That morning, when the crew boarded their skiff, each one had made the Catholic sign of the cross. Now I understood why. As I boarded that morning, I noticed that we had no life vests or any other safety equipment in our heavily loaded fishing skiffs. It hadn't seemed an issue then.

I remembered boot camp at Parris Island back in 1970. We were taught what they called "drown proofing." I'd never thought I'd need it. Now I gripped the gunwale tightly and prepared myself for the inevitable flip. I looked at the captain. The man was reading the waves and maneuvering his boat this way and that way as a skier slaloms down hills and powdery slopes.

a smuggler and his wife

Our lives depended on his skills and a tired 45 horsepower outboard motor. One misread of a wave or inaccurate positioning of the boat within a swell and over we would go. If the motor quit, there'd be no keeping control: we'd capsize and drown.

With all the necessary maneuvering, we were making agonizingly slow progress. Off the north shore of the island, I saw a jutting line of rocks. The mass of each giant wave pounded so hard against these rock walls that spray shot straight up and disappeared into the dark sky. It was like a reverse Niagara Falls. I'd been to Niagara Falls, and as impressive a sight as it was, this was overwhelming.

And then, suddenly, we were on the sheltered side of the island and motoring towards the pier. I was awestruck and full of gratitude.

"Carlos! Captain!" I shouted. "I'll get everyone rooms for the night. Stay here and rest!"

I couldn't stand the thought of them going back out into that weather, into Calypso's spinning sea.

"No senor." Carlos shook his head. "We must go to catch fish."

He was so matter of fact. I felt a surge of desperation.

"Please! Don't go back until the weather clears and it isn't so rough."

He smiled at me and patted my shoulder as if to convey something I couldn't understand. We pulled up to the pier and I shook hands with the captain, then shook hands with Carlos and patted him on the back in a sort of hug. I really did feel a kinship with him and wanted to show this somehow. I gave him a small wooden and steel knife I kept in my survival kit. It was somewhat ornate and somewhat antique but most importantly, it could be handy. He nodded and smiled at me again.

"Good luck, amigo," he said.

I climbed out of the boat and onto the pier.

"Yes, amigo. You too."

I waved as they pushed off from the dock. The captain steered his tiny ship back toward the shifting horizon. I watched as they slowly faded from sight into white caps and swells, then turned to chart my own course toward the little city waiting behind me.

I found the closest restaurant, downed several gin and tonics and waited for the rain to slacken. The warm liquor burned my throat and the sheer thrill of life was still coursing through me after surviving such a commute. The effect was adrenaline, of course, but there was more, more than a hit of coke or puff of good herb. Being tossed in a tumultuous ocean and then precisely delivered to safety had left a sense of insignificance I'd never felt, but at the same time made me feel how significant it all was — how significant life was. No, it was not adrenaline, but more like the rush of euphoria one feels when they fall in love for the first time.

I walked over to where the ferry docked. I bought a ticket and boarded the next boat to the mainland, then caught a cab to the Plaza Caribe Motel in the heart of the old downtown district of Cancun. I needed a shower and some rest. It was four in the afternoon. I fell into an exhausted sleep to the sound of rain falling outside my window.

Early the next morning I bought some clothes at the motel shop. The weather had cleared and I walked about two miles to the local telephone company office, which had a room with a couple of operators and some phone stalls.

The Plaza Caribe was a modern motel by Mexican standards, and my room had a phone in it. One of the cardinal sins of smuggling, however, was using the phone in the room or any phone in the motel to make calls, especially international calls. The motel operator could easily listen in on a call, become suspicious, and tip off the police. The phone company was the best of my choices.

First, I asked the operator to place a call to Johnny's number in Belize. I paid her for the call and walked to the phone she designated. When she buzzed the phone, I quickly picked it up. I could hear the ringing and then the voice on the other end.

"Hello." It was a familiar voice.

"Johnny, it's Jim." The excitement on the other end was a welcome sound.

"Billy, er, Jim! Man we thought you were dead! Where the hell are you?"

I gave him my location and explained I needed a Mexican visa and a ride — and quickly. He took down the vital statistics of my alias identity.

"Jim, Ramon will need to stop in Chetumal to pick up a visa and then he'll come and get you."

"I'm at the usual motel. Room 9. I'll be waiting there or by the pool."

I needed to get back to the compound, where I could feel at ease. Perhaps the Mexican authorities knew about the plane and its missing pilot.

I then gave the operator Earl's number in the States.

"Earl, it's Jim."

All I could hear was laughing and yelling. Earl was easily excitable and I guess this was a call that might have produced that in anyone. I could picture his smiling face.

"Damn Jim! We thought you were long gone! Why you want to scare us like that?"

I was taking a chance talking on Earl's phone, but desperate times called for drastic measures. As part of our crew his phone could be tapped but I had no choice.

"Earl, I'm okay, but I need you to do something. Write down what I'm going to tell you."

It took him a minute to get a pencil. I glanced around the room to see if anyone looked interested. They all seemed to be going about their own business. Earl gave me the go-ahead.

"Call Johnny and make sure he has my correct name, James Gordon Lang, DOB: April 18, 1947, Birthplace: Harrison County, Mississippi," I waited a moment, "Do you have that?" I needed to make sure everything matched my fake ID on the visa Johnny was procuring for me.

"I got it, Jim. I'll call him right now."

I was nervous about the visa and didn't want any more problems when I got to the Belize border.

"Thanks, Earl. I'll call you tomorrow from Johnny's."

Earl had been brought into the cartel along with Timbo about the same time by Freddie. They were both from the Century area and had similar south Alabama drawls. I knew he'd follow through on my request.

I spoke in code to my friends as much as possible. They knew that I stayed at the Plaza Caribe a lot, so I didn't have to give the name of the motel over the phone. I could see the operators from my phone's position, and it looked like they were too busy to be listening in on my conversation. I got up from the chair and split from the telephone building. As soon as I got outside, I felt safer. I decided to walk back to the motel even though my legs and feet were still hurting and walking would kill more time while waiting for Ramon.

It was a productive morning and everything was falling into place. It was about a twenty-minute walk back to the Plaza, and I was ready to eat. Tacos are the breakfast of champions in Mexico, and I was starving. I then headed back to my room for another shower. I napped, woke, and smoked a joint, looked out of the window and watched the people at the pool. Ramon was traveling from Orange Walk to Cancun with a stop in Chetumal to clear Immigrations and Customs. It would be a hard six-hour trip. Johnny would need to scramble around and get organized before he could send him. While in Chetumal, Ramon would have to get with their Mexican Immigrations contact to obtain a visa for me without me being present. I estimated I was looking at eight to ten hours waiting — if there were no problems.

I went outside to the poolside bar and grill and ordered a Sol beer with lime. Fajitas sounded good, so I ordered those too. I relaxed and enjoyed the beer, the food, and a cage full of colorful tropical birds flitting their wings and sunning themselves. I reflected over the events of the past couple of days and counted my blessings.

January 26, 1990

I haven't heard from Billy since Saturday a week ago and that hasn't bothered me until Tom came by today. His exact words were, "Kay, I don't want to upset you and you shouldn't be upset because Billy is okay now."

"Okay now?" I said. I was holding onto the back of the chair. "What the hell does that mean?"

"Well, Kay" he says, "I guess Billy had a, you know, a crash-landing several days ago on a beach not far from Mexico and was lost until he could find his way back to civilization and call his contacts."

"He ... he crashed? He was lost! Is he hurt?"

"Actually, Kay, I don't have the details, but I'm sure from what I've heard Billy will be getting in touch with you as soon as he, you know, gets back home."

When Tom left I just slumped in the chair. Does this mean Billy needs medical care and can't get back right now? Oh God, please be with him, take care of him. Please don't let him die. I don't know what to do. Do I go to Belize? I don't even know how to contact any of the people that work with him now. Everybody else's dead or in prison.

A little before sunset Ramon and another of the loading crew showed up, all smiles. Ramon handed me my visa. I offered to put everyone up for the night in Cancun to celebrate my rescue but Ramon thought it best to get back to Belize. We bought some beer and ice and were on the road to Orange Walk. I told them my story and Ramon told me his.

"After you took off with the load, we went back to the compound like normal. About ten that night, we were all waiting on the phone call that would tell us it was 'Miller Time.' When Freddie did call, he wanted to know what the problem was and why you hadn't left yet. Johnny told him you had left on schedule. He didn't say anything except, 'Are you kidding me?' Johnny told him we would keep our ears open and call if we heard anything. You called four days later."

We drove straight to Orange Walk with no problem at the border. I went to bed dead tired at about 1:00 a.m. and woke up around noon the next day when Johnny arrived at the compound. I told him the story, and he told me what he'd seen on Mexican TV that morning about the downed airplane. There was nothing reported about the pilot.

We had to get me back to the States and make a little money in the process. Johnny and I could try and get a plane in Belize or Freddie could find a plane in the States and come down to pick me up with the next load of pot. After several days, we weren't making any headway at either end. My five thousand dollars was just about down to nothing, so I decided to return to the States and get the plane myself.

I didn't like the idea of testing my fake ID. On the other hand, I didn't want to stay in Belize and wait for Freddie to someday find a plane. My partner was no go-getter, and it might be a month or longer before he came up with something, if ever.

I called the States and got Earl to agree to meet me in Cancun. He was to bring ten thousand dollars with him, five for me and five for Johnny to offset some of the expenses for the lost load.

I met Earl at the airport in Cancun and Johnny's man took us to the trusty Plaza Caribe. From there, Earl and I went out to the old town Cancun strip, picked out a restaurant and ordered drinks and a meal on the open-air patio. I asked Earl the question that had been in the back of my mind for days.

"No one called Kay, did they?"

Earl looked a little sheepish. He took his cap off and scratched the bald portion of the top of his head. I don't think I ever saw him with that cap off.

"Yeah, I think Freddie called Tom in Lake City when you didn't show up. Freddie told him to go by and let her know that you were lost, but I don't know if he did."

We turned the subject to what we needed for a smooth border crossing. Earl dropped his voice a little.

"When I was in the Marines back in the seventies, I was stationed at San Diego and we'd go to Tijuana all the time. All we had to do was walk across."

"You sure that's all there is to it? You walk across with no questions asked?"

"Well, okay," he said. "They may ask you if you're an American, or do you have anything to declare, but that's all."

"Fine," I said. "We're going to Tijuana first thing in the morning."

We had a plan, which gave us the rest of the night to party in Cancun. I was celebrating the fact that I hadn't managed to kill myself and a guy can't do that by himself. After the night out on the town, we got a night's sleep, got up early the next morning, had a good breakfast in the motel restaurant, caught a cab to the airport and bought tickets to Tijuana.

January 30, 1990

Tom hasn't heard anything else from Billy's contact in West Florida. I'm going crazy with worry. Tom said they told him Billy was alive, but is he injured in some way? Who is taking care of him if he is? Would he risk going to a hospital if the injury was bad enough? It has been 9 days since the crash and nothing else from them. Surely Billy knows they've told me about the crash. If he could call, he'd have called to let me know something by now. I haven't slept well. I feel like a zombie in class and Debbie has asked me several times if something is wrong with me.

I need to know something.

We were staring at the American/Mexican border. I told Earl to walk across and report back what happens on the Mexican side and on the American side.

"Damn Jim. That's silly and a waste of time. Just walk through with me."

But Earl was not a fugitive and had nothing to lose. He was wanting to get back to Pensacola and party. I can't blame him but I was not going to risk my capture for a night at the strip bar.

"Earl, it's you who's wasting time. I'm not going through until you get back with a full report."

Reluctantly he headed out across the border while I watched. The man was of average build and blended in with many of the Mexican nationals as he approached the boundary. I had just started looking around for a place to wait on him when I saw him coming back.

"Damn, Earl, that was quick. There must have been nothing to it."

It had been around twenty years since he'd crossed there, and it was not how he remembered. Everyone was getting stopped and questioned on the Mexican side, so he turned around before they could ask him. Earl was not a chance taker, so he wasn't going to push the issue.

"My visa says that I walked across the southern border of Mexico from Belize into Chetumal yesterday." I looked glumly at the Mexican border post. "Now I'm at Tijuana wanting to walk across the northern border the next day. They're going to think I'm one hell of a walker."

There was nothing illegal about walking across the border but doing it too often might raise a guard's interest. The Mexican side might alert the American side to check the "walking man" a little closer than usual. I hadn't survived a crash and epic skiff ride through a storm so I'd get hung up for walking across the border.

"Earl, let's get a room and think about this."

We got a room in Tijuana and had a big supper and a few drinks. Not long after supper, I started having stomach pains. I went to my room to try and get some rest but was back and forth to the bathroom all night. By morning I was weak and exhausted, I'd made my decision.

"I don't like Tijuana, Earl. We're going back to Cancun."

At the airport we bought tickets and boarded the same plane that we'd flown in on the day before. During the trip back to Cancun, Montezuma's revenge was hurting me so bad I thought I would die. After one of my many trips to the airplane's lavatory, I leaned over to Earl.

"I'm catching the first plane out of Cancun back to the States. Don't care where that might be. I'm not dying in Mexico. I'm gonna die in the States or on a plane out of Cancun, whichever comes first."

Earl just laughed.

"Come on, Jim. It can't be that bad. Let's spend one more night with our little friends we met in Cancun."

"You do whatever you want, but the only way I'm spending another night in Cancun will be if I miss the last plane out."

I was feeling a little stronger by the time we landed but not enough to change my mind. There happened to be a plane leaving for Houston in thirty minutes. I turned to Earl.

"You riding or staying?"

"I'm going with you, buddy."

We had just enough time for me to buy a Cancun cap, bag, and one shirt. I put the shirt on and loaded the bag with some of my dirty clothes. Maybe I'd look more like a tourist.

We landed in Texas in the early evening. Immigration was not busy during that time, so we were able to walk up without waiting in a line. I held my breath and gave the officer my entry card and he typed it into the computer.

"Welcome back, Mr. Lang."

We found a flight leaving for Pensacola from Houston in twenty minutes. We arrived in my beloved home state around nine that evening.

We'd flown from Tijuana to Monterey to Cancun to Houston to Pensacola. A good day's flying by anyone's standards. Now the only problems facing me were the loss of a $80,000 plane, being a smuggler without a plane again, and letting Kay know I was alright. I'd start working on those problems as soon as I got some rest.

February 1, 1990

Buddy came by today. His message was, "Meet Billy tomorrow at your Mama's." Well, at least he isn't dead or in a coma. I'll know something tomorrow. Thank you, Lord, for watching out for him. I'm leaving first thing in the morning for Vernon. No school for me.

February 2, 1990

Not a scratch. No, I take that back. I think his knuckles were scratched. It took him 12 days to let me know something. He said he had to wait in Belize on some money to get to Mexico. Then he had to go to Cancun, then Tijuana, then back to Cancun to try and get through the border. Then, when he did make it to Pensacola, he needed to take care of a little business before he could see me. I was okay, he says. Why was I so worried?

How can I love him one minute to the point of thinking I'll die from worry, then want to kill him or at least put him in the hospital? His explanation of why it took him so long to let me know something makes me want to scream. How is it that I can love then hate him with an equal passion? It is that fine line again, between love and hate. Billy has a knack of staying right on the border of each with me.

12

I was a witness to my own ticking clock on a train that never changed direction, that circled viciously without a stop, with nowhere to get off.

I'd survived. The little Century cartel was still in business but it faced some new hurdles. Getting another airplane was one of those. Basically, we could buy one, ask Robert if he had anything available for rent, or dig out my magic key ring and subscribe to the unauthorized borrowing plan.

I discarded the idea of buying an airplane because it brought back memories of a recent, expensive, and overly-long train ride. I rejected renting from Robert because of the risks involved: apart from serious maintenance issues, there was no telling who had been making use of Robert's airplanes. They were most likely smoking hot and even more likely to be under surveillance or have a tracking bug on board.

I went with the key ring plan. As in the past, I would leave the plane at a location where it would be easily found and eventually find its way back to its rightful owner, no major harm done.

The biggest drawback to illegally borrowing an airplane was me standing out on a ramp in the wee hours of the morning going through key after key until I found one close enough to pick the lock. As a fugitive who had already pressed his luck, I lacked the necessary enthusiasm.

I decided it was a job for Wolfman and got in touch with him. I wanted him to find a nice 210 or 206 somewhere in the southeast. He'd grab it for me and meet me at the Brewton airport. I'd take it from there. His pay would be in cash or a piece of the load at a discounted price.

Wolfman needed work. He lived in Tennessee, so he agreed to meet me in Florida the following week. I gave him the address of the Red Roof Inn close to the University Mall in Pensacola.

"I'll see you at lunch time next week at Bennigan's," I told him. "We'll iron out the details and I'll give you the key ring."

Kay hadn't taken the beach crash well. Our anniversary was near and I needed to make it up to her somehow. I knew it was hard on her, never knowing whether I was dead or alive. When things did go wrong and she knew about it, she'd worry until she saw I was alright.

I was ready for the million questions I knew she'd have when we met in Vernon after my return and, sure enough, her questioning about the crash was tougher than most prosecutors could come up with. After the barrage, she started to cry and begged me to stop smuggling. I put my arms around her.

"You are going to end up dead," she sobbed. "I can't go on like this. I don't care if we have to live in an igloo in the middle of Alaska. I need to be with you."

All I could manage was my usual.

"Don't worry, Baby Love. Everything will be alright."

I didn't know how to fix our situation. I had no responsibilities when I was apart from Kay except smuggling and keeping myself entertained. She shouldered the responsibilities of everything else. I finally convinced her that we only had a few days and shouldn't argue. It was the roller coaster ride of life, but she loved me, and I loved her. I was pretty sure she wasn't leaving me, but how far could one woman be pushed? I knew I had to be close to crossing the line with her. Something had to change but I couldn't see how.

February 15, 1990

When Debbie came by to pick me up for school this morning, she said Billy had called and wanted me to meet him at her house tomorrow between 4 and 5 p.m. The rest of the college crew didn't have school tomorrow so I will drive over to class in Jacksonville myself and then to her house.

I've been thinking quite a bit about my marriage. I don't see how it can survive at this rate. It can't be healthy for me mentally and does Billy even really care anymore? I don't know. His actions make me doubt that we still have a relationship. I'd rather live alone than suffer like I have been doing. I know it is our 19th anniversary coming up but the way I've been feeling, it may be our last.

February 20, 1990

I stayed with Billy until this morning and then drove to my class in Jacksonville from Gainesville. We had a suite at the motel, and I'd cooked several meals for us there in the room.

It wasn't all fun and games. I found lipstick on a cigarette butt in the ashtray of his car while I was waiting for him to get the room. I'd been flipping the cover up and down on the ashtray on my side of the door when I happened to see the butt sticking out. His explanation was that when his friends thought he was dead, they'd been driving around partying in his car in his memory. It was probably one of them. He expected me to believe that his so-called friends were partying instead of looking for him when he was supposedly crashed in an airplane. What I could more easily believe was that one of his own party girls had left it and he'd failed to get rid of the evidence.

But what difference does it all make? If he can't see the ridiculousness of these scenarios, I'll never be able to explain it to him. I just continued my silence until the following morning. Problem was, he acted so pitiful yesterday, still maintaining his innocence,

I finally caved in. I could either stay and put up with his antics and be somewhat happy at times or be miserable without him.

I drove back to Pensacola thinking about my family and life — one shit storm after another. Every solution I came up with led to prison and the possibility of 15 to 20 years behind bars. I knew it was getting closer, probably just a matter of time before it caught up with me.

Two weeks later, Wolfman called Earl. He'd found a 210 in Enterprise, Alabama and was going out that night to try the keys. The next day I drove to Enterprise and after lunch, we went out to the airport and drove slowly around the prospective airplane. It looked good, but I wanted to check out the avionics. Wolfman dropped me off at the perimeter of the airport around 1:00 a.m. I walked straight to the plane, stuck the key in the door, opened it, and gave the cockpit a once over.

It was an averagely equipped 210 with no surprises. I was familiar with everything it offered. I walked back out to the road and waited for Wolfman's next pass, then returned to Century and used a payphone to give Freddie the news and call Johnny in Belize.

"Johnny, we're ready to work again. Can you send someone up to collect a down payment?"

"Yeah, but ..." His tone was tinged with hesitation. "I didn't make any money on that last load, so I'm going to need a larger down payment."

"Okay, Johnny. Send your man up here right away. We'll send him back with thirty thousand."

I spent the next day or so bar hopping at the local Pensacola hot spots, then got bored and decided to take a drive over to the beach. Heading down US 98, I passed a quaint little beach motel where Kay and I had stayed back before I was on the lam. Emotions flooded over me as they had that day I crashed on the Holbox beach and the night I'd spent in the jungle. She was there even though she was many hundreds of miles away.

I turned the car around and parked. I needed to quell a dull emptiness swelling in my chest and I smiled as I entered the lobby. Maybe I could recapture what we'd shared there. I went to the same little poolside bar and ordered a drink. I ate at the same restaurant where we'd once enjoyed dinner. I imagined how we'd laughed, talked, and made love. My heart ached. I could no longer outrun the grip of loneliness. It wasn't the same and nothing would ever be the same without her. No one and nothing could take her place. I missed my family more and more, Kay and my kids. I thought about the times I could have spent with them, hearing about their joys and fears, good days and bad, ideas and aspirations. I'd often busied myself with other *things*, things I wanted to do. I was absent for so many moments, even when I could've been there, and now I felt the weight of regret. I was physically sick with remorse. I wanted so desperately to do it all over again, to turn back time. I was a witness to my own ticking clock, seeing the time slip beneath my cemented feet. I was on a train, on tracks that never changed direction, that circled viciously without a stop, with nowhere to get off. The view from my window was always the same, unfulfilling and miserable. I told myself to think rationally. I told myself this was no time for feeling sorry. The facts were non-negotiable: I was a federal fugitive. Reminiscing and wishing things were different didn't change anything.

I checked out the next morning and returned to Pensacola.

Flying High with Gringo Billy

March 1, 1990

I received a call this afternoon. It was from my friend Ann at the high school. Amy was failing a class. Failing? She was student vice-president of the school! What the heck? I made an appointment to see her teacher. Amy said she didn't know why she had an F; he was just a bad teacher. After the meeting I surmised that it was a conflict that was not going to be resolved between the two. Neither he nor Amy are going to give an inch so we've decided to change teachers. No sense fighting a losing battle for the rest of the year.

As soon as Johnny's man arrived, I gave him the money and made sure he was aboard an airliner back to Belize. I returned to Century and dug the old bladder tank out of storage to extend the range of the plane. This 210 had no Flint tip tanks. I looked over the bladder, pump, filters, valves, hoses, and fittings and decided to replace the fuel pump. I bought a 12-volt pump, removed the old one and attached the hoses to the new one. It was a simple job, but when I'd finished, I had a small roll of thin white tape left over. This made me curious, so I unfolded the directions. Steps 3 and 4 explained how I should have wrapped the threads of the male fittings before screwing them into the pump. I thought about this oversight for a moment and decided the tape was unnecessary. The joints were screwed in good and tight and there was no way that it could leak.

The bladder assembled and the airplane located, I was as ready as I could be. I called Johnny to see how it was going on his end.

"Give me three days and call me back," he said.

I let Wolfman know that I would probably need him to deliver the plane at Brewton airport soon. I would be back in touch in three days and I wanted him ready to go. Three days later, Johnny and I discussed logistics.

"I'll be ready to load you tomorrow at 7:00 a.m. local time," he said.

"Johnny, I'm gonna need one more day because Wolfman still has to get our wings and I'll need to bladder it. Can I see you the following morning at 7:00 a.m.?"

"Okay okay."

I called Wolfman.

"I need you to be at the airport at daylight in the morning. I'll be there with my 2-meter radio waiting for you. Gotta make it daylight or close to it. I want to be out of there before any of the workers show up."

"Okay, Billy. I'll grab it first thing in the morning."

I got a room in the Brewton area and called the Century boys to put them on standby at the Jay hangar the next morning. They knew the drill and would have the hangar doors open, ready to park our new wings.

If all was cool, we would remove the seats, install the bladder, fill it and the wing tanks with fuel for a scheduled 1:00 am departure the next morning.

After a good night's sleep, I woke early, ate a quick breakfast, and drove out to the airport shortly before daylight. I was delighted to find the airport completely deserted. I parked and waited. A nice 210 was right there on the ramp. Too bad I didn't have my keys, I thought. I could easily acquire that pretty number sitting all alone. Of course, I'd need someone to drive my car away from the airport.

In the midst of this fantasy, I realized the sky was getting lighter and the sun was going to break the horizon at any moment.

"Come on, Wolfman," I thought. I was hoping to simply jump in the cockpit and take off while he hopped into my car and drove the hell out of Dodge before any witnesses could appear. I sat in the parking lot, waiting. An hour passed and no Wolfman. I called him on the radio, hoping that he was close enough to hear me. No response. Some of the airport workers began trickling in for work. The access road soon featured a short caravan of automobiles, I cranked my car and left.

For the next thirty minutes, I drove up and down the highway running along the perimeter of the airport property, listening to dead air on my radio hoping for Wolfman to break through. I scanned the sky.

I found a wooded area close to the airport and decided to park for a moment. I stayed close to two hours. There was no mistaking that Wolfman was a no-show. Something was wrong. I went to a nearby payphone and called his motel room in Enterprise. He answered on the first ring.

"Wolfman! What the hell is wrong? I've been waiting for hours!"

"Yeah, right, Billy." He was mumbling. "The man that was, ah, going to drop me off at the airport. He, ah, he chickened out. Hey, don't worry, Billy. I found another guy who'll do it first thing in the morning."

I agreed, hung up, and drove to another payphone to call Johnny and let him know that we'd be late by a day. If there were any more problems, I'd call him before he moved the pot out to the landing strip. I returned to the motel and rented my same room for one more day. I was upset but I was used to delays. I took a deep, deep breath.

I might as well have saved that breath.

Early the next morning, Wolfman followed the same script.

"I'm about tired of this horseshit, Wolfman," I said. "I'll

have Earl drop me off at your motel and you can drop *me* off and I'll get the damn airplane tomorrow."

I called Johnny and assured him this would be the last delay. I called Earl and let him know I needed him to take me to Wolfman's motel in Enterprise, and then drive my car back to Century. Wolfman and I spent the rest of the day at a country bar outside of Enterprise, drinking beer and shooting pool.

"That stupid chicken-shit friend of mine!" Wolfman shook his head. "Billy, can you believe it? That guy was too damn scared to drop me off. Stupid chicken-shit friend!"

I looked at him. Hard to imagine how anyone could be too scared to drive by an airport and let someone out of the car.

"Don't stress it Wolf," I advised. "It's moot now."

"It's what?"

"It's come and gone, Wolf."

"Stupid chicken-shit friend" Wolfman said again.

The next morning about an hour before daylight he dropped me off at the little Enterprise airport. I walked straight out to the airplane, opened the door with my key, got in, cranked it up, taxied out and took off into the night sky.

The 210 seemed to be in good shape. I flew around checking her mannerisms until daylight, then called Earl on the radio.

"Everything cool down there, Earl?"

"Come on in, man."

I set our new 210 softly on the ground at the Jay airport. Earl and I closed the hangar doors and installed the bladder. We drove back to Century.

I called a meeting of the crew but Freddie wasn't part of it. He'd failed numerous drug tests and been given a choice of rehab or prison. He'd apparently decided rehab was the better choice.

I mapped out my plan for the men. We'd unload and abandon the plane on a gas pipeline in the Blountstown area.

"The gas company keeps a well-maintained right-of-way. The stretch I'm thinking about is where the pipeline goes through a large, wooded area of scrub oaks. There's a dirt road nearby. It's about a mile long and leads to a paved state road. You could probably sit out there for a week without anybody coming by."

Everyone nodded in agreement.

"So I'll need y'all to hook the horse trailer up and drive out to the pipeline after I take off. If you see any scrub oaks you think my wings won't clear, chop them down, then wait for me to show up with the load."

March 15, 1990

I took the girls prom dress shopping in Jacksonville this past weekend and they wore me out. I bet we went to at least 10 different stores and they tried on 25 dresses a piece. Kim decided on a red mermaid fitted dress, Amy a white dress with gold trim and Amy Doub a royal blue one. The prom isn't until next month, but it's important to make sure you get the right one and let it be known so no one else will get that one. Oh, to be young again! What I would do different!

I saw Billy the other night. He'd been driving around looking for airplanes and we met in Alachua. He looked tired and he's lost some weight. I don't know if it's the drugs, no sleep, the stress of smuggling or what, but he seems like he's aged 5 years since I saw him last. I'm sure it's a little of all of that. I even saw a sadness in his eyes that wasn't there before. I know we both have regrets, but I'd never actually witnessed any in Billy. Maybe that's what I saw in his eyes: regret. Whatever it was, it was affecting him physically and mentally. I'll pray for him tonight and pray that God will somehow fix this situation that we find ourselves in before it kills one of us.

A clear, chilly mid-April morning. Earl and I drove to the hangar, opened the doors, and rolled out the plane. I hopped in and began the engine start-up procedure. When I turned on the fuel pump, nothing happened. I flipped the switch off and back on again. Nothing. I did this several times. Finally, it caught, and the fuel pressure gauge came to life. I started the engine, let it warm, and ascended into the night sky, heading for Belize.

I'd been airborne a little over ten minutes and was about to level off at 10,000 feet when I smelled gasoline. Not unusual, but maybe a little strong. I got out my flashlight and checked all the fittings to the bladder and hoses. All good. I picked up the pump and every fitting was leaking. The tape, of course, the tape I'd decided not to wrap around the fitting's threads. I hated the idea of turning back but as soon as I did, there was another problem. How could I find the little grass strip with no lights and no useful moon? Could Earl still be in range? Could he have left his 2-meter radio on? I picked up mine.

"Earl?"

A crackle of static.

"Yeah, Billy?"

"Come on back, Earl, I'm headed back too."

The landscape was mostly black below me but I navigated back to the general area of the strip.

"Earl, go to the west end of the strip. There's a big oak tree that overhangs there. Park just east of it and point your headlights eastward down the strip. When you get there, start flashing your lights so that I can see your location."

A few minutes later white headlights flashed.

"Okay, man. Leave those lights on now so I can see down the strip."

I came in right over his truck and touched down on the lit part of the open field, dust and dirt flying up behind. We put the plane in the hangar and headed to Earl's house.

Johnny was growing tired of delays and so was I.

Earl and I fixed the fuel pump leaks by wrapping the threads with tape as I should have done in the first place. However, I had to flip the switch on the booster pump for five minutes before it started. This was unacceptable because it would almost be impossible to start a hot fuel-injected engine without having a fuel boost pump to purge the fuel lines of air. I didn't know if the problem was in the switch or the wiring connectors. I didn't have a lot of time for troubleshooting, so I ran another wire from the hot side of the pump through the firewall into the cockpit. Whenever I needed a boost, I could stick the bare end of the hot wire coming from the fuel pump to the 12-volt battery that operated the bladder pump. Nothing could stop me now.

The next morning about 1:00 a.m. we rolled out the 210. I cranked it up and took off for Belize.

I often did a line of meth to keep me awake on these trips, but I'd been so busy dealing with the little mechanical issues, I hadn't packed any and had to use cocaine. The problem with cocaine is that it's easy to do too much and get wired out, though I preferred flying a plane wired to falling asleep in midair. As a result, after using coke on and off for 14 hours, my touch down at the pipeline site in Florida was not my typical landing. I was still hyped and I bounced her quite high on the landing. I shook my head vigorously, shouted at myself, gripped the throttle, and got my aircraft under control, salvaging the landing. I shut the engine down and sat still for some long moments.

The job was done but the completion process seemed to me full of complications and risks. It wasn't as satisfying as it should have been. Maybe it was just the many tiny frustrations. Or maybe there was something more to it than tape.

June 1, 1990

It was Kim's 18th birthday two days ago. It doesn't seem like that long ago that I myself was eighteen and so naive. I hope I've taught Kim and Amy more than I knew at that age. I was no more prepared to meet the world than a 12-year-old. Then at 19 I married Billy. Wow. Would I do it differently if I knew then what I know now?

Kim and Amy Doub's graduation was nice. My sister and Greg came to support her, along with Billy's family. Amy helped on the field with graduation since she's an officer. I knew it wouldn't happen, but I had wished somehow Billy would show up. Someone would recognize him if he tried to mingle with the crowd but if he had just driven up and sat in the car — just to be there. Of course, I know that would never enter his mind. I wonder if he ever thinks about things like I do. He'll never be able to get back some of the memories he's missing. Does that bother him like it does me? Kim and Amy Doub went to a graduation party afterward and finally made it home about 2 a.m. and I'm letting them sleep in after the big night. I've rented a condo at the end of June for a week at Summer House in Crescent Beach. Billy said if he can work it out, he'll meet us during that week. I just need to get away from Lake City, the house, the people. The girls will go to the beach and I'll sit by the pool and read. Reading fills most of my nights. I read books by Danielle Steele and like authors. I try to lose myself in the books, to think about other people's dreams and problems.

The weeks following the pipeline load were busy ones for me. Freddie was out of rehab, but sticking close to home with Sweet Pea, and by all accounts doing heroic quantities of drugs. I delivered pot to Randy in the Montgomery area and drove up to Atlanta to visit my old friend, Dog and give him some pot. While

I was there, I paid Wolfman for his services and gave him some extra pot to help him out.

On the drive back I went through Blountstown and picked up a local newspaper. To my surprise there was no mention of an abandoned airplane being found on a nearby pipeline route, but when I returned a week later, there was the story. The plane had been spotted by law enforcement aerial surveillance whose mission was to look for pot patches. The story made no mention of the fact that the plane had sat out in the open — on a pipeline, no less — for the better part of two weeks.

When I'd distributed all the pot and collected all the money and paid everyone associated with the load, I knew I'd need to go airplane shopping. I called Dog again at his apartment in Buckhead, Atlanta. It seemed that Wolfman was staying with him — good news because I didn't have too many trusted friends left and we needed to talk about our next project.

I arrived as they were about to walk up to a bar and grill to get a bite. I tagged along and we found a quiet table where we could talk. At some point in the conversation, Wolfman dropped his voice.

"Now that I've got a copy of your airplane keys, I'm going back to Tennessee to start looking around. I'll need to contact you when I find one."

I took a minute to consider what Wolfman was asking. In all the months as a fugitive, I'd never told anyone other than members of our little cartel how to get in touch with me.

"You're right," I finally said. "I'm in Pensacola at least once a month and I always stay in motels around the University Mall area. I'm a regular at Bennigan's restaurant. All the bartenders know me as Jim, so just call there and ask them to relay a message."

After a few drinks, we headed back to the apartment. It was night by this time, and there was no one out and about. Dog and Wolfman had been arguing at dinner like brothers fighting over a toy. In the parking lot, however, it escalated into a fistfight. Wolfman, being younger and far less intoxicated, got the best of Dog but the older man never gave up and remained defiant to the end. After a few minutes of push and pull, they were both slumped over, trying to catch some air. Wolfman, panting and sweating, pulled himself off the ground, stumbled to his Chevy Suburban and headed back to Knoxville. No further words were spoken.

Dog and I partied hard over the next few days and we were still partying when we got the call. Wolfman had been arrested. Apparently, he'd driven back to his house and got into another fight, this time with his live-in girlfriend. She'd called the cops in what was looking to me like a pattern among my people. The cops discovered he was a fugitive and locked him up without bail.

I hung up disconcerted. This was another friend down and, just as bad, locked up in that cell with Wolfman was information about my hangouts.

I announced I'd be leaving the next morning, but even after this ominous news about our buddy, Dog didn't let up on the hard stuff. He settled back on the couch and partied on alone. Then, like he'd forgotten something on the stove, he jolted up from his slouch and stood rubbing his chest. He stretched and shook himself as if to force himself awake.

"You okay, Dog?"

"I don't feel well," he said, sort of mumble. "I'm going to lie down."

I watched as he sat down on the bed. He exhaled as if he was completely out of breath shaking his head as he sat there.

"Do you need to go to the emergency room?"

"Hell no, I don't need no damn doctor. I just need to ride it out."

He laid back and appeared to go to sleep. I went back to the living room. After an hour or so I stuck my head back in and called to him. No answer. I went over to the bed. Dog's eyes were open but it was a blank stare. I put my hand on his chest but there was no movement. I tried some CPR. Too late.

I called his son, JD, in Orlando and told him I had some bad news. His father had passed away and I couldn't wait for the authorities to arrive. I told him I had to go, and I was sorry for his loss. His son knew how to get in touch with Dog's ex-wife there in Atlanta. I hated leaving him but at that point there was nothing I or anyone could do for Dog.

I went straight to my car and hit the road. My lifestyle was no different than Dog's and he was only a few years older than me. Staring into my friend's dead face, calling his son, realizing my own clock was ticking, it scared the hell out of me. I drove south to Jacksonville.

June 19, 1990

Billy showed up at the beach condo last night. I knew something was wrong by the way he was acting. It wasn't until we went to bed that he told me another one of his friends, a guy named Dog, had died. I didn't know him, but he died while Billy was with him and that really got to Billy. He had to call the guy's son and tell him, then he drove straight here. What will it take for Billy to realize that this lifestyle will kill him too if he doesn't change? This is about the fourth or fifth friend who has died as a result of drugs and the lives they're living but yet they can't turn it loose. They love it more than they love anything else. Are they afraid to grow up, to be adults and have responsibilities?

He's staying the rest of the week. Thank you, Lord, for watching out for him when I cannot.

June 30, 1990

Billy and I decided to stay together for another few days. The girls went back to Lake City and we headed to St. Simon and Jekyll Island for a couple of nights. After he made a few calls this morning things changed. I watched the transformation of my husband within minutes. Billy went to make the phone calls and Jim Lang returned. He said, "I've got to get back tomorrow." He was distant and antsy at being confined to the room and the car. Our conversations were short, no laughter or joking around anymore. It's like he cannot wait to get me back to Jacksonville where we left my car so he can return to his other life — his life without responsibilities and a wife to confine him. I feel like I've served my purpose for this crisis in his life. I've gotten him over his bump in the road and he's ready for the excitement to return. That desire I cannot fill, or he will not let me fill. It would mean him growing up, becoming an adult, taking on obligations that he is just not ready to do.

Before he left, we decided that he'd come home for a week in late July or August. It's a risk but one that we'll take.

I drove back to Montgomery to visit Randy and catch him up on the recent misfortunes. He was ready, willing and able to help me in any way he could. Of course, he was also our biggest customer and would be interested in maintaining his supply of pot, but he was also dependable. I didn't want to lose him.

Wolfman's arrest left me in charge of finding an aircraft, so Randy and I took a ride that night down to the Troy airport to scope out prospective airplanes. We were there less than thirty minutes when the local sheriff pulled in next to us. We exchanged pleasantries and moved on. We traveled around for a few more nights until we ended up at Eufaula, Alabama, where we found a capable Aztec and a Cessna 206. Both airplanes could do the job and I had no problem fitting the keys. The airport was just a nine-iron shot away from an Alabama Highway Patrol station, so we took care of business swiftly and were in and out without being noticed.

I still needed to meet with the unloading arm of the cartel and plan with them where we would meet. As before, we'd be abandoning the borrowed aircraft and couldn't use the Blackwater unloading strip. I needed a new location.

I left Montgomery and on the way to Century, I stopped and called Johnny and told him to send his guys up to collect a down payment.

I called Joe to let him know that, even though we are not using his Blackwater farm for the unload, I'd still like his help. I drove to his farm and picked him up. We meandered over to the Apalachicola area and combed through a large forest. There were plenty of roads crisscrossing and no houses around for miles. There were so many roads that would suit us, getting lost would be a possibility. In the end, we decided on a road close to the main highway.

I was pleased. We had a safe spot to unload and had found a couple of good airplanes. I especially liked the looks of the Aztec and looked forward to flying it. A week later Johnny's man arrived. I fixed him with the $40,000 deposit and sent him back to Belize with a message that I would call Johnny as soon as possible with a date. I bummed around Pensacola until it was time to head over to Lake City. Meanwhile Kay and I had concocted a sort of 'hide in plain sight' plan where I would sneak into the house and stay for a week without leaving. I was excited. She was excited. The thought of sleeping in my own bed for a little while was overwhelmingly comforting. I couldn't wait to get there.

July 7, 1990

Amy turned 16 on the 4th — my firecracker baby. We bought her a black 240 SX for her birthday. Just like Kim, she was one excited young lady. It has been a week or so since I've seen Billy. I wish he could have seen his daughter's face when she got the keys. She almost gave me a heart attack when she test drove a standard shift. She let off the clutch and we bunny hopped in between new cars barely missing several until I could get her to stop the car and get out. She needed an automatic, no doubt. I have no patience to teach her to shift gears. That should have been her dad's job, but he wasn't here. Another memory he'll miss out on. He should be home for a few days in a month. I hope nothing spoils our plan. I want him home!

July 9, 1990

I began my summer dance practice this week. We have two weeks of practice and then camp for four days. This will help keep my mind off the fact that I still have a month before I see Billy again.

July 28, 1990

I'm exhausted. We finished camp and our weeklong practice after camp to learn all the dances for football season. I need a vacation.

August 5, 1990

I registered for my college classes for this semester today. Debbie and the other girls are riding separate from me now as they are in their final semester at the university. I will be driving every day starting on the 20th. It will be hard, but I can do it. Next week Billy will be home. Home. Will he ever be able to call it home again?

August 12, 1990

Billy is home. I picked him up at Debbie's house last night and he parked his car at the back of their house. I could tell how happy he was as we drove to the house and I was as thrilled as he was. The girls fixed him some party food for his homecoming. It was so nice to crawl into bed with my husband and in our house.

August 13, 1990

Billy's parents came over. It has been 28 months since they've seen him. We haven't told anyone he's here except his parents, my sister's family, and the three girls. I can't allow myself to be caught up in this moment because I know this joy will be short lived and soon it will be over. Soon this normal happy life will fall back into the crazy rat race of a life we've allowed ourselves to be part of.

August 14, 1990

I took Billy back to his car tonight. We kissed goodbye and he told me he would see me soon. He echoed my feelings that we couldn't go on living like this, that he missed our home, his family, and me. I know he meant it but how do we escape this terrible fix that we're in? He said he'd figure it out.

It had been so long. The old neighborhood was just as I remembered: serene and comforting. Each bend of the road that led me home filled me with a sense of peace. Kay drove and I felt like my old self as I lay back in the seat watching the branches of the ancient oak trees careen over our car as we passed, their shadows a familiarity I hadn't even realized I missed.

It ended too soon. Kay drove north — back to our home, back to our girls, back to the solo life of a mother and wife of a fugitive. I drove west to Pensacola. My heart was heavy but I tried to hold on to the precious time we'd just shared and refocus my thoughts on work.

Within a couple of days of my return, I contacted the crew and we had a meeting set up to make sure all our equipment was in good operating condition. I went over each step of the procedure. Randy would drop me off at Eufaula airport after dark and I would pick up the Aztec. I would fly it to a remote grass strip, gas up and then take off for Belize.

Someone was living in a house trailer on one end of the strip. This person didn't own the property but he did know Timbo on the unloading crew. He was willing to look the other way while we gassed up and installed the bladder tank — provided we kicked a little cash his way and were gone by daylight the next morning.

I was ready.

"Hey Johnny, are you ready for us yet?"

"No man, I'll need at least three more days."

"Three more days? What the hell for?"

Johnny was almost always operational but suddenly he needed more time.

"Ah, just because, Billy. We're going to use the old strip, the cane field road in the San Lorenzo area. Call before you come."

Three days passed and I called back.

"I got a problem down here, Billy. We need to delay a while."

"Johnny, what's going on? Tell me."

"Okay, okay." He breathed audibly into the phone. "A guy crashed his plane out near San Lorenzo. It's crawling with police. I'm going to call you back in another couple of days."

A few days later, it was the same situation. The police were monitoring all strips in the San Lorenzo area, which was known to be used by smugglers.

Meanwhile, Freddie was back from rehab but said to be making up for lost time. A clue to his state of mind was his purchasing Sweet Pea a handgun.

"She needs protection when I ain't around," he said.

"The only person she's gonna shoot with that gun is you," I said.

Two weeks later, after one of their fights, she unloaded on him as he was running down the hall. The bullet went through his shoulder and came out his arm. They took him to the hospital with the gunshot wound. Convicted felons are not supposed to have firearms and I never found out how he escaped a fifteen-year sentence on a parole violation charge.

"I got out of it," he told me. "Don't worry about it."

But I was worried about it. Cops had to be watching him more closely than ever. And if he had another dirty urine, his parole officer wouldn't be experimenting with rehab again. Under any Freddie scenario, I was doing the job of two men.

September 2, 1990

Our house was broken into a few days ago. I was at school and when Kim came home from her classes at the college someone had broken the front door side panel window and came into the house. It couldn't have been too long before she got home. The house was turned upside down. The drawers in the bedrooms had been gone through and dumped on the bed and floor in all our rooms and some of the drawers and cabinets in the kitchen and living room had been trashed. Nothing was taken. None of my jewelry nor any of the girl's jewelry was missing. It was as if someone was looking for something specific, not necessarily to steal valuables. It's been a couple of weeks since Billy was here and that's probably not a coincidence. Billy's dad put in a motion-sensor light on the front and back porch and that makes me a little more secure. I just can't figure why someone would take the chance of getting caught by the law breaking into someone's house and then not take anything. Unless it WAS the law. Maybe someone tipped them off that Billy had been here. Maybe one of Billy's new associates?

I was going to tell him about the break-in, but he didn't call today. Hopefully, he'll call next week. The more I think about it, the more I'm convinced that it had to be someone looking for information. The only other explanation would be that Kim came home while they were in the house and surprised them before they could take anything, and they ran out the back door. To make matters worse there was someone in Gainesville that killed several students in their dorms over the past two or three days. That's only 40 miles from us. They still have no idea who the killer may be.

It was September and I was getting low on money. I called Johnny.

"Hey, amigo. Listen. Since the police are hanging out at San Lorenzo and our other strips are under surveillance, how about we do a hit and run at the Orange Walk Municipal Airport? I can bladder the airplane with enough fuel, I won't need to fuel up in Belize. I can land without shutting the engine down, throw in the pot, and take off before a welcome committee arrives."

"Hm." Johnny thought a minute. "Okay, I am willing to do it. When can you be here?"

"I need to crunch the numbers, Johnny. I need a bladder tank big enough for a round trip."

I tallied the mileage and capacities of each plane and decided that for round trip fuel capacity it was best to use the 206. I had been looking forward to testing the Aztec but this was business, not pleasure. I'd need a two-hundred-gallon bladder and the only place I knew I could get one was a little aviation shop in south Miami that was out of business.

My Miami connection was a guy named Howdy. I'd met him back in the late '70s when I first started to smuggle but we'd lost contact in recent years. Fortunately, our mutual friend Randy could reconnect us. I talked to Howdy and he amicably suggested I come on down so we could talk. "It's been forever," he said. I left that same day.

My travels were bringing me closer to Gainesville and the closer I got, the more I thought of Kay and our little rendezvous. It had only been a few weeks since I stayed at the house, but my carousing wasn't numbing me anymore. The misery wasn't something I could mask.

September 10, 1990

Greg called me after I got home from school today and told me Billy wanted to meet at the barbeque place tomorrow afternoon. He'd be there by 4:00. I had to go to Jacksonville first to take a test in one of my morning classes but I'll skip the class in the afternoon and head over to Gainesville. I just now walked over to Billy's parents' house to let them know I wouldn't be home tomorrow night. Even though the authorities think the suspect in the Gainesville murders is not in the area, it still makes me terrified. The three girls would be home alone. I was contemplating not going. The girls said they wouldn't go out. I have a gun and they said they wouldn't hesitate to use it if they needed to.

Still, there's this atmosphere of fear. I still haven't made up my mind.

I exited the highway to meet at our usual location. "Our usual" had become a little motel in the sleepy town of Alachua, right along 441 and just across from Sonny's Barbeque. I was anxious to see my girl and feel her warmth. I wanted to tell her everything plaguing my mind and I wanted to tell her I may be ready to try her "igloo idea" if she was still willing. I was stopped at one of the only red lights in town and to my surprise, there were police everywhere. It looked like something big was going down, and I surely did not want to get caught up in a roadblock or a license check. I made my way to the motel and hung out until Kay arrived.

September 12, 1990

I met Billy last night in Alachua. He was watching the news when I got there and we talked about what happened in Gainesville and he was as concerned as I was about leaving the girls alone. I told him I'd left them with the gun and let his dad know I'd be gone.

Finally, I told Billy about the break in. His first impression was that it was the law. He had no idea who might have tipped them off. He told me he was headed to Miami to get something for an airplane. It would probably be a couple of weeks before I heard from him again because he has several jobs coming up after he gets back from Miami. We're going to eat breakfast at the Waffle House in the morning and I'll take off to Jacksonville for my classes.

I had three girls, three people in my life that meant everything to me. I should be the one keeping them safe and watching after them. Instead, I had to depend on Kay. She was managing her responsibilities and mine, all the while trying to stay strong for me in my moments of weakness. Lately, there'd been so many. I felt the heat of the law closer than ever. I felt the weight of my decisions, the desperation for time. I wasn't ready to give up though. As always, Kay revived me. It was a short visit — only one night — because Kay was nervous about leaving the girls alone. But I needed to get to Miami and get that bladder so I could make some money.

I arrived in Miami early on the afternoon of September 12, 1990 and checked into a motel. I lay down on the bed for a quick nap and woke up in the middle of the next morning. I went straight to a payphone and called Howdy, who gave me the address of a big trailer he owned out near the bay in Miami.

We met and got along well. Howdy agreed to source a two-hundred-gallon bladder for me, and as he was leaving to do this, he turned back to me.

"By the way," he said, "you're welcome to just stay here at the trailer. Maybe we could do some boating. My boat's docked at the marina."

He was back in an hour and he'd already got someone looking into my bladder tank request. It might take a week or two. I suggested we take that cruise he'd mentioned.

We cruised down to Bimini and did a little snorkeling, checked out the nightlife, then motored over to the Keys and back up to Miami. Howdy was well off and he showed this ole country boy the sunny side of South Florida. I don't say I was totally happy, but I was entertained and glad to be doing something other than the motel circuit around Pensacola. Two weeks later, Howdy's man showed up with the two-hundred-gallon bladder. I left Miami early the next morning for the twelve-hour drive back to Pensacola.

September 25, 1990

Next semester will be my internship. I got confirmation today that I'll be doing it with a teacher friend of mine at Columbia High School. I'll be taking over her classes, teaching three honors American history courses, two leadership courses, and one African American history course for the semester starting in January. I can't wait. I'm really excited, and I hope it will give me the possibility of a job there in August. I'll take my teaching test in June after my internship. If I pass, I'll be a certified teacher. My classes this semester are going well. I have solid Bs in all four of the courses. I'll be 40 at my graduation and finally where I probably should have been in my twenties.

I drove straight to Joe's, our farmer friend. Joe had been helping with the unloads since the Cotton Patch fiasco. He had just moved into the small block house at the strip after separating from his wife. His family had grown cotton and peanuts and he'd done the same all his adult life. Now he was in the yard working on his tractor when I arrived. The guy's tall, lean form was bent over the fender of the tractor.

"Hey Jim!" He looked up and his brown hair blended with his farm-tanned face. "I was just thinking it was about time for me to be seeing you. How about a beer?"

It wasn't often that you saw Joe without a cold one in his hand and today was no different.

"Yeah, Joe. I'll have one. I've got a little something in the trunk I need you to help me with if you have a minute."

I needed Joe to buy the necessary hardware for the bladder tank. We stretched it out on his sparely furnished living room floor and went over the fittings, pipes, hoses and fuel pump. While we were working, Joe suddenly straightened up and sort of squinted at me.

"Billy, ah, our friend Freddie, he's going through a full-blown relapse, man. Thought you should know. He's been using, like, *way* more than before. But anyway, thing is, Freddie wants to see you. Guess he, like, he needs to borrow some money."

I shook my head.

"That's not good news, Joe. I'm sure the heat's still on Freddie's house. No way I'm going over there."

"Yeah, I get it. He just wanted me to let you know."

I didn't want to let Freddie down. Maybe I could talk some sense into him, help him slow down a little. It had been weeks since I'd seen him and I did need to catch him up on what was happening. Also, we needed to go over the books from the last load so I could throw them away.

"Let him know I'll meet him at Bennigan's for lunch tomorrow," I said finally.

I slept at Joe's house that night and got up a little after 8:00 the next morning. Joe had already hidden the bladder in his attic. He'd soon be on his way to deliver my message to Freddie and then get the hardware. I thanked him, told him I'd be back to see him in a few days, and headed to Pensacola. Killing time until my lunch appointment, I stopped for breakfast and then went by the University Mall game room to play the pinball machines. I just wanted to keep a low profile and get this next job done.

As noontime approached, I drove over to Bennigan's. I took an inconspicuous spot at the end of the bar, grabbed a handful of peanuts from the communal bowl, and ordered a beer on tap. I sipped slowly and snacked on peanuts. Forty-five minutes passed. I was wondering if Freddie was even going to show. I ordered a sandwich and taken my first bite when Lori, a DJ from Solid Gold strip club, came in. She looked around and spotted me, waved and smiled as if she'd been looking for me. She came right over and sat down.

"Hey Jim," she said. "I'm supposed to meet Freddie here. You seen him?"

"I'm waiting on Freddie myself," I said. I took another bite from my sandwich.

"Oh yeah?" said Lori. "He let me know he was having lunch here and said it was okay, me borrowing some cash from him."

Odd, since Freddie was borrowing money from *me*, the main reason for our lunch appointment. Anyway, that was their business. Lori and her husband partied a lot with us both at the strip club and elsewhere. They often provided us with party supplies if the price was right.

"I guess you might as well join me for lunch," I said, already taking my last bite.

Lori dropped her voice. "You got any cocaine on you, Jim?"

That was odd too, because I was usually the one asking her or her husband this question.

"I do — and some killer homegrown pot," I said. "When Freddie gets here, we can go for a ride, smoke a joint and do a few lines."

As I finished this sentence, Freddie walked in, saw Lori and me at the bar, and came over. We shook hands and he sat on the stool next to me.

"Hey Jim, how about buying me lunch?"

"Sure, Freddie."

"Did Joe tell you I needed to borrow a thousand?"

"Yeah, he did."

It was only a couple of months earlier that we'd split $200,000 profit from the last load. As usual, I'd divided the earnings equally between us even though Freddie hadn't participated. For me, *not* having him at the site and *not* piloting was worth it. He'd become too much of a risk factor and I'd started to think of him as a decoy. If he was at home and the law was watching him, they wouldn't be watching *us*. Anyway, if he was blowing through $50,000 a month without any smuggling expenses, he was doing a lot of drugs.

"Sure man," I said. "Order something and I'll get your grand from the car." I pushed my plate aside. "I've got a couple of ounces of homegrown we can smoke and a line or two of coke we can do before I leave to meet Randy up in Alabama."

A good friend had given me the pot. I wanted to take an ounce of it down to Belize so Johnny could see the high-quality product he'd be competing against in the American market.

"I'll get the money from the trunk." I slid off the bar stool. "We can take my car for a little joy ride." I needed to get on the road to Montgomery and this would speed things along but I was also looking forward to a joy ride. My day was planned so my mind was clear.

I went out to the parking lot, still wondering how Freddie could be out of money. The math was baffling, no doubt about it. I'd have to ask him for an explanation when I handed him the loan. I opened the trunk and reached into my overnight bag, grabbed the wad of cash, the cocaine, and the pot. I closed the trunk, opened the driver's door, dropped the thousand in a litterbag, stuck the pot under the fold-down armrest and put the cocaine in my pants pocket. I closed the door and turned to walk back into the restaurant.

A non-descript man about my build was walking towards me, then he was taking large strides, then he was at a full run less than twenty feet from me and then he was pointing a large caliber semi-automatic pistol at me. He was excited, maybe even scared. We made eye contact.

"Put your hands up in the air! Don't move!"

Law enforcement was the last thing on my mind. I experienced a crazy impulse to run away from this scene, it was so unreal. I looked around the parking lot. Faces were coming out from behind unmarked cars, all of them in a blur. Plain-clothed law enforcement officers, weapons drawn and pointed at me, circled from every direction. It would be suicide to run. Even if the first guy missed, they couldn't all miss. And anyway, I was very, very tired of running.

I slowly raised my hands and looked over to Bennigan's windows. I didn't see any of my friends.

September 27, 1990

I should be studying but I just don't have it in me this afternoon. Got some dinner started and read for a while. Found myself looking at the clock, sort of expecting the girls any time now. There's a lot to do around here and I'm generally pretty good at keeping up but some days you just need to take some time for yourself. Billy should be back from his trip to Miami by now. Unless he's on a pot run, I should hear from him this weekend for sure. Maybe we can take off for a little adult time before long.

END

The Cast

Johnny, exporter who loved the ladies. Indicted by U.S. courts in multiple cases of conspiracy to import and distribute marijuana. Never arrested or convicted. Still flourishing in Belize.

Doc Philpot, who understood the value of medication. Never convicted of any crime. Lived out his life in Lake City and died of a heart attack in the 1990s.

Ruben Rivero, a pilot less careful than myself. Pled guilty to multiple charges of importation and distribution of marijuana. Testified against me at my trial. Served five years in Federal prison. Died in a helicopter crash while showing off to people on the ground.

Big B, who had the magic key ring. Pled guilty to numerous charges of importation. Testified against me at my trial. Served seven years in Federal prison. Died of natural causes.

"Don Boyd", chicken and tobacco farmer. And enthusiastic good Samaritan. Testified at my trial as a government witness.

Buddy Davis, who was made of the right stuff. Did not testify against anyone. Convicted of conspiracy to import and distribute marijuana and served thirteen years in Federal prison. Passed away from cancer July 31, 2022.

Ronnie, who helped me retrieve and store the Flat Tire load. Never charged for any marijuana-related offence. Still living in Lake City.

Robert, who furnished the Aztec and the 206 connection. Convicted of conspiracy to import and distribute marijuana. Did not cooperate with government prosecutors. Served sixteen years.

Dog, who never knew when to stop. Sorry I missed his funeral, but he'd understand.

Mark, who was a good guy and our main pot buyer. Died of a drug overdose, September 14, 1987. Missed his funeral too.

Frenchie, who landed on his well-shod feet. Convicted of conspiracy to deal weapons, importation and distribution of marijuana. Testified against me as a state witness at my trial. Sentenced to thirty-three years in federal prison but only served four.

Freddie, my eager partner. Probably figured he was facing parole violation charges after Sweet Pea shot him. Decided to turn state witness on his co-conspirators and may have had a little to do with my arrest at Bennigan's. Formally arrested after my trial and pled guilty to conspiracy to import and distribute marijuana. Served a mere eight years in Federal prison and survived his relationship with Sweet Pea. Nice guy otherwise. Died of cancer in 2016.

Glen, who preferred the flip-flop as a style. Pled guilty to numerous conspiracy and importation charges of marijuana and cocaine and testified against me at my trial. Served some six years in Federal prison. Still sunning in Daytona.

- **Wolfman**, who was still learning. Turned out in court to be his own chicken-shit friend who was afraid to steal the airplane. Convicted of importation and distribution, testified against me in my trial, and possibly helped law enforcement arrest me at Bennigan's. Served six years in Federal prison.

- **Art**, who I met in prison. Hooked me up with Pete and helped me purchase aircraft. Not convicted of any crime. Lives in Detroit.

- **Pete**, who came to own a lot of planes. Not convicted of any crime. Lives in Detroit.

- **Ramon**, **Tommy**, and **Enrique**. Hope they're all still well in Belize.

- **Arnie**, who I'd trusted with my aircraft maintenance since I was sixteen. Died of natural causes.

- **Mick**, who was Arnie's son and worked in the shop with him. Did not testify against me in my trial but cooperated with authorities about his involvement with the 210. Not charged.

- **Blaine**, who was the mechanic at the west Florida grass airstrip where we kept our Aztec. Testified against me in my trial. No charges.

- **Randy**, who was a major pot buyer in Montgomery. Pled guilty to conspiracy and importation of marijuana. Arrested after my trial and turned state witness on co-conspirators. Served some seven years in Federal prison.

- **Sweet Pea**, who needed some target practice. No doubt still being sweet somewhere, after her fashion.

Timbo, who was the subject of Sweet Pea's discussions with the cops. Pled guilty to conspiracy and importation of marijuana. Arrested after my trial and turned state witness on co-conspirators. Served three years Federal time and currently serving time on other charges.

Earl, who flew down to Belize with money after I crash-landed. Arrested after my trial and pled guilty to conspiracy and importation of marijuana. Did not testify against anyone. Served eight years in Federal prison.

Joe, a farmer who owned a bolt cutter and a trailer. Arrested after my trial and convicted of conspiracy and importation of marijuana. Did not testify against anyone. Served thirteen years in Federal prison.

Lori and the Solid Gold Dancers, who knew a few moves. Questioned about me prior to my arrest at Bennigan's. Presumably knew of my approaching arrest but didn't bother to tell me.

Carlos, who liked me. Please send him my regards if you come across him on the Holbox beach.

About the Authors

William Dekle, the son of a north Florida businessman and part-time farmer, was born in Gainesville in 1949 and as a teenager fell in love with flying. Kay Dekle, born as Cathryn Jenifer Sistrunk in Lake City in 1950, was the daughter of well-to-do parents and dreamed of a quiet life in a house with a white picket fence. They married in 1971, had two daughters, divorced and re-married.

Following a short but modestly successful career flying pot from Belize to Florida, Billy Dekle was arrested in 1990, tried, and received two life sentences without chance of parole plus eight thirty-year sentences plus ten years of supervised release. In 1991 Kay Dekle became a teacher and over the next thirty years rose through the Columbia County School System to become the Director of Secondary Education while raising the couple's daughters. After twenty-five years in federal penitentiaries, Billy Dekle received clemency from U.S. President Barack Obama.

The Dekles live in Lake City, Florida. Their daughters and grandchildren live nearby.